Jan 2017

D1251244

Because of Annie

Unlocking the Mystery of Life after Death

BOB HARRISON

BALBOA.
PRESS
A DIVISION OF HAY HOUSE

Balboa Press books may be ordered through booksellers or by contacting:

Balboa Press
A Division of Hay House
1663 Liberty Drive
Bloomington, IN 47403
www.balboapress.com
1 (877) 407-4847

Printed in the United States of America.

ISBN: 978-1-4525-8680-9 (sc)
ISBN: 978-1-4525-8682-3 (hc)
ISBN: 978-1-4525-8681-6 (e)

Library of Congress Control Number: 2013920735

Balboa Press rev. date: 11/26/2013

Dedication

To my wife Annie of 39 years: a beautiful lady that touched so many hearts. I found it special how her humanity, compassion, and ability to see through her pain allowed her to reach out and touch the hearts of others.

Though her tears were many, she'd always find a way to display her trademark smile.

Annie, I will love you forever. xo

To My Beautiful Daughter Melissa: She was the light, a beacon of hope, and her momma's peace through an unforgiving storm.

Blood Cancer/Multiple Myeloma: Loss of a Loved One; Patients in Treatment; Survivors & Supporters. *You Are Not Alone.*

Teddi Ann Raffail: A very inspirational person and friend that took the time to encourage me to write this story every step of the way. When I wanted to give up she was always there in the distance saying, "Keep writing Bob, Annie's story needs to be told." I will forever be grateful to her.

Special Thanks

Cancer Center of Kansas, Wesley Medical Center---Eight Tower Cancer Ward, Via Christi St Francis---Stem-Cell Transplant Ward, Heartland Cardiology, Family Medicine East, Total Homecare, the Leukemia and Lymphoma Society, Wichita EMS, Wichita Fire Department and all the oncologists, doctors, nurses, radiologists, medical staff, as well as the medical support folks.

Our families and friends for their supportive visits, letters, cards, and phone calls.

Introduction

Ann Elizabeth Barber (Harrison) was born on December 12, 1949 in Chelmsford, Essex, England.

As a young teenager in England she worked for the Marconi Company, which was involved in the effort to break the German codes for the British Government during WW11. She was also the young lady they used as their model when getting color resolution correct on the new color televisions. In addition, she put together some of the PC boards that went on our Apollo 11 mission to the moon in 1969.

The journey Annie is going to take you on is very tragic and filled with true love and some challenging events that in many cases will defy logic. My goal is to reach out to each individual reader and speak to you on a one-to-one basis. I know the basic needs of individuals vary, but I have no doubt that somewhere in this story there is a message for you. Seek it out and find it. Hopefully, it will make a positive difference in your life.

Over the first three months of Annie's illness the nurses at the cancer center started calling her their little miracle girl. On many occasions I'd hear them say to other patients; "There she is." When other cancer patients understood the magnitude of what she went through those first few months, they were inspired and many were able to find a new sense of hope.

Annie was known throughout the medical community for her strength, courage, and kindness. However, part of her legacy would have to be her trademark smile. Through her pain and tears she would always find a way to bring out her smile. In two of my sympathy cards, one from Dr. Moore Sr.'s office and one from Dr. Assem Farhat's office, they made mention of the fact that she was always smiling. Those were two very special gentlemen in her life.

Annie was a beautiful lady, and over our thirty-nine-year marriage I don't believe she had an enemy. Everybody just seemed to be drawn to her. Her humanity—well, let's just say the world lost one of its great humanitarians when she passed. She seemed to love everybody; and it didn't matter what color your skin was, how much money you had, how you dressed—if you needed a friend, she would be there. I used to say to her, "Annie, you can't solve the world's problems. The tears you shed for humanity is causing you so much pain and stress, it could one day be your downfall." I'm sure her empathy towards others contributed in some way.

I also believe it's possible that Annie was destined for a better place. Annie didn't believe in God or going to church. She described religion as a "total load of rubbish." In some ways, that's what makes this story so unlikely, and perhaps unique.

As I walk you through her journey, over time you will see a pattern start to form. Was she receiving miracles, or was it just simply coincidences? This is a complex story in that it enters into the realm of possibilities that science will not often acknowledge. I want you to be the judge.

Soul Mate

I always found it interesting how two people meet, fall in love, and start professing they've found their "soul mate." Here's what I believe. When you're in love and call yourselves "soul mates," that's probably meaningful to the relationship at the time; however, if you're not there in the end when the going gets tough, those words become meaningless. Annie or I never used those words. As it turned out in the end, I was Annie's "soul mate."

Wishes of a Loved One

As Annie's caregiver it was very important for me to know what Annie's wishes were, not only during her illness but after death. She had a last will and testament which was durable and contained the necessary medical directives for me to make decisions on her behalf if she couldn't.

It was a special moment when a doctor looked at Annie and asked a question about an upcoming procedure or medication changes, see her eyes glaze over, then ask me what I thought Annie would like to do. I always knew what she wanted. To live as long as she could, but under no circumstances be resuscitated if her heart stopped. She made me promise I wouldn't let her die in the hospital, and to have her cremated as soon as possible so she didn't have to stay in the morgue too long. She wanted her ashes taken back to her motherland

England, and sprinkled in the crematorium's beautiful rose garden, where she could rest with her mother and two sisters.

When Annie died, some people would say, "What's the rush, you're stressing out! She doesn't know what's going on anymore."

I'm not saying they're wrong, but Annie's wishes were sacred to me. Otherwise, what's the point of making wishes? She trusted me in death to do as I promised; I fulfilled that promise with pride and integrity.

Multiple Myeloma

The Leukemia & Lymphoma Society recently put out these disturbing statistics. Every four minutes, one person in the United States will be diagnosed with a blood cancer; every ten minutes one person will die from a blood cancer. It's estimated that one million people in this country have blood cancer at any given time. Blood cancer is the leading cause of cancer deaths in the United States.

Since this book deals with a rare form of blood cancer, I thought it would be useful for the reader to have a basic understanding of the disease. But, before I tell you about the disease, I'd like to share some potential life saving measures with you.

Annie was diagnosed with one of the many blood cancers of which many are curable if caught in the early stages. Over a year before Annie's diagnosis she wasn't feeling well. In January, February, March, and April of 2008, Annie broke one rib each month for no apparent reason. She was also suffering from anemia, and was very tired, with easy bruising. Her blood was unstable at times, in one way or the other. "As there is no prescreening for blood cancer, family doctors have a difficult time making a diagnosis."

If you have symptoms such as Annie, coupled with your blood being too thick, or your blood counts are unstable with deficiencies showing up with no real solution to the problem, be proactive and ask for an appointment to go see a hematologist/oncologist as quick as you can. He or she will do a study of your blood, and most likely a twenty-four hour study of your urine. If you have multiple myeloma, it might not be showing up in your blood; but through sensitive testing of the urine, they can tell by the abnormal protein levels that you have a problem.

At that point they will do a bone marrow biopsy, which will give the hematologist a definitive answer on whether or not you do in-fact have blood cancer.

We know now that Annie was fighting multiple myeloma when her ribs started breaking. Breaking bones is a classic case of stage 1 or early stage 2 of the disease.

Remember, this could save your life, or certainly prolong it. How do I know this? It happens every day in the world of blood cancer. The oncologists see new patients that are literally dying, as you will see was Annie's case. Annie probably couldn't have been saved from this cancer, but if caught earlier, most likely she would have lived two to five years reasonably well, received a full or partial remission, and not have suffered from all the nasty side effects of the cancer such as: broken bones, pneumonias, shingles, low platelets and other related illnesses prior to the end stage of her cancer. Keep what I just spoke about in mind as you read chapters two and three. You'll get this message loud and clear. I know I can't bring Annie back, but if I can keep just one person from living the story you are about to read, "She will not have died in vain."

Multiple myeloma is very destructive to one's immune system. The patient is quite often one germ away from a life threatening event. In addition, the bones in the affected areas eventually become very diseased and brittle.

Multiple myeloma starts in the bone marrow from malignant plasma cells. I'm sure most folks haven't heard of this cancer. When it affects different areas of the body, it's called multiple myeloma. The disease is terminal, metastatic, and not curable, but treatable. When the disease is localized to one part of the body it's called myeloma. Approximately twenty thousand new cases are diagnosed each year.

Most people diagnosed with multiple myeloma have a reasonable chance of getting a full or partial remission at some point. Average life expectancy is two to five years, with about 35 percent living as long as five to seven years, and a few folks surviving as long as ten years or more. However, it is not considered curable and most likely will be back.

There are no known causes of multiple myeloma; however, the scientists believe the most probable causes are exposure to certain pesticides, chemicals, high doses of radiation or Agent Orange. It was noted that after the atomic bombs were dropped over Japan, there was a very high incidence of myeloma within the local population. This isn't the sort of radiation you get from X-rays.

Myeloma usually doesn't target people who are under forty years of age. It happens, but is rare. The average age when the disease seems to manifest is normally 50 years old and above. Annie was 58 years old when diagnosed. Here's the breakdown: African Americans are two times more likely to get the disease than Caucasians. The risk factor for Asian Americans and Hispanics is significantly less than Caucasians. As you can see, with the risk factor being so low for Asian Americans, perhaps radiation does play a role in the development of this cancer.

Multiple myeloma is staged in three stages. Annie was diagnosed with aggressive stage three, symptomatic multiple myeloma. That is probably as bad of a diagnosis as there is with this cancer. Her bone marrow, which was her lifeline for receiving all of her blood cells was over 80 percent cancer, which meant she was surviving on a thread.

Keep in mind, multiple myeloma is not usually fatal in itself. Complications due to multiple myeloma are usually the culprit. Three of the leading causes are pneumonia, shingles (germs in general), and low platelets.

In multiple myeloma, the disease takes the calcium from the bones and puts it into the bloodstream. That is why the bones of patients with multiple myeloma break easily. Annie fell into that category from the day she was diagnosed.

The word "symptomatic" when attached to this disease is significant. Some of the symptoms I could treat at home and some I couldn't. For example, kidney and bone diseases are symptoms, as is anemia. I studied the disease online, and from booklets put out by the Leukemia and Lymphoma Society that I obtained at the cancer center, as well as listening to Dr. Moore Sr. There were times when I just wanted to pick up the phone and call emergency services. However, I never panicked. I simply fell back on my knowledge and understanding of the disease, and many times was able to resolve the problem and get her feeling better without medical intervention.

Here is some food for thought that transpired while I was with the USAF, stationed in England. On a bright sunny day Annie, and her sisters Tracy and Wendy, spent the day sunbathing in Wendy's backyard despite strong government warnings to stay indoors. On that day, the radioactive cloud from the Russian reactor explosion was over England. Wendy died in December 2001, Tracy died in January 2002, and Annie in November 2010. What's ironic is that Tracy was 40 when she died, Wendy was 50, and Annie was 60. All were so young! They were different cancers, but who knows? I'm sure the scientists would say that was not possible, but I believe it is worthy of mention.

Leave all the technical associations of this disease to the scientists and your oncologist. The things that Dr. Moore Sr. said to me in the beginning were way over my head. But in layman's terms, he told me what to pay attention to. First and foremost, as a caregiver, it truly was about the numbers attached to the blood counts. Remember, this is a blood cancer.

Here is how they get the numbers. Quite simply, blood is drawn from your arm, or a finger stick is done. With the blood, they do what is called a CBC, which stands for complete blood count. The hemoglobin (or HGB), as well as the white blood cell count (or WBC) and platelet count, will be the numbers you need to watch. When the laboratory does your blood count make sure you get a copy for your records. That way, as you learn more about the disease, you can track your progress. As you read the story, you'll know exactly what I'm talking about.

Normal hemoglobin (HGB) is 12 to 16. That is in accordance with the laboratory reports I have on Annie. The red blood cells that are traveling throughout your body contain hemoglobin. Essentially, these two elements are responsible for delivering oxygen throughout the body and expelling carbon dioxide via our lungs when we breathe out. When your HGB is low, as was in many cases with Annie, you can be anemic, very tired, and sometimes a bit breathless. In Annie's case, when her count dropped to 5, she became very dehydrated, delusional, and looked very pale. Anytime Annie's HGB was below 8, she would get a blood transfusion, which made her feel better within four to six hours. Also, she would get EPO injections to help boost her red blood cell count.

Normal white blood cell count (WBC) is 4 to 8. I've looked at many of Annie's laboratory reports from various laboratories, and that seemed to settle in as a good average. White cells are a part of your body's immune system and are your soldiers. They go to battle for you, fighting the enemy (infection). When Annie's WBC got down to 1, being around her required total cleanliness, and wearing a mask and gloves when making contact with her. We did that many times. When her count was 1 or lower, she was given a G-CSF injection in her tummy to help boost the count. At that point, she was one germ away from a catastrophic event. When the white count is high, that indicates the possibility of an infection in the body.

Normal platelet count is 150,000 to 450,000. Over the 30 month period, when Annie received platelets, there are only a couple of times I can remember or can see on paper where they actually worked. From about the halfway point of her disease, my greatest fear was that the lack of platelets would bring her down. Her platelets were always low. Annie also had isoantibodies, making it very complicated. They would recognize her transfused platelets as being foreign, and destroy them. In Annie's case, when her platelets were down to 10,000, they would transfuse her. Instead of going up, they would often go down, or the gain would be insignificant. However, Annie's inability to take platelets wasn't normal, and dying from low platelets is rare. They usually work for most folks and can be life sustaining when needed.

Contents

Chapter 1

Consultation

June 16, 2008: We got up this morning both feeling anxious and apprehensive. I remember trying to make conversation, but the mood was too awkward. The reality was setting in that we would soon be on our way to the cancer center. Looking back on Annie's extensive health issues over the past year gave me an uncomfortable feeling. It was obvious she had some medical issues, that for whatever reason her general practitioner, and the specialists she'd been seeing, could not diagnose. I'm sure we were both hoping for the best, but from the worried look on Annie's face, I believe she was expecting the worst.

A short time later we arrived at the cancer center and checked in. We were placed in a waiting area that was large, seating thirty to forty people, and was relatively full. It didn't take long for us to realize that we were surrounded with so much sadness. Annie pointed to a lady and said, "Look at her, bless her heart, she's really struggling."

Personally, at the moment I wasn't concerned about the other patients in the room. But as my gaze shifted to the lady, I took a good look at her, and my emotions went through some changes. That's when I realized we were on the outside looking in, and the thought that we might soon be on the inside looking out changed my views.

Annie was an extremely compassionate person, and I believe I was trying to look at the other patients through her eyes. I was starting to understand rather quickly that the folks in this room were all part of a larger family, and for the most part lived on hope.

Eventually, a nurse took us back to the laboratory where Annie had her initial blood draw. After her blood was drawn, the nurse escorted us to one of the patient rooms and checked Annie's vital signs. She left the room telling us that Dr. Moore Sr. would be in soon. The room was small, about 10 by 12 feet. We were sitting along the North wall facing South. Annie and I both noticed the South wall was ornately decorated with large and small shadow boxes filled with different species of some of the world's most beautiful butterflies. I couldn't help but wonder if the butterflies weren't peace in the face of such adversity. For that short moment in time, I think the butterflies allowed us to communicate and escape to a part of our minds where there was no thought of cancer.

When Dr. Moore Sr. came in the room, his first words were, "Ann, have you been feeling sick lately? Have you had a cold or any fever?"

Annie replied that she hadn't been feeling well, but she didn't believe she was sick.

This short, stocky man had a strangely curious look on his face as he walked by us towards his desk saying, "That is strange," but really didn't elaborate.

That's when I asked the question, "Dr. Moore, have you ever seen blood like Annie's?"

My heart sunk when he looked at me and replied, "I see it every day Bob, that's what I do."

Cancer was not mentioned as he needed to do a bone marrow biopsy to find the source of Annie's illness. At that point, he opened the door and yelled out two words, "Bone marrow!"

Shortly after, a nurse came in pushing a stainless steel cart. It happened so quickly, I believe she was waiting outside our room for the call. The cart had a tray on top with some strange looking instruments—a rather frightening sight. One of the instruments was long and narrow with threads on the end. That was to be used like a cork screw to get inside the bone to the marrow. The nurse helped Annie onto the bed and laid her on her right side. They used sterile cloth to drape over her hip, leaving the target area open. They gave her a local anesthetic to numb the area. I positioned myself up near her upper body, put my right arm around her neck, and held one of her hands with my left hand, knowing it was going to be painful.

When Dr. Moore Sr. finished the procedure, my hand was numb from Annie's squeezing. The only thing I heard from her through that whole process was when she said "Ouch!" a couple of times.

The process took about half an hour. Before the doctor left the room, he looked at Annie and remarked, "Ann, I think Bob took this procedure worse than you did."

I had tears running down my cheeks, and probably for the first time in my life, I felt her pain. It really pulled at my heartstrings watching her go through the procedure, and I suppose in the back of my mind I was very fearful of what they might find.

He told the nurse to clean her up and told us that we could expect the results in about seven days.

Dr. Moore Sr. was kind. He didn't make a big deal out of the lab report one way or the other. We assumed that he was going to be absolutely sure of her biopsy results before he spoke.

The ride home from the cancer center was very awkward. Our drive through suburban Wichita was a non event, but it was now difficult for both of us not to notice the kids playing, and couples walking hand in hand in happiness, while we were left wandering in the darkness.

We really didn't know what to say to each other. Annie simply sat and stared out the window, her eyes gazing from one area to another, obviously deeply in thought. She had a strange calmness about her as if she had resigned herself to the fact that she probably had some sort of cancer. As for me, I felt rather numb, but remained focused on driving through heavy traffic and getting us home safely.

When we arrived home, Annie would normally get out of our vehicle, look at our beautiful two story home, all our trees, shrubs, and greenery, then give me instructions on the many jobs she had in mind for me to take care of. Not this time. Her mood was solemn as she took a slow walk into our home.

Our Home

As the sun started to set, it became apparent to me that our lives were changing. The unspoken words of Dr. Moore Sr. were driving our emotions. I didn't know what the unspoken words were, but somehow I think Annie knew.

When we went to bed that night, I gave her a leg massage, as over the past several months her legs had been hurting. She fell asleep, not mentioning the day's events.

The next few days were much the same; they were filled with a quiet calmness, and our own anticipation of the biopsy results that would be coming our way in a few days. For whatever reason, we didn't speak of Annie's first appointment, but once again, I think the unspoken words or Dr. Moore Sr. were locked in the forefront of our minds. What was he going to say?

Chapter 2

Diagnosis/Prognosis

J une 19, 2008: At approximately 11:00 A.M., I was sitting in my office at our antique shop when the phone rang. It was Tracy, Dr. Moore Sr.'s nurse. She asked me to take Annie to the cancer center at 3:00 P.M. to see Dr. Moore Sr. I instinctively knew that we were in trouble, as the results were supposed to take seven days, but it had only been three days.

I asked her if it was bad news. (What I am going to tell you next is pretty accurate—some conversations one doesn't forget).

She simply said, "Your wife has multiple myeloma."

I remember getting very anxious, and with an elevated voice, I asked her, "What is that?" I had never heard of multiple myeloma before.

"It's cancer of the bone marrow."

I asked if she was going to be okay. "What's the prognosis?"

Tracy said in a soft voice, "It could be three or four weeks, maybe a little more," depending on whether or not she could take treatment and how well she responds to the chemotherapy.

At that point I started crying profusely. I just couldn't wrap my head around that sort of news.

She kept saying, "Please calm down."

I was a mess! I kept saying, "What will I tell Annie?" It's only 11:00 A.M., and her appointment isn't until 3:00 P.M.

Tracy told me to tell Annie she has a blood disorder and that Dr. Moore Sr. wanted to talk to her about it. Tracy indicated that she had spent two days going over Annie's medical records, and couldn't figure out why she was still alive.

Apparently, in her words, I was a very fortunate man to have her this long. What a nightmare! Panic was starting to set in and I didn't know what to do! My emotions were so elevated. I sat in my office for a while, then walked around our large antique shop for at least an hour, just trying to focus. The tears were flowing, when it suddenly dawned on me that all the beautiful antiques I was surrounded by were now meaningless.

A lady came in the shop, looked at me, and asked me what was going on.

I told her, and she replied, "Oh my God, I'm so sorry," and then left.

That was my welcome to the world of cancer.

By 1:00 P.M. I had gotten myself together and called Annie. I told her what Tracy told me to say, which wasn't completely truthful, but I didn't have the courage or words to tell her the devastating news. Annie said she would be ready when I got there.

I told her I would pick her up around 2:15 P.M. Of course, I wanted to run to her, but I knew if I did she would put two and two together, then panic would set in. She needed to hear it from her doctor.

Annie was always a lady of many questions, and why she accepted the reason she was going to the cancer center without wanting to know more of what Tracy had to say, will remain a mystery.

Maybe there is some truth in the statement that Annie's sister Wendy made to her before she was diagnosed with cancer. She said to Annie, I'm sorry, but I'm going to take you through a long dark tunnel. "I have cancer."

Annie told her not to be silly, and that she didn't have cancer.

Wendy explained to Annie that when their baby sister Tracy was diagnosed, she spoke of an unusual odor about her. Wendy said that she too could smell a strange odor.

I wondered if it was possible that going to the cancer center triggered Annie's senses and she could smell an odor too.

Annie never said a word to me about our previous visit, but it certainly seemed at the time she knew something I didn't.

When we arrived at the cancer center they had a room reserved for us. It was the same room we were in on our previous appointment. We went in, sat in the same chairs, while the nurse took her vital signs.

Shortly thereafter, Dr. Moore Sr. came in, rolled a stool over and sat in front of Annie. I'll never forget the look of dismay on her face when he gave her the diagnosis.

He told her she had multiple myeloma, and that it was terminal, metastatic, not curable, but treatable. He further stated that multiple myeloma has three stages, and that her cancer was in stage three, with her bone marrow being over eighty percent cancer.

I guess it would be like someone offering you an apple when you were starving; eating eighty percent, then giving you the core.

While Annie was talking to Dr. Moore Sr., there was a knock on the door. When he opened the door, Nurse Lisa, a well-dressed lady, came walking in. Lisa was the nurse in charge of putting new patients on the clinical trials.

Lisa spoke to Dr. Moore Sr. about the requirements for the clinical trials, and some new changes coming out.

Dr. Moore Sr. seemed a bit agitated when he asked her to go see if Mrs. Harrison would qualify for the clinical trials.

Raising her arm and holding up what I believe was a copy of the current laboratory report, Lisa told the doctor that based on Annie's HGB being so low, she would not qualify for the clinical trials.

Without hesitation, and a strained look on his face, Dr. Moore Sr. said, "Well then I will transfuse her!"

Lisa simply nodded her head in acknowledgement of the doctor's words, and left the room scampering down the hallway to her office.

After Lisa left the room, Dr. Moore Sr. explained to Annie that her best hope for survival would most likely come from the clinical trials, potentially using new drugs that weren't on the market yet.

But it seemed Dr. Moore Sr. was in a bit of a dilemma. Apparently he needed to start chemotherapy right away, but once he started giving Annie chemotherapy, she would no longer be eligible for the initial phase of the clinical trials. He also said that once placed on the clinical trials, most of the treatment for the disease is free.

After his short but to the point conversation with Annie, he excused himself and left the room for a few minutes.

After he left the room, Annie and I just sat there quietly staring at the wall. I tried to reflect on what we had been told, but other than the key points, I don't remember much of anything that was said during the first half of the appointment. Annie appeared to be in shock, and I knew in her mind her life was spiraling out of control. Her eyes looked so empty and sad as she stared straight ahead at the butterflies on the wall. As I stared at her emptiness, I wasn't sure what to say to her, but knew I had to say something. I got on my knees, put my hands on her cheeks, looked her in the eyes, and said, "I promise I will love you, take care of you, protect you, and won't let anyone hurt you." At that point she lowered her head down to mine, and we simply held each other and wept.

I was sitting beside her holding her hand when Dr. Moore Sr. came back in the room. The first thing he did after looking at Annie and me, without saying a word, was walk over to his desk and get us a tissue. He then rolled his stool back over to us and started revealing his strategy. We had just started talking when Lisa returned.

Lisa told the doctor that the study had been shut down for two weeks, but when it reopens, Annie would be eligible.

He looked straight at Lisa, speaking with a very elevated voice, and hitting the table with his fist he let these words fly; "I don't have two weeks, I don't even have two days!"

It was apparent from his frustration and tone in his voice that Annie's fate had already been sealed. It wasn't a matter of whether she was going to survive, but rather how *long* she would survive.

I have a copy of his progress notes dated June 19th, 2008. "I hope to get started by next week on treatment of this unfortunate patient."

While we were in his office, he noticed that Annie kept rubbing her right hand. He asked her if her hand was hurting.

In a soft voice, she told him "It was very painful."

He checked her hand and told her she appeared to have carpal tunnel syndrome, which he said was caused by amyloid buildup around the nerves of her hand.

Amyloid is basically malignant plasma cells creating an abundance of abnormal protein that deposits in the body's tissues. If the deposits reach any of the body's vital organs, they can block the organ, causing the organ to fail. The kidneys are the most likely target and should be watched carefully. It was just another one of those things we had to worry about.

He picked up the phone and called Dr. Lucas, a specialist on carpal tunnel syndrome, and explained his suspicions to him. Dr. Lucas set us up for a consultation on the 24th of June.

Eventually we started talking about his strategy, which was going to be two different types of chemotherapy. His first choice was IV Velcade, which was a very good drug for the disease, but hard on platelets. That would be administered on Monday and Thursday of each week at the cancer center treatment room via an IV. During that same period, Annie would take melphalan, which was an oral chemotherapy, administered one pill a day for four days in conjunction with Velcade. Melphalan has rather nasty side effects so he decided to give her only one four-day course. He also prescribed pain medications; one 15 milligram extended release morphine tablet every eight hours, and Percocet 7.5/500, one to two tablets every six hours as needed.

Dr. Moore Sr. told us of another chemotherapy drug called Revlimid, which is taken orally. Relatively new on the market, the drug is tightly controlled and very expensive. I guess it was the gold standard drug for multiple myeloma, and was used in some of the clinical trial patients in combination with other drugs. It was a cleaner drug, and the side effects weren't as bad as those of the other drugs. At the time there were only a few pharmacies in the country that carried it.

After a lengthy discussion with Annie about the drug, he looked at me and said, "I doubt your insurance will cover it."

I immediately saw a worried look come over Annie's face. I told her not to worry, when we eventually ran out of money, we would refinance our home and get more. This was so typical of cancer, as treatment is very expensive. Sadly, I knew this wasn't going to be a long-term illness as Annie was too sick.

Dr. Moore Sr. asked me to accompany him down the hallway so we could check on my insurance coverage.

As I walked, it occurred to me that this would have been a very difficult visit for Annie without me, for many reasons. At the moment Annie was just trying to come to terms with her emotions, and answering questions about our insurance coverage was not something she needed to be concerned about. Her plate was full! When the doctor and I walked out of the room, she was just sitting in her chair staring at the colorful butterflies. Her eyes looked so empty, I'm sure she was looking through the butterflies into the unknown, as it would be hard to see the beauty in anything when surrounded by so much darkness.

The big question, the one I instinctively knew seals many cancer patient's fate, and always comes right after the diagnosis, was now coming to visit Annie and me; "What sort of insurance coverage do you have?"

I knew I had heard that question before outside the world of cancer, but at the time it was meaningless to me. Now I was feeling the panic and the worry of not knowing how good, or how bad, our insurance coverage was. One way or the other, the answer to the question would potentially give her more time, or her journey would be over very quickly.

Dr. Moore Sr. guided me over to one of his secretaries, and had her send a request to TriWest seeking approval for the Revlimid. To our surprise the drug was approved immediately. It was a "high-five" moment.

I'm a veteran with twenty-four years of military service, and was told when I enlisted that I would have health care for the rest of my life if I served my country over twenty years. That also included my spouse, and children until they became adults. It appeared that the promise made to me all those years ago was being kept.

Dr. Moore Sr. gave me a big smile and guided me to his office, sat me down, and thanked me for serving my country. I guess he just wanted to do that in private.

He said, "Bob, I wish everybody had insurance like yours, we could help so many more people."

Dr. Moore Sr.'s statement was very moving to me, as he said it with such strong conviction towards helping others.

He asked me some questions about Annie's medical history, and then walked me back to her room.

When we walked into the room with smiles on our faces, she was just sitting in her chair, still staring at the butterflies. As her head turned our way I knew immediately from her body language, as our faces came into focus, that she sensed the good news.

Dr. Moore Sr. looked straight into her eyes and told her the drug had been approved, and in her case offered the best possible chance of getting some sort of remission.

Annie's response to the good news was a beautiful smile that seemed to light up her face. I desperately wanted this moment for her, and it was wonderful seeing her smile.

He explained to me that Annie was very fortunate, as the sad truth is, when a person gets the initial cancer diagnosis many insurance plans will only approve the cheaper chemotherapy drugs. If the cancer doesn't respond to the low end drugs, depending on the type of insurance coverage one has, they may be elevated up a level to the next drug. By the time the patient is elevated to a drug that gets a response to the cancer, it's sometimes too late for a cure or extended survival.

As we were getting ready to leave the room, I glanced at Dr. Moore Sr. who was still sitting on the stool with his head down, appearing to be deep in thought. I heard him mumble some words under his breath: "God help us if she can't take Velcade." When he looked up, he saw me staring at him with inquisitive eyes. He said, "It's nothing Bob, I was just mumbling under my breath."

I got his message!

June 20, 2008: As today was a Saturday, I was surprised that we had several appointments at the Wichita Clinic. Once we arrived at the clinic and checked in, Annie was taken back to radiology by a nurse. She was having a metastatic skeletal survey to find other areas where the cancer was located. They essentially X-rayed her entire body.

When the technician returned Annie to me, she had a concerned look on her face when she asked me, "Does the doctor know about this?"

For an instant I was stunned. I looked at her and said, "Know about what?" It was as if for that split second, I had forgotten that she had cancer. I quickly gathered my thoughts and told her he knew, but apparently was looking for the various locations.

That sort of set off more alarm bells in my head, as technicians don't usually comment on X-rays.

In addition, while at the clinic they drew nine or ten vials of blood for analysis, and did an EKG to check her heart function. Her kidneys and liver functions were screened as well.

It was obvious to me after all the testing on Saturday that Annie and I were in this way over our heads. What was most troubling to me was not understanding the disease, and the fear of the unknown.

From Annie's lack of communication with the healthcare professionals, I think she was just trying to come to terms with her illness. She wanted me to take charge of her chaotic life for now, which was my promise to her; and one I intended to keep.

June 23, 2008: I called Dr. Moore Sr. and told him how much pain Annie was in. She was suffering from severe pain in her bones.

He said he wasn't surprised as he has seen the skeletal survey, and decided to up her dosage of extended release morphine tablets. She would now be getting two 15 milligram tablets every eight hours.

The pain in Annie's hand was a real problem and a constant reminder of the uncertainty of the new journey she was on. At times she would stand behind one of our dining room chairs, sedated from the drugs, using her good hand to hold onto one of the chairs for stability, while continuously shaking her other hand as if trying to shake the pain away. Sometimes that would go on for over an hour and be repeated throughout the day and even into the night. I was always standing beside her, or behind her, giving her additional support as she would literally fall asleep while standing. She was so tired, but due to the relentless pain, going to bed was not an option at times. We were both very tired, but managing as best we could.

June 24, 2008: I took Annie over to see Dr. Lucas, who took some X-rays and spoke with her about the surgery. Annie wanted the surgery as soon as he could do it, as she would have rather lost her hand than fight that sort of pain. Her surgery was scheduled for the 7th of July, which I felt was too long of a wait, but apparently until all her test results were in there would be no surgery.

Annie was starting to get tired and the fatigue factor from all the pain, stress, medications, and her worsening condition was starting to set in. But we couldn't afford to look back, as we weren't going that way. Our only choice was to keep pushing forward.

June 30, 2008: Today we met with Dr. Moore Sr. at the cancer center in regards to Annie's skeletal survey. Having a reputation of being a no-nonsense type of person, Dr. Moore Sr. laid everything on the table.

He told us her X-rays showed she had bilateral fractures in both femurs from the disease. Also, she had multiple myeloma in her skull, spine, hips, and ribs. Her skull was peppered with multiple myeloma lesions, but her kidneys and other vital organs were functioning adequately.

At that time, the possibility of using radiation therapy in the future was discussed. That would possibly destroy the tumors in her hips, but also adversely affect her blood counts. He set her first chemotherapy date for July 7th, 2008.

It seemed reasonable to me that if you were just told you had bilateral fractures of both femurs you would find the nearest chair and sit down. Annie wasn't like that! When we left the cancer center she walked very slowly, with me by her side. I understood her decision of not wanting to get into a wheelchair, as in her mind it would reinforce the fact that she was now slipping further down the slippery slope she was on. I really didn't want her to walk on fractured femurs, and I told her I didn't think it was a good idea, but loving her the way I did, well, I guess it just got in the way.

Dr. Moore Sr. would like to have started the chemotherapy earlier, but her condition was such that he had to wait until all her vital organs were checked for damage from the cancer. Sometimes cancer is diagnosed at such a late stage, there is nothing they can do. His window of opportunity was very small, but he was jumping through it. Annie's treatment, once started, would be difficult for her to tolerate and very aggressive; but would offer her the only hope of any length of survival.

Dr. Moore Sr. had the Revlimid ordered that day, but the pharmacy couldn't ship until they were able to talk to me. I called the company later that day and verified all of the information. I had to talk to three different folks to get it ordered. It would be delivered by FedEx to my doorstep, and I had to be there to receive it. It was still going to be a couple of weeks before they could ship

Even though Annie wasn't a believer, she was on many prayer chains. She was in a battle for her life, and she knew it. We both humbly accepted anyone and anything that might give her an edge.

At this point in her illness, Annie was dealing with her elevated emotions, and I believe, starting to grieve. It was very painful watching her, knowing that any logical conclusion would indicate that her condition was only going to get worse.

Chapter 3

Chemotherapy

July 7, 2008: Today started off with me giving Annie her pain pills and her first dose of melphalan. We had a bite to eat, then departed for Founders Circle where her outpatient surgery would be preformed.

At 9:00 A.M. I checked Annie into the surgical department where she had surgery about an hour later. After surgery, while Annie was in the recovery room, Dr. Lucas came out and told me the surgery went very well and that it was in fact amyloid wrapped around her nerves causing all the pain. He asked me to bring her back on the 16th of July for a follow-up.

Later in the afternoon I took Annie over to the cancer center for her IV Velcade and Prednisone. The latter tablet was a steroid Dr. Moore Sr. added on the 3rd of July. He also gave me a prescription for nausea medication as Annie was feeling very nauseated.

It was becoming apparent that I would soon be a primary caregiver as well as manager of our chaotic lives. With the impending doom and gloom staring us in the face every day, it was becoming increasingly difficult trying to stay focused in order to meet her daily needs.

July 8, 2008: Annie had her second dose of melphalan today, and with that being such a nasty chemotherapy, I knew she would be feeling the effects soon. With the two chemotherapies she was on, her blood counts would soon be dropping. Chemotherapy drugs don't have the ability to identify good from bad blood cells, which can cause many deficiencies in the patient's blood over a short period of time.

Today our daughter Victoria flew in from Alabama for a week. Not realizing how ill her momma was created a very humbling experience for her. This early in the cancer there wasn't much laughter, just an overwhelming feeling of uncertainty.

July 9, 2008: Annie had her third dose of melphalan today, and seemed to be tolerating it for the moment; but it was obvious that Annie's condition was deteriorating as her bone disease was getting worse, and her pain level was intensifying.

I called Dr. Moore Sr. and spoke to him about her intensifying bone pain. He decided to add one to two 15 milligram immediate release morphine tablets every four to six hours. Annie was now essentially on over 200 milligrams of morphine a day, plus Percocet as needed.

Dr. Moore Sr. told me our objective at this point was to stay ahead of the pain. He indicated that if I let her pain get out of control and had to play catch up, that it could be very dangerous, potentially leading to drug induced problems.

He further stated that Annie was in trouble and, "Pain pills are the least of our worries." He had to somehow stop the cancer.

Before he got off the phone he asked me how Annie's hand was doing. I told him it no longer appeared to be painful, but that she was hurting in so many other places I wasn't sure she would even notice.

July 10, 2008: Annie was starting to get very tired, anemic and was suffering from further nausea. The nausea medication helped but didn't stop the burdensome feeling of nausea. Her blood counts were now in free fall and dropping rapidly. I gave her the fourth and last dose of melphalan this morning along with her steroid.

At 1:30 P.M. we drove over to the cancer center for her IV Velcade.

July 12, 2008: Today I had to take Annie to the infusion center for two units of blood, as her HGB had dropped below 8.

The infusion center was a room about 40 feet long, 18 feet wide in places, and facing South. The first thing you saw when you entered the room was the nurses' station located on the East wall about halfway down. The West wall of the room was lined with large recliners for folks having treatment to sit in. Each little treatment area had a television mounted near it, and a privacy curtain. The South wall was full of large windows and treatment areas with recliners too. A small portion of the Southeast wall had a couple of larger private treatment areas with just a few recliners and a bed in each area. The room was staffed by three nurses who were kept busy by the volume of patients coming in for transfusion or other blood work.

We were now dealing with two major problems. The cancer was compromising her bone marrow in such an adverse way that it was stopping the bone marrow's ability to produce an adequate amount of healthy blood cells. The cells that were produced were mostly malignant plasma cells, and of course the chemotherapy was killing the good and bad cells. She was extremely tired, but I knew the blood transfusion would soon start filtering more oxygen to her body, which would help her feel better in a few hours.

Annie's nephew Andre flew in from England today as Victoria would be returning to her home in a couple of days. When Andre arrived in Wichita, I'm sure he had no idea of the trauma he would witness, or the short term role he would play in helping me care for Annie.

July 14, 2008: We went to the cancer center today for a CBC and her next dose of IV Velcade. It was obvious that the Velcade was having a very adverse effect on her platelets as they were now at the critical low stage. The low platelets took my caregiver duties to a whole new level. It was now very important that Annie didn't fall and bang her head as that can often lead to a brain hemorrhage, which is usually fatal.

From this point on things would start going tragically wrong for Annie. It's difficult to accurately describe on paper the emotional roller coaster we were on and just how extreme her caregiving would become. Her struggle for survival was going to be tough, tragic, and full of love and companionship. Even though we didn't know it at the time, through the many tragedies, Annie and I were going to become one. Our love for each other would have no boundaries.

Chapter 4

Broken Hip/Femur

July 16, 2008: When I woke up this morning I was feeling a bit uneasy, but wasn't sure why. As I fixed her some breakfast and gave her medications to her, a strange feeling came over me. Over the past few days I had become increasingly aware that we were now approaching the end of the first month post prognosis, and pushing the limit of what science gave as a reasonable expectation of her life expectancy. It was as if a lingering fog was all around us and not willing to dissipate. My senses were on high alert, but I didn't have a clue what I was looking for. It seemed for the moment we were living day by day, or perhaps hour by hour.

Annie had a 1:00 P.M. appointment this afternoon to see Dr. Lucas for a follow up on her hand. I wasn't too worried about it, as I had cleaned and bandaged it several times. It always looked good and appeared to be healing well.

It was around noon when Annie decided to go upstairs and get dressed for the appointment. Due to all the pain medications she was taking, her fractured femurs, and her low platelets, I walked up the stairs with her to make sure she didn't fall. I held onto the rail with my left hand, keeping my right arm around her waist. When we arrived upstairs she went into the bathroom to have a quick shower. We had a chair in the shower stall where she could sit and get washed. When she was finished I helped her out of the shower and wiped her dry.

With Annie wearing a draped towel, we walked over to her walk-in closet where she picked out a nice outfit, then sat on the bed while I helped her get dressed. When she got up, she walked over to the foot of our bed with me by her side. I was standing beside her at the foot of our bed while she was looking in the mirror and combing her hair. As she turned to the right, she didn't pick up her right foot. She tried to slide it on our plush green carpet. I heard a snap then heard Annie scream. I immediately grabbed her and held her steady. She was crying out, "Oh no, I didn't need this!" Her voice was very audible, and then she said, "This can't be happening to me!" "What am I going to do?"

I helped her onto the bed using pillows to take the pressure off her right leg and hip. I remember saying in a soft voice, "Don't move Annie, I'm going downstairs to get you some more pain medication."

Andre was sitting at the dining room table, and didn't know what to do. He heard the commotion upstairs and asked me how he could help.

I told him to stay put for a few minutes, while I ran back upstairs with three 15 milligram immediate release morphine tablets, and gave them to her with some water. I knew it would take about fifteen minutes for the pills to start working.

While waiting for the morphine to kick in, a couple of things were running through my mind. I'd been trying to keep her off her feet as much as possible due to her fractures, but as soon as I turned my back, she would be up moving around. She knew the potential consequences of walking, but being an extremely independent lady before the cancer she misguidedly thought she would be fine, and I suppose I did too. My position as her caregiver was not to bark orders at her, but to guide her as best I could based on my understanding of what we were dealing with at the time.

I was starting to realize that cancer patients don't come with instructions.

I'd learned many lessons from Dr. Moore Sr., and knew the potential consequences of this event. With her bone marrow being over eighty percent myeloma, and being in stage three with her cancer, she could very well be in "End-stage multiple myeloma." It was a horrible thought, and was now becoming part of my natural thought process. I knew if it were to be the case, her bones would just start breaking, and chemotherapies, blood transfusions, and life-sustaining medications would just stop working. That was a real possibility, but it really didn't matter what I or anyone else thought. Annie was on an unchartered journey, with a strong will to survive, and in my heart I knew she had only just begun to fight.

I purposely waited for the morphine to take effect before calling the paramedics. She was already on plenty of pain medication, but when the bones broke she needed more. I wanted to make sure her pain medication had taken full effect before EMS arrived. I knew when they started moving her it would be very traumatic and painful for her.

When I told her I was going downstairs to call the paramedics, she said, "I don't want to go to the hospital!" She indicated that she wanted to go see Dr. Lucas and make sure her hand was okay.

I looked at her and said, "Are you serious?" She was very serious.

I tried explaining to her that I couldn't get her down the stairs. It would be 11 steep steps down, a right turn, and then 3 more.

Her tears were flowing when she said, "Please Bobby, you can do it, Andre can help."

Right or wrong, I just wanted to respect her wishes. At this very moment, I sensed Annie's life was reeling out of control. Every day just seemed to get worse. As for me, it was just a deep heartfelt pain seeing the woman I loved for so many years suffering in such an unimaginable way.

I agreed, and gave Andre a shout-out. He ran up the stairs and into the room. Luckily, he's a tall and very strong English lad. When I asked him to help me take Annie downstairs, he looked at me like I was out of my mind. I told him I knew what he was thinking, but we were going to get her downstairs, into the vehicle, and take her to see Dr. Lucas.

I could see the pain in his eyes as he stared at Annie. He lowered his voice, and in a barely audible whisper said "Okay mate."

I called my daughter Melissa, who was her mom's nurse at Family Medicine East, and worked for Dr. Terry Klein, Annie's newly assigned family doctor. I told her about her mom's accident and that I suspected some bone breakage. When I said we were taking her mom to see Dr. Lucas she was a bit resistant at first, but when I told her it was her momma's wish she immediately got on board with the decision.

I called the receptionist at Dr. Lucas's office and told her of the situation. She told me to get her there as quick as possible and to be very careful while moving Annie.

I should have known Melissa would use her job to network this event. Dr. Lucas was waiting for Annie and seemed to know the whole story when we arrived.

My strategy for moving her down the stairs was to gently help her stand on the floor with no weight on her right leg. Her right arm would be over my left shoulder, while her left arm would be over Andre's right shoulder. Getting her to the stairs was relatively easy; but getting her down the stairs was a whole different issue. When we got to the stairs I looked down, then looked to my left at Andre. His eyes had an expression of apprehension, but I knew he was okay. Still, I got the sense that this was going to be a daunting task.

As we navigated our way down the stairs, very slowly, one gentle step at a time, I hung onto the rail tightly with my right hand, which gave us all a sense of stability. The further we went down, the more confidence we gained with every step we took. We were able to move her with minimal pain, and surprisingly everything went okay. I knew once we got to the bottom of the stairs it was a simple left turn, then about five feet to the front door.

From that point on it wasn't too difficult getting her to the car. What I failed to realize was that we had a large Toyota 4Runner that sat very high off the ground. Getting her into the vehicle would have to be thought out very carefully.

When we arrived at the vehicle the first thing I realized was that I didn't have the keys. I had Andre put his right arm around her waist and hold her stable, so there was no pressure on what I thought to be a fractured leg, while I ran in the house and grabbed the keys.

When I got back to the vehicle it took me less than a minute to plan a strategy. After we positioned Annie with her back to the front seat, I held her in place while Andre climbed into the back seat. He reached out over the front seat and put his hands under her arms at her shoulders. He was able to lift her just enough that she could place her good hip on the seat while I gently lifted her legs into the vehicle. It wasn't easy, but we were able to get her in the vehicle without much pain. During this process I knew we had to be very careful as her good leg had a fractured femur too, but fortunately it was holding up.

It was a six-mile drive to Founders Circle, and I think she felt about every bump along the way. When we arrived I was able to park in front of the doors and go inside to get a wheelchair. Getting her out of the vehicle was just as hard as getting her in, and this time all the pressure was on her broken leg. It was challenging, but we managed fine.

Once inside, I filled out a couple of forms, then took her straight back to where she was put inside a patient's room. A nurse came in, took her vital signs, and asked a few questions.

A few minutes later Dr. Lucas walked in, sat down in front of Annie, and started removing the bandages from her hand.

He said, "I understand you have hurt your leg." Before Annie could even reply, and before he finished unwrapping her bandage, he instructed the nurse to take her to the X-ray room. He wanted an X-ray of her leg and hip immediately.

I pushed Annie down three short hallways to the X-ray room, escorted by the nurse. From that point the nurse pushed her into the X-ray room and I followed. The X-ray machine had a very long and hard flat surface. With her diseased bones and fragile condition, I knew it was going to be very difficult for her to lay down on that hard surface. The two X-ray technicians and I managed okay, but it was very painful for her. I saw it as simply another sad reality of her cancer.

I'm sure the technicians had no idea what to expect, but I suspected it wasn't going to be good as I had heard the bone break.

As it turned out, it was very serious. The socket on her right hip, which the femur was attached to, had completely broken off taking some of the hip with it. Her femur was cracked down toward her knee. The X-ray technicians, obviously seeing the seriousness of the injury, didn't move her off the table until Dr. Lucas and an orthopedic surgeon, Dr. Pence, had a chance to look at the X-rays. From that point on things started moving rather quickly.

It wasn't long before they brought a bed into the X-ray room. At that point I started focusing on making sure her transition to the bed was completed without making her injury worse. The bed was lowered to the same height as the X-ray table, and the two X-ray technicians and I worked as a team to get Annie on the bed with as little pain as possible.

She was then moved to a separate room where they started IV fluids to keep her hydrated and to help stabilize her body.

The nurse came into the room and told me that Dr. Pence had been in consultation with the hospital and Dr. Moore Sr. As soon as a room was available, Annie would be transported to the cancer ward, Eight Tower, Wesley Medical Center.

While in the room, Dr. Lucas brought in Dr. Pence and formally introduced us to him. He told us he has known Dr. Pence for a long time and that he is an excellent orthopedic surgeon.

It was then that Dr. Pence showed me a paper copy of the X-ray of Annie's hip.

It was shocking to look at! A part of the femur up near the top was broken off and had jagged edges protruding out near the surface of the skin. The top part of the broken femur was still attached to the hip socket, which had broken off and still had a small part of the hip attached. The femur and socket were leaning away from the main part of the hip and seemed to be suspended by air.

Not long after they left the room, the paramedics arrived and transported Annie to the hospital while Andre and I followed in the car.

I probably should have called the paramedics, but as it turned out, we did the right thing. EMS has a protocol and always straps the patient to the gurney. That would have been very painful for Annie, as no one knew the extent of her injuries.

Being moved around by two guys that loved her as much as Andre and me, she was never in danger of getting hurt.

Emergency rooms are very busy, and in Annie's condition, being moved from bed to bed, as patients often are, would have been very difficult and painful for her. Our lack of understanding of how bad the situation was allowed us to take our time and handle her with care.

I was starting to learn that I might have many difficult decisions to make, and once made, I needed to stay the course. Sometimes, what seems to be the wrong decision turns out to be a good strategy. We were very fortunate that, in this case, it worked for Annie.

Chapter 5

Surgery

The trip to the hospital appeared to go well, as the paramedics drove relatively slow, probably to keep Annie from bouncing around.

The slow ride to the hospital gave me time to reflect on the day's events. It was very difficult watching Annie suffer the way she was. It hurt me deeply! Still, I had no choice but to be strong, alert, and take control of the situation and not let it control me. I knew now, beyond a doubt, the only way I could create any reasonable expectations for Annie to feel safe was to learn all I could about the cancer, and start controlling each event as they happened.

When we arrived at Wesley Medical Center, Annie was taken to a private room on Eight Tower, Cancer Ward. The paramedics and nurses took their time figuring out the best way to move her to the bed. They decided to leave Annie on the bed sheet used on the gurney, and by holding onto the four corners of the sheet they could lift her up gently, transferring her to the bed without hurting her. It was a real relief when she was lying safely on her bed. She was in a lot of pain, and I could see the confusion in her eyes over what had happened today. At times like that I just wanted to wrap her in my arms and make the pain go away.

Today I started coming to terms with my new role as her primary caregiver. I would be forever by her side and keep a watchful eye over her; and as her caregiver I would be as much involved in her care as the nurses and doctors.

Dr. Pence came up and visited with me a short time later. It seemed we had a serious problem with Annie's platelets. They were too low for surgery, leaving the potential for uncontrollable bleeding. If she started to bleed during surgery, they might have difficulty stopping it.

Dr. Pence said he was going to order two units of platelets tonight and see how she was doing in the morning.

I stayed up most of the night watching her and trying to get a grip on my emotions. It occurred to me that the longer we waited for surgery, the greater the risk of her developing an infection, which is common in multiple myeloma patients.

July 17, 2008: This morning, her platelet count hadn't improved at all. I was very disappointed, and anxiously awaiting the arrival of Dr. Pence.

While waiting for Dr. Pence to arrive, Dr. Moore Sr. walked in. He examined her like he always did and asked her a few questions. Due to the IV Dilaudid, she didn't have a clue what was going on. We were able discussed the platelet problem and the risk of holding surgery off too long. At the moment, there appeared to be more questions than answers.

Dr. Moore Sr. told me she would get her last dose of Velcade today, and I'm sure that was in response to her falling platelets. During these first few weeks his strategy apparently changed. He was hoping he could use the Velcade with the new drug Revlimid. That would have given him two powerful weapons to fight the cancer.

I couldn't help but remember the statement he mumbled under his breath earlier when he was planning his treatment strategy; "God help us if she can't take Velcade." That was now a reality. It was a big setback, but regardless, he had to stop the cancer!

Dr. Moore Sr. looked at me rather curiously and said, "If Ann broke her hip at home, how in heaven's name did she get to Founders Circle?"

When I told him the story, he laughed out loud and said, "That's the craziest thing I've ever heard of."

I couldn't agree more.

When Dr. Pence walked in, he was disappointed too. The decision was made to once again hold off on the surgery and give her more platelets. As the day went on, I started to notice she was getting more uncomfortable with pain. Imagine, your femur is shattered and broken off at the hip and your bones are badly diseased from the cancer. Anytime we tried to get her to eat or move, it was difficult and very painful for her. Melissa and Andre helped me as best they could, but in her broken condition there wasn't much anyone could do at the moment.

Annie was precious to me, and I went to great lengths to keep her comfortable. I was slowly coming to terms with her illness, and understanding the most powerful weapon I had was my love for her. Looking at her laying in the hospital bed broken and defenseless just made me love her more. I was starting to understand that my role as her caregiver and husband was not going to be defined by her cancer, but by my unconditional love for her.

This evening, Nurse Colin came in and inserted a catheter that was attached to a bag to collect her urine. With her broken hip and femur the bed pan was not an option.

Annie's face was starting to show signs of more pain and stress, which was indicated by her wrinkled forehead. I talked to Colin and asked him if it would be possible to up her pain medication. Annie was already on IV Dilaudid, which is several times stronger than morphine and was running through her system at all times.

He said he would check with the doctor and see if he could increase the dose.

After Colin spoke with the doctor, he came back to the room and told me the doctor wouldn't increase the dose for fear she wouldn't wake up. But he did agree to attach a PCA pump, which is a stem like object with a button on top, which she could push when she needed more pain medication. The pump was placed in her left hand and set at fifteen-minute intervals. Once pushed, she would get a pain medication boost. If she pushed it again, anytime during the fifteen-minute period, it wouldn't administer any further medication.

Later that evening when Colin made his rounds, he noticed that the button had been pushed a few times.

He asked me if she had been pushing the button, and I told him, "No."

Colin told me in a diplomatic way that I was defeating the purpose of the button as she would push it herself if she gets in enough pain.

I understood, and it never happened again; but if I saw her thumb making the motion of pushing the button down, I'd place her thumb over the button and simply tell her when she needed more pain medication to push the button. Annie was unconscious, but I'm sure she could hear me as on occasion she would push the button down.

July 18, 2008: I was starting to get frustrated and confused, as the platelets she received yesterday didn't work either. I assumed they would raise her count and get her out of the danger of bleeding, and then the surgery could take place to mend her broken bones. But for some reason they weren't working, and no one was saying why.

When Dr. Pence came in, he said he would try them one more time, and if the platelets worked or didn't work, surgery was being scheduled for 8:00 AM tomorrow.

Later that afternoon Dr. Pence came back up to Annie's room, this time to visit with me. Once again he said the new platelets hadn't worked and her risk of infection from the injury was now elevated. He also stated that due to the low platelet count, this was going to be a high-risk surgery.

Thoughts were starting to swirl through my head as I knew even if the surgery was successful, once she has been opened up, her risk of getting an infection would soar. Germs just seem to find their way into open wounds, especially in a hospital environment.

Taking another crash course in cancer and its effects through a traumatic situation was hard to deal with. Dr. Pence held off on surgery to give her the best chance of survival through platelet transfusions, and in the process they didn't work; now we have an elevated risk of infection as well as the low platelet count. I didn't see this coming and I'm not sure they didn't either.

My daughter Melissa, Andre, and I were very uncomfortable with the upcoming procedure, however, there were no other options. The three of us sat with her that night and just loved on her. She had been in the hospital for three days, and asleep most of the time. So we really didn't get to visit with her very much. Dr. Pence was hoping that if she came through surgery okay, they would be able to back off on the pain medications and she would start waking up. It never really occurred to me that once the hip and leg were repaired, her pain would subside. I know that is common sense, but for me, it was difficult to rationalize anything that was going on at the moment.

July 19, 2008: At 7:00 A.M. the medical staff arrived to take Annie to surgery. It was a rather helpless feeling following them down to the waiting area as she was in and out of consciousness and didn't have an understanding of what was going on. While giving her hugs and wishing her well, we didn't know if we were actually saying good-bye to her. It was difficult releasing her to surgery, as our emotions were elevated, and we were all worried about the outcome.

It did occur to me that some folks might have felt like we were being a bit dramatic, but try to remember this; when you have been told that your loved one is going in for a high-risk surgery, the odds aren't in their favor. It's a troubling experience knowing her life was hanging in the balance, and she was going to need some help. With raging cancer running through her blood stream, and low platelets, there was no guarantee she would get through the surgery.

While in the waiting area, it was obvious we weren't the only ones worrying about a loved one. It's a strange feeling watching doctors come out of surgery and discussing the results of a procedure with family members. At one point I saw one couple crying, and although I didn't know the circumstances, I felt for them. I'll admit it left me wondering. Was that going to be us? It was just a natural thought process and very difficult to escape from.

The surgery took about three hours, and by the time it was over there were only a few folks left in the waiting room.

We were standing in the hallway when Dr. Pence came out of surgery. We watched him walking down the hallway towards us.

Dr. Pence is a very stocky man, not too tall, and one of those doctors that moved rather slowly, with his head down, as if deep in thought. As he walked toward us there was no doubt we were all waiting for him to raise his head. Melissa was standing there with tears running down her face, while Andre and I were just very anxious.

Once he raised his head, he greeted us with a grin saying, "The surgery went well, and we used Amicar to help keep the bleeding under control."

We were so excited and hugging each other, until he said, "We're not out of the woods yet. She must be carefully monitored a couple of days for infection." He then started explaining to us that the cancer had compromised her immune system, leaving her more vulnerable than a normal high risk patient.

We really didn't need to hear that, but as I was learning it was best to be as honest as possible with the patient and their loved ones.

Dr. Pence showed us a couple of black and white pictures of her new hardware. There was a stainless steel ball that looked to be wired into the damaged hip and socket. Extending down from the ball was a steel rod that went within a few inches of her knee. It looked awkwardly strange, but he said it would hold her together fine.

When Annie started waking up, she was in a great deal of distress. Her pain level was very high, but she couldn't tell us where she was hurting. I called the nurse into the room. She recognized her distress very quickly and called the doctor. Dr. Pence upped her pain medication, but told the nurse that sort of pain can't be from the surgery. It has to be from something else.

July 20, 2008: This morning Dr. Pence came in and examined Annie. After the examination, with a puzzled look on his face, he told me the pain seemed to be coming from her back.

He walked back to the nurses' station and had them order an X-ray of her spine. About an hour later two X-ray technicians came into her room with a mobile X-ray unit.

The technicians had a very difficult time trying to take the X-rays as Annie was in so much pain. When they tried to move her in place for the X-ray she couldn't handle it. Every time they raised her bed and tried to put her spine against that hard plate, she would scream out in pain.

Recognizing the problem, I asked one of the technicians if I could hold her back and spine about a half-inch off the hard plate while they shot the picture. They weren't thrilled about my idea, as I suspected there may have been some liability involved in me getting radiation too. In the end, I gently held her back and spine off the bed, allowing just enough room for the plate to fit. They were then able to take the X-rays, and Annie wasn't in as much pain.

Awhile later Dr. Pence came in with some sobering news. After viewing the film, he said it showed she had several compressed fractures of the vertebrae, and in essence her spine had collapsed.

In consultation with several doctors the decision was made to perform a procedure on her called vertebroplasty, as surgery was out of the question. Tomorrow morning they would be doing the procedure.

We now had a definitive answer as to the source of her pain. A collapsed spine opens up many possibilities to pain, discomfort, as well as potential nerve damage that can affect many parts of the body. According to Dr. Moore Sr. many patients that suffer from multiple myeloma, and have a heavy burden of tumors in their spine, often suffer this fate. It was just another sad reality of the cancer, and at the moment it was just another step further into the unknown.

July 21, 2008: Once again they wheeled Annie out, this time down to radiology where Dr. Berger injected bone cement through small holes in her skin, into her various fractured vertebra. They used some sort of X-ray guidance system to know where to place the needle. The cement dried quickly and formed a support structure within the vertebra, which helped provide her with strength and stabilization. It didn't leave her pain free, but stopped the excruciating pain she was feeling.

Around lunchtime the doctors started cutting back on her pain medication. It wasn't long until she started waking up and became reasonably alert. One of the first things she did was have a good cry. She had missed the last few days, and was now realizing her mortality was staring her in the face. She was also trying to come to terms with the fact that she would be wheelchair bound for the foreseeable future.

Around 3:00 P.M. Dr. Moore Sr. came walking into our room. He indicated he was in the area and thought he would stop by and check on Annie.

Annie was reasonably alert at the time, and as he checked her over, they were having a little chat.

After listening to her heart he told Annie he was going to lower the bed a bit to check the veins in her neck. After checking the veins a frown came over his face. He told us that Annie might be in congestive heart failure, as she appeared to be drowning in her own fluids. He told her not to worry, he would give her cardiologist a call and let him sort it out.

Approximately fifteen minutes later the PA assigned to Annie's cardiologist came over. She didn't say much of anything, other than tell us that Dr. Farhat would be over soon. His office was located just across the street from the hospital.

When Dr. Farhat came walking in he was his usual bubbly self, and always smiling. His initial evaluation of Annie was that she was indeed on fluid overload; but he couldn't quite figure out why. He then did something very strange. He pulled her bed away from the wall a bit, went around behind the bed and got down on his knees on the floor. In an instant he popped his head up with a big smile on his face, and said, "I found the problem!"

The catheter bag was full of urine, which was backing up in her system. He immediately got a nurse in the room to empty the bag. Then he ordered two shots of Lasix, which is a diuretic, that would force the fluid out of her body into the catheter bag. The shots were to be administered six hours apart. He said that should take care of the problem, as he didn't believe it was anything to do with her heart.

Before he left, I asked him what it was about the neck that indicated she was on fluid overload. He showed me the two large veins, one on each side of her neck, that were bulging out. Apparently the bulging veins are a sign of fluid overload.

He also had me stand by her bed and listen to her rapid and shallow breathing.

He told me that was a sign of fluid overload too, and as with the arteries, must never be ignored by me. That type of situation would be a medical emergency and is actually not that uncommon with cancer patients.

I was sitting there with Annie, and didn't even realize what was going on. If Dr. Moore Sr. hadn't came in, who knows what might have happened.

I wasn't upset, as I looked at it as more of a learning experience. This was something I really needed to know, and because it was caught early, posed no real threat to Annie. I knew if it ever happened again I wouldn't miss it.

July 22, 2008: Today they tried to put her into a wheelchair in order to get her moving. She was way too weak, which was a concern as one of the leading causes of death in multiple myeloma patients is pneumonia. Annie hadn't been mobile for a while and was at risk of an upper respiratory infection.

This afternoon, after a teary goodbye with Annie, Melissa took Andre to the airport to catch his flight back to England. It was time for him to go home too.

Andre was a real blessing to me, and without him, this whole event from the day Annie broke her hip and femur may have turned out less favorable. Annie and I were very grateful for his help and encouragement throughout this event. We both loved that boy.

July 23, 2008: Today Apria Healthcare delivered a hospital bed, a wheelchair, a portable potty, and a sundry of other things to our home. Melissa met them, made sure everything was set up, and that Annie's bed looked beautiful when she came home.

Melissa had went shopping prior to the bed arriving and purchased colorful sheets and pillowcases for this strange new bed that was going to be the focal point of our living room.

Over the next three days many attempts were made to get her mobile, but with no success. Annie was essentially disabled, but very appreciative to those that tried to help her get moving. Annie knew this was her new reality and really didn't question it. She wasn't angry or despondent; she just wanted to go home.

July 25, 2008: The hospitalist doctor met with me this morning and told me we could go home. He said there wasn't anything else they could do, and that she was a very sick lady, although stable. He also discussed the seriousness of having low platelets with me, but said that if she started spontaneous bleeding from low platelets, even in the hospital they wouldn't be able to stop it. His statement gave me a strong sense of insecurity, but left little options. As long as she was on chemotherapy and fighting aggressive cancer, I knew things were not going to get better in the short term.

As her caregiver, I knew I could keep her safe and comfortable at home and there were things I could do to stimulate more movement. Although it wasn't going to be easy, I was up for the challenge. Annie was going home, and at the moment we were excited and nothing else seemed to matter.

The ride home was slow, as I took great strides in missing all the bumps in the road. Every now and then Annie would crack a grin; She was going home.

We didn't say much, and we didn't have too. We both knew and understood she had just fought a noble battle for her survival, this time coming out on top. We were very happy this event ended in our favor, but were under no illusions, as we knew there was still a war to fight. However, at the moment we were home, and just like the many other cancer patients we met, we were living on hope.

Chapter 6

Home/Post Surgery

July 25, 2008: When we arrived home today, our home looked different, but beautiful. We now had a brightly colored hospital bed in our living room with a portable potty. I positioned the bed in a way that would allow her to see out of our large picture window facing West. It also allowed me to see her face while I was lying on the sofa, which would be my new bed as long as she was in her hospital bed. Having a visual of her face and chest was so important, as the amount of pain medication she was on could cause shallow breathing and lead to further complications. I had to be aware of that at all times.

When things started settling down I realized that, as her caregiver, I had my work cut out for me. There would be little help, and I was pretty much on my own. It was a challenging thought, but I was going to keep my commitment to her no matter how difficult the journey.

A short time after I had Annie comfortably resting in her hospital bed, I had to attach a large piece of four inch thick foam rubber to the inside of her legs by straps that would run from her groin down to her ankles. It was approximately four inches wide in the groin area, and spread out to about eighteen inches at her ankles. She had to wear that for a few days while in her hospital bed to maintain stabilization of her hip and femur. The fear was that her movements while she was sleeping might somehow upset the new hardware attached to her hip and femur.

It wasn't long until I realized I had a problem. So the question became, how was I going to get her on the bedpan without hurting her? The portable potty was not an option and each time I tried to lift her onto the bedpan it was so painful for her I had to stop.

It was now time to become an engineer. I asked her to be patient with me, while I sat on the sofa and figure out a solution. It took me a while, but I figured it out. I knew that she was weak and wouldn't be able to help me much due to being on all the pain medications. For my theory to work, I knew I would need her help.

I devised a system where I'd put my right arm under her legs just above the knees and with my right hand I held onto her left leg. My left arm was placed across her back, just below her neck. I'd then gently roll her over on her left side, foam rubber and all. Once she was rolled onto her side, she'd place her right arm over the top bed rail extending it down to her elbow and hold herself in place while I positioned the bedpan. I'd then gently lower her down onto the bedpan. It wasn't easy or pain free, but it worked. The real challenge was that the procedure could be necessary three or four times an hour. Annie couldn't stay on the bedpan long as it was too painful on her back.

She often suffered from diarrhea and constipation from all the medications and chemotherapy she'd been taking. So it really was a continuous effort and a bit of a nightmare at times, but we muddled through.

Over the past month I'd learned many things, but the challenges surrounding getting her on the bedpan required a lot of tender loving care. They say, "Love always finds a way," and so far, so good.

My biggest concern at the moment was all the pain medication she was on. I knew I had to stay ahead of the pain, which wasn't easy. With the amount of morphine she was on, the dangers from over medicating were very real. Just one extra pill could tip the balance with catastrophic results. I had many sleepless nights where I'd force myself to stay awake so I could keep an eye on her. Annie's cancer was simply eating away at her bone structure in places, causing pain and suffering that was horrible at times. She was hurting in so many places that it was difficult figuring out how to make her comfortable. At this point in her illness I was learning that solid pain control was equally as important as stopping the cancer.

I broke down and called Dr. Moore Sr. and spoke to him about Annie's pain level. As her husband and caregiver it was getting increasingly more difficult watching her suffer in what I felt was just simply an inhumane way. There was no doubt in my mind that the level of morphine Annie was on bordered on an overdose; but there had to be something they could do to help with the pain control. After our visit he decided to up her pain medication by prescribing a 25 milligram Fentanyl pain patch to be changed every seventy-two hours. Knowing Fentanyl patches can be very dangerous, I went online and studied their side effects. The side effects weren't any worse than those of the morphine, and when used correctly, they provide break through pain control for pain that comes on despite round the clock treatment with pain medication. The Fentanyl patch appeared to be exactly what I was looking for to aid in her pain control.

Dr. Moore Sr. explained to me that with Annie's heavy tumor burden, broken bones, and lesions from multiple myeloma, she was going to be in considerable pain; and all the pain medication she was on was how multiple myeloma patients in Annie's condition were treated.

He made it very clear to me that Annie had a very aggressive cancer, but hopefully over time the upcoming radiation treatments and the new chemotherapy would start destroying the tumors and relieve some of the pain. I think his thoughts were that if he could keep her around for a while, and get her on Revlimid, we still had a fighting chance for some sort of remission. Her treatments and pain control were going to be very aggressive, but they had to be.

I knew that over time her pain medication would build up in her body tissue with the potential consequences of a fatal overdose. For me it was a real balancing act, as excessive amounts of narcotics often lead to labored breathing and sometimes completely shut the body down.

Once again as her caregiver and husband, when asking for more pain medication, I had to be fully committed to her care. Pain control was paramount to my humanity, and this new level of care I was going to provide for Annie was all about love. When you really love someone it's amazing what you can do when the chips are down. Annie was on all sorts of medications, with many different side effects, but I knew that if I paid attention I would detect any impending emergency and deal with it.

At the moment, everything surrounding her cancer always seemed to be difficult or offered many challenges. I was starting to get angry at how inhumane this disease really is, but I was not going to give into it. I was going to get stronger, more knowledgeable, and help her fight this wretched disease on a more level playing field.

Each day, Annie received her last doses of medicine at 12:30 A.M. She would have her generic medications, a Xanax, a sleeping pill, and her morphine. Sometimes in the night she might need an extra morphine, which meant I definitely couldn't lie down as I had to be aware of her breathing at all times. I didn't mind, as Annie wanted to live, and as long as she was willing to fight, so was I.

Once she had her nighttime medications, I knew if she was going to have problems, it would be during the first couple of hours. I would usually sanitize the kitchen during the wait as I had a good visual of her from there. On the nights I felt she was safe, I'd lay on the sofa and rest, which was usually around 2:30 A.M. On the nights that her breathing became labored, I would sit in the wheelchair beside her bed and stimulate her by talking to her and rubbing her head and neck. What that basically did was annoy her. Sometimes her pretty little eyes would come open, she'd look at me, and I knew what was coming. In her weak little voice she'd say, "Would you leave me alone? I'm trying to sleep." Further, "Now look what you've done, you've woke me, and I won't be able to go back to sleep." Her predictable words always made me smile, knowing my mission was accomplished. We now had normal air movement again. Sometimes, I would do that on and off all night. That was such an important part of caring for her. If her labored breathing became too low over a period of time, her vital organs could become oxygen deprived and start shutting down, or her breathing would simply get too low, and eventually stop. With that much morphine, anything was possible. It was very worrisome for me at times, but the reward of getting to spend another day with her made it all worthwhile.

With our new and unique sleeping arrangement, when I laid down to rest at night, the last thing I saw before I fell asleep was Annie's face as she slept silently on her hospital bed. On many occasions when I woke up in the morning I would just lay on the couch staring at her and loving her. Eventually she would awaken, look in my direction, and as her eyes came into focus with mine she'd give me a beautiful smile and say, "Hi babes."

I always smiled back saying, "Hi sweetie."

That greeting was replicated many times throughout our journey and created moments of tender love that made me wonder what I could do for her today to make her day just a little bit better.

Her cancer was bringing us together in a way that quite simply created a very new and spontaneous love. At this point we'd been married 37 years, and were now experiencing a love affair that would change our lives, creating a new meaning in our lives for the word "Love." We always loved each other, but my feelings were that we were now on the verge of capturing something new, exciting, and very rare in the world of mortality: "The Perfect Love."

Annie was not one for pity parties, but during this timeframe she was on so many heavy drugs, that this one evening she felt like she'd just had enough.

I was standing in the kitchen doing my chores when I heard her cry out that she just wanted to die. I walked in the room and said to her, "Having a little pity party are we?"

She looked at me and said, "No. Bobby you don't know what it's like laying here in this bed, in pain, and feeling miserable all the time. I just want to die." I pulled the wheelchair over to her bed, sat beside her and put her hands in mine, then told her I wanted her to do something for me.

She said in a pitiful voice, "What's that?"

I looked straight into her eyes saying, "Go ahead and die."

Her reply was a sharp and sorrowful "What?"

I then repeated myself. "Go ahead and die, you have my permission."

She started crying and laughing at the same time saying, "You know I can't die."

"Annie, you're just having a bad evening."

I sat down beside her bed in the wheelchair and made a fuss over her for the rest of the evening until she took her medication and went to sleep.

The next morning when she woke up she looked at me with a smile saying, "Hi babes, do you remember what I said last night?"

I acknowledged her with a smile.

"Well I've changed my mind."

"I thought you would." We then had a good laugh.

One of the things Annie always loved about me was my sick sense of humor. I believe that was one of my finest hours. As strange as it may seem, I knew exactly what I was doing and the results were predictable. I knew Annie didn't want to die, and once again, I found a way to make her laugh.

So far, I've only addressed medications and her bedpan, but my duties entailed so much more. Annie needed to live in as germ free of an environment as she could. I had to keep the home as free of germs as possible, as well as do the laundry, cooking, paying the bills, and more. I was pretty much run off my feet for a while, until I realized making up a schedule would help organize my days. I got as much help from Melissa as possible, but she had a full-time job and four children. Plus, she worked around sick people all day and there were many days when she was just too infectious to come over.

July 28, 2008: A home health company was assigned to Annie in an effort to monitor her progress and give us some emotional support. Their responsibility was to send a nurse over a couple of times a week to check Annie's blood pressure and temperature. It was basically a well-being check. They were also responsible for her physical and occupational therapy, but it didn't work out very well for us, as Annie was just too sick. The company wanted us to work off their schedule, but when a patient is as sick as Annie, and spends so much time at the doctor's office, it's not possible. Beyond that, the company said her bones were too painful and brittle for any form of therapy. In other words, they were afraid they would do more harm than good.

Later that day we went to see Dr. Moore Sr. He wrote in his progress notes: "Unfortunately, the blood counts are down. I am going to delay, for another week, the start of her new treatment." As the new chemotherapy was her only hope in stopping the cancer, we were both worried about the delay, but we never questioned the doctor's decision.

August 5, 2008: Dr. Moore noted, "Called Mr. Harrison today, told him that her platelets are still down." He also stated, "The patient will have further problems, I am sure, with the radiation therapy that she started yesterday." Radiation as extensive as that of Annie's was expected to lower the counts even further, which it did.

He further stated, "I told Mr. Harrison to start cycle one of her new chemotherapy tonight."

Revlimid was to be administered orally in pill form, 25 milligrams daily for twenty-one days, then seven days off. Decadron tablets would be administered orally at 40 milligrams a day, on days one, eight, fifteen, and twenty-two of the cycle. His strategy of giving Annie the highest dose recommended for both these drugs was to increase her chance of survival. Decadron is a steroid, and form of chemotherapy. It's very helpful in controlling multiple myeloma and isn't hard on platelets. However, it does cause a whole slew of other problems.

His last noted comment really concerned me as he noted that he would stay with this dose until he sees if he gets a response.

I knew if the new chemotherapy didn't work, we were out of options, and the battle would be over quickly. I was worried, but didn't tell Annie. I just stuffed it inside of me and acted like the words of Dr. Moore Sr. were never spoken. I was not going to let the cancer control me.

It was very difficult giving your loved one a pill that might ultimately be fatal, but on the other side of the coin, it's hard to justify not giving it to her as it might help. This was quickly becoming an insane journey and very challenging. It seemed we were struggling with something unpleasant every single day. Sometimes, before the end of the chemotherapy cycle, she'd tell me her stomach felt like it was on fire, and I'm sure it did. I always gave it to her around 10:00 P.M. so any side effects would be minimal, and occur while she was sleeping. It didn't cause her too much nausea, and she was going to keep her pretty hair. It's just one of those pills that affect your blood counts, which leads to various other problems. It always seemed to be a vicious circle.

The one thing I did during the day and in the evening was speak to Annie often. I'd walk over to the bed and say, "Are you okay?" She'd let me know in one way or the other. She wouldn't eat much, but loved Breyers Ice Cream and raspberries. She liked bagels, toast with marmalade, and things like that. I knew she wasn't getting enough calories, but there was nothing I could do.

August 6, 2008: Today I received a call from TriWest Healthcare Alliance. The lady introduced herself as Carol Vannoy, RN, saying she would be Annie's case manager. What a blessing! I asked her questions about our insurance coverage for financial reasons, and in an effort to find out the level of care Annie would get as we moved further into the world of cancer. She said that at TriWest they have a motto: "Whatever it takes."

Each time Annie was hospitalized, the hospital received a letter from TriWest giving them the authority to do whatever it takes to care for her. If I ever had a problem with Annie's care, I'd call her, and she'd get on the phone and sort it out. She called us about every other week to check on Annie. Sometimes the call would be in reference to something she saw in the medical notes on Annie that came to her. I usually spoke to her, as Annie didn't really know much about what was going on with her care.

August 8, 2008: Today Annie finished her first week of radiation. It's been a really tough week for both of us. Just getting her washed and dressed each day, as she was not mobile, was difficult at best. I had to slide her out of her hospital bed each morning and into the wheelchair. I'd help her get washed, which was easier to do when she sat in the wheelchair. I'd help her get dressed, then give her a bite to eat or a BOOST to drink. BOOST is a high-protein drink, which is basically equivalent to a small meal.

Each morning I'd wheel her out to our vehicle, and once we got there, I'd open the door, then bend over so she could put her arms over my shoulders. I'd very slowly help her stand, and while doing so, my left foot would push the wheelchair out of the way. As she got near the standing position I'd rotate her body so that when she sat down her bottom would be on a cushion on the car seat. She'd put her right hand in the handle on the inside of the vehicle above the door for stability. My left hand would rotate the back of the cushion toward me, while my right arm under her legs guided the legs inside. I could have had some help on occasion, but the more hands involved the more likely she'd get hurt, as we were working in a very small area. Anytime we headed for the car, to us, it was our day out. Annie and I loved getting out, even if we were only going to a medical appointment; and we were learning just how important the little things in life truly are.

On the 11th through the 14th of August, Annie went to radiology/oncology for radiation therapy. On three of those days she had laboratory work at the cancer center. Each day she received an injection to boost her white cell count, and a different one for her red blood cell count. It was becoming apparent that they were not working as her blood counts were in a free fall. Annie was always having problems, and watched closely. At the moment she was going through some tough times.

August 15, 2008: Annie and I had been moving along, struggling through each day. Today the perfect storm seemed to hit. Events were about to unfold that would leave Dr. Moore Sr. scratching his head in dismay, and it appeared the tide was starting to turn in a way that I'd never have thought possible.

Chapter 7

Miracles or Coincidence

August 15, 2008: I rolled off the sofa around 7:00 A.M., woke up Annie, put the coffee on, then went to her closet and picked out a couple of outfits for her to choose from.

The past few days she'd been feeling worse than normal, but with no fever, congestion, or obvious symptoms, I assumed it was from all the radiation and chemotherapy. This was to be her tenth and last day of radiation.

I walked over toward her hospital bed, and from a distance of about 10 feet away, I held the two outfits up and asked her which one she would like to wear today.

She looked my way, staring at me, but not saying a word.

I said, "Annie, are you okay?"

She simply said, "I can't see them."

I responded, "What do you mean you can't see them?"

She said it once again. "I can't see them."

As I walked over to the bed, I could feel the anxiety flowing through my veins.

I asked her if she could see them now, and she said, "No."

So I laid each outfit out across her lap and let her touch them, explaining what they were.

She said "Bobby I can make out the color, but I'm not sure what they are."

I don't remember the top, but she picked her yellow track pants to wear, which were nice and very comfortable.

That was one of the few times over the thirty months she didn't have a morning wash. I got her dressed and into the wheelchair. By then it was around 8:00 A.M. I pushed her to the dining room table, made her some toast and placed it on a colorful plate thinking she'd be able to see it better. I sat the toast down in front of her with a glass of milk, and while making my toast, she asked me for her milk.

I said "Annie, it's right in front of you."

Her little hand was moving around trying to locate the milk, but she couldn't see it, or find it. Alarm bells were going off everywhere in my head, but I had no idea what was going on.

I decided that after breakfast we'd go to her appointment early as her radiology/oncologist was Dr. Rine. He had an extensive knowledge of blood cancer, and my thoughts were that he would know what to do.

At approximately 8:45 A.M. our doorbell rang. It was a nurse from the home health agency making a well-being check on Annie. She'd been over a few times before.

After she walked through the door, she walked over to Annie at the kitchen table saying "Hi Annie." Annie sat in her chair quietly, motionless, and didn't make any attempt to communicate with the nurse. The nurse sat down in one of the dining room chairs to the left and beside Annie.

She said to Annie, "Do you remember me?"

Annie replied, "No."

I spoke up telling the nurse that she probably can't see your face well enough to recognize you.

The nurse asked me what I meant, so I told her about the clothes and milk.

The nurse and I were having a discussion about her condition when Annie abruptly said, "I don't want to go to the hospital!"

The nurse told her she probably should go get checked.

Annie looked her way saying, "But I don't want to go."

For whatever reason, the nurse went against her own better judgment and said to me, "Why not give it until Monday, and see how she's doing then?"

I was shocked at her request, and said something to the effect; she can't even see you, surely you see the seriousness of this event, knowing her illness.

The nurse then asked Annie if she would go to the hospital for Bobby.

I was very vocal when I said, "For me, this is not about me! Annie is very ill."

At that point I basically dismissed her saying, "I will take care of Annie." This was a Friday, and knowing how fast blood counts can drop, I was concerned that it was a blood issue, requiring immediate intervention. I felt bad for dismissing the nurse, but she had to know in this case Annie's wants were secondary to her needs.

Around 9:15 A.M. we left to go get her last radiation therapy. Annie was pretty limp, and weaving in and out of consciousness, but with some difficulty she still responded to my commands. It was tough getting her in and out of the vehicle as we were still dealing with the diseased bones. With her head hanging limp against her right shoulder area, I had to hold her head up with my left hand and push the wheelchair with my right hand. That worked okay inside the hospital with the hard floors, but outside I didn't have the strength to do that on rough surfaces, so I used my left waist line as my left hand. This was just another one of those sad realities of being a caregiver.

It seemed, as I crept further into the world of cancer, I was literally being schooled on just how cold and cruel the world of cancer can be.

As Annie's caregiver, I didn't expect much help from others, and as a rule didn't ask for it. But I was learning just how important of a role caregivers play in caring for cancer patients. In Annie's case, I was now her eyes, ears, and voice to the world. I was aware that I had made some mistakes over the past two months. However, my role as her caregiver would not be defined by a mistake; but it could be defined by lack of trying, or caring for Annie. I wasn't going to let that happen.

When we got inside the radiology clinic, a nurse took one look at Annie and moved her straight back to the treatment area. When she returned, she said they'd made Annie comfortable, and Dr. Rine would call me back to the treatment area when he was done.

I was sitting in a large waiting room, staring out a wall of windows at people coming and going. I saw one couple holding hands and loving on each other. At that moment, I felt the first signs of grief coming on. At this point, I knew with certainty our lives were going to change forever. All I could do now was to care for her and give her as much love as humanly possible. While my mind was wandering, I was relieved to hear the nurse's voice and then see her arm motioning me to come over so she could escort me back to the treatment area.

She took me through a couple of large doors into a room where Annie was waiting, bundled up with a blanket, her head hanging limp, and sitting in her wheelchair. Dr. Rine was standing a bit to her left, arms folded, looking down and staring at her. He was a tall man and had a strong presence about him.

My words were quivering when I looked at him and said, "I think she needs some blood."

He answered back, "I think it's a whole lot more than that."

I could see the concern in his eyes, and hear it in his voice.

He asked me if I'd like him to call the laboratory and get her blood drawn for analysis.

I told him we had a 11:15 A.M appointment at the cancer center for laboratory work and I was going to go ahead and take her there.

We left radiology and drove to the cancer center, which was only a couple of minutes away. When we got there she was basically nonresponsive. I struggled, but got her out of the vehicle, into the wheelchair, and wheeled her into the cancer center where we took the elevator to the third floor.

Shortly after I checked her in we were directed back to the treatment area. It's a very large area and has many rooms that will hold two or three folks at a time, while taking chemotherapy or other treatments. Annie was placed in a room by herself where she was immediately surrounded by nurses.

As luck would have it, Dr. Moore Sr. was off that day. A group of nurses looked at Annie and told me to take her to the emergency room immediately.

I said "No!" I wanted them to draw her blood for a CBC, and show me her blood counts as she was at her scheduled appointment. My concern was, that if her white count was down, being around a bunch of sick patients was very dangerous for her. It was only two weeks ago when her white count was under one, that she essentially had no immunity to germs. It can take a long time to see a doctor in the emergency room and it's always full of people with various illnesses.

One of the treatment nurses walked down the hallway and asked Dr. Moore Sr.'s nurse to come visit with me.

When Nurse Jenny arrived, she stooped down beside Annie's wheelchair and said, "Annie, do you know who this is?"

Annie said in a low whispered voice, "Sandra, Sandra," who's one of Annie's sisters in England.

Nurse Jenny said to me, "She doesn't know who I am."

I responded by saying, "She doesn't know where she is either."

Jenny looked up at me with puzzled eyes, then stood up and started walking down the hallway to place a call to Dr. Moore Sr., who immediately ordered a CBC on Annie.

Her blood was drawn a few minutes later, and having an independent lab on the hallway, we'd see the results within fifteen minutes.

In the hospital or emergency room even under extreme conditions, it can take over an hour to get the results back.

When Nurse Jenny received the results she took immediate action and called Dr. Moore Sr., informing him that her blood counts were terribly low. Her HGB was 5, while the normal range is 12 to 16. A number that low would indicate the vital organs were probably not getting enough oxygen to sustain them over a long period of time. Her platelets, blood-clotting mechanism were at 2,000, whereas the normal range is 150,000 to 450,000. She was at high risk of bleeding or having a brain hemorrhage. Her white count was very low too, which elevated her risk of infection. Her potassium and magnesium levels were well below normal. She was also extremely dehydrated, which is an emergency and can become life threatening over a short period of time. Annie was in trouble and we all knew it.

Once I heard the results, the words I heard this morning from the Home Healthcare nurse could not be erased. I couldn't even imagine the consequences of leaving her in that condition over the weekend. I couldn't have lived with myself if I had kept her home and something happened to her. I sensed she was very ill, but I had no idea it was this bad.

After Dr. Moore Sr. received the results, he had the nurses scrambling. They got her on a bed and attempted to start IV fluids. The first nurse tried to start the IV, but the minute she put the needle in, the vein collapsed. She tried a couple of times, but the veins wouldn't hold. The next nurse that tried was unsuccessful too. They called another nurse over, who was said to be one of the best when dealing with difficult IVs, and she was successful. Those three nurses were highly skilled nurses and starting IVs is part of their daily routine. Sometimes, when a person is badly dehydrated, this is what happens. Veins can collapse as fast as the needle goes in, and once the magic line of being too dehydrated is crossed, it can be very challenging bringing a person back.

I learned something that morning, something I shall never forget. You *cannot* drink your way out of dehydration and must have IV fluids. Without the immediate intervention Annie received, we may have crossed the threshold of no return within the next few hours. The consequences could easily have been fatal.

Just after the nurse got the IV started, Melissa showed up. I'd called and told her what was going on, while requesting her presence as soon as possible. After we spoke for a few minutes, I dismissed myself and went outside the cancer center and sat on the lawn in front of a big oak tree. I called my friend Darrell, and cried like a baby. I always called him or his wife Jan when I was struggling. By this time it was afternoon, and with all the anxiety I'd just been through, I guess I needed to have a good cry to release some of my emotions.

It's very difficult watching someone you love continually living on the edge, especially when you don't know which way they're going to fall. My mind was on overload due to my limited understanding of the disease, and seeing the affects it was having on Annie. She had already lived past her prognosis and I knew her situation was bad. So the question, "Is this it?" was always on my mind. It wasn't always like that, but when it was, times were very tough. It was becoming apparent that cancer sets the scene for many emotional traps. I was starting to understand how well I dealt with them would define my success or failure as her caregiver. And I truly believe, in my mind, failure was not an option.

Multiple myeloma is all encompassing in that it not only creates tremendous stress and pain on the patient, it's quite happy beating the caregiver and all the loved ones down too. At the moment we were at the beginning of a raging storm, with unknown consequences. The question was, how much damage would it do?

They left Annie on the IV fluids for a few hours, trying to hydrate her. They were having trouble getting her a room on the cancer ward, Eight Tower. Annie's continual high risk of infection meant she always had to have a private room, which often meant shifting several folks around to fit her in.

It was around 3:30 P.M. when the decision was made to take her over to the hospital via wheelchair, with IV fluids running. A tunnel runs from the cancer center to Wesley Medical Center, which is where the cancer ward is. When we finally made it to the hospital it was around 4:00 P.M. We sat in a private waiting area for about an hour, until they found her a private room on the birthing ward.

Around 5:00 P.M. Annie was pushed into a large private room on the birthing ward. The nurse put a mask on her to protect her from germs and had Melissa and I wear one too. It wasn't long before a person showed up from the lab and drew Annie's blood. The blood would have to be typed and cross matched to tell them what red blood cells she needed. It usually took about an hour to get the results back, and based on her blood type, platelets or blood could be ordered.

Annie needed blood, but as her platelets were critical, that created a much greater risk factor, so they ordered her platelets first and started transfusing them at 8:51 P.M. When the results filtered down to me, they had moved up from 2,000 to 6,000, which was still very critically low. One unit of platelets should have a response of around 15,000 new platelets or more. That wasn't good news, and certainly not what we needed to hear.

Not long after Annie arrived at the birthing ward her pain level started increasing rapidly. I told the nurse it was time for me to give Annie her pain medications. The nurse told me I couldn't, due to numerous hospital rules. They would have to get in touch with her oncologist and order the appropriate pain medication from their pharmacy. I stood my ground with the nurse and directed the conversation in a way that would insure she called Dr. Moore Sr. and advocated on Annie's behalf. It wasn't more than a few minutes before a compromise was reached and she made the call to Dr. Moore Sr. When she got off the phone, she came into the room and told me to give Annie's pain medications to her. I thanked the nurse and then gave Annie her medication.

My orders were literally to stay ahead of the pain and Annie was certainly hurting, even though she was only semi-conscious. If I didn't do something soon, I'd get behind the power curve on her pain control. I certainly understood the nurse's rational for not wanting me to give her the medication, as she needed to be in control of any medication Annie took while in her care. I also understood that those two immediate release morphine tablets I gave Annie would quickly ease her pain, which would allow her to relax.

As Annie's caregiver, while she was in the hospital it was important that I didn't ever give her any medication without permission. I had to negotiate with the nurse but I got my permission, and both the nurse and I knew she had taken those pills. That stops the potential for an overdose or other medication conflicts.

Around 9:45 P.M. Annie was wheeled out of her room on the birthing ward and, while in the same bed, moved up to Eight Tower, cancer ward. Melissa and I walked with her and were by her side when she arrived at her room. The nurses asked us to wait outside while they got her settled in. I told them about her fractures, ensuring they'd be careful moving her to another bed, and the two 15 milligram morphine tablets she took and when. While we were waiting outside, what I assumed to be a hospitalist doctor came in with another nurse. We had no idea what was going on in her room, but there was a lot of activity with a sense of urgency.

While Melissa and I were waiting out in the hallway, we were both very tearful, and as we discussed the day's events our attention became focused on a figure at the end of the west hallway. At the end of the hallway, where it intersects with the north and south hallways, we both saw this big-framed nurse go walking by heading south. She stopped, looked down the hallway at us, then kept on going.

I said to Melissa, "Did you see that funny-looking hat she had on?" It was like the old-fashioned 1950s nurse's hats.

Melissa looked at me puzzled and said, "I did!"

About that time, out of the corner of my eye, I saw her coming our way. As I shoved Melissa into Annie's room, I was saying, "Don't look now, but she's coming our way." She was a short, older looking lady and I guess the thought of her being Annie's nurse was worrisome to me.

As you walk into Annie's room, which was facing north, on your immediate right was a large bathroom. Once you move past the bathroom, you're in her room, which was about the size of a small bedroom. Annie's bed was against the north side bathroom wall, so she couldn't be seen from the outside of her room.

Melissa and I were standing about five or six feet from her bed and facing her. There were a couple of people standing in the doorway and I could see the nurse with the old-fashioned hat standing behind them trying to look over their shoulders.

All of a sudden she just pushed her way into the room and moved herself over to Annie's bed. At that time Annie was unconscious. She put her hands on Annie's cheeks and said, "God loves you so much, you're such a beautiful lady." She said that a few times, repeating herself. That was a jaw-dropping moment for Melissa and I. She then said a long, and what I felt was, a very powerful prayer. She stayed by Annie's bedside for a while, quietly talking to her. I don't know what she was saying, but I'm sure it was spiritual. Just watching the delicate way she touched Annie gave me chills.

A few minutes later Annie's nurse came walking over to Melissa and me. She told us they'd done all they could for now and that the blood would be arriving soon, so they could start the transfusions. She told us Annie needed at least three or four units of blood.

I asked the nurse how she was doing and she replied, "We don't have any expectations either way. She's a very sick lady, but hanging on." It was all about the numbers; the blood counts had to come up soon, as Annie was compromised in many ways at the moment.

As the nurse walked away, the nurse that was praying for Annie walked from the bed and over to us. The first words out of her mouth were, "You must be the family."

I told her we were and that my name was Bob, and Melissa was my daughter.

She identified herself as Beverly, and told us, "On my way to work tonight I had a premonition from God that I was going to meet someone very beautiful and special." She looked straight into my eyes and said, "I believe I just met that person." She then put her right hand on my left shoulder and her left hand on Melissa's right shoulder squeezing rather tightly, but affectionately.

She told us we're going to get through this event, as she didn't believe God would send her to visit someone that was going to die.

She asked me what her name was, and we told her in unison, "Annie."

Beverly remarked, "I believe she needs some work."

Beverly indicated that this wasn't her area of responsibility, but when she got through with her shift, she'd come back and check on Annie.

As she walked out of Annie's room, Melissa put her arms around me and said, "Daddy, we just met an angel."

I felt as if something very special had just happened, but I wasn't ready to make that leap. I knew instinctively that over time this night might play a significant role in Annie's life; or was it my emotions wanting me to believe there was some sort of intervention playing a bigger role here? I must admit, I did find Beverly's words to Annie very comforting. But it left me wondering if Annie was aware of her presence, or even heard her gifted words.

At 10:40 P.M. Annie started receiving the first of many blood transfusions, which gave me a huge sigh of relief. I knew that would be like a two pronged attack as it would increase the flow of oxygen to her vital organs and tissue, while helping with her hydration issues too.

August 16th, 2008: Around 1:00 A.M. Beverly came back into the room, said a prayer for Annie, and then sat and visited with Melissa and me. She wanted a little history on Annie to include whether or not she believed in God.

I told her she didn't believe in God and, in fact, was a lifelong atheist.

She then focused on asking me the question, "How about you Bob?"

I told her from a child up until the 7th grade my family took me to Sunday school and church every Sunday. I had an understanding of the Bible and God, but never pursued my religion after we moved to California while in the seventh grade. This was probably due to the fact that my parents stopped going to church.

I will admit, I was very interested in what I saw and felt, but with the understanding that I was an emotional wreck and open to anything that might help Annie in whatever form it took on. I wasn't going to get in the way!

I said earlier that Beverly had a premonition she was going to meet someone very special that night. On this second visit, she told us what attracted her to us. Apparently she was looking down the hallway as they were preparing to push Annie into her room, and saw a glowing gold ring around the top of Annie's bed. She indicated she knew then, beyond a doubt, who she was going to meet that night.

I gave her statement some thought, and realized she rather forcefully entered Annie's room as if on a mission. She obviously had no doubt that Annie was a part of her premonition, and she wasn't going to be denied.

At 1:40 A.M. Annie started receiving another unit of blood. The two units of blood would only bring her count up to about seven, which is below the threshold for needing a transfusion. She would need another couple of units to get her blood up to a stable number. The nurse checked her vital signs; she was still stable.

Throughout the day things weren't getting any better. She had additional blood transfusions at 8:15 A.M., 7:55 P.M., and 10:25 P.M. She also had platelets at 11:49 A.M. and 5:13 P.M. Her platelet count at 2:11 P.M. was 8,000. Her platelet count at 10:25 P.M. was 6,000. It was pretty obvious to me the platelets were not working adequately.

Beverly stopped by around 3:00 P.M., spoke to us a bit, and then said a prayer for Annie. She was getting ready to start her night shift and said she would check on us throughout the night.

August 17, 2008: Annie received another unit of platelets at 12:42 A.M., and then again at 9:15 A.M., which only made things worse. Her platelet count fell to 3,000. I don't want to underemphasize the danger Annie was in. Due to her critically low platelets, her life was hanging in the balance.

It was now midmorning, and Annie was awake and feeling a bit better. The IV fluids had taken care of the dehydration, and the blood transfusions were giving Annie a small jump in her red blood count. With the boost in her red blood cells, Annie was becoming more alert and aware of her situation. Her breathing was less labored, and her facial color was better. She was even using the portable potty with our help. When using the portable potty it was absolutely essential that we didn't let her fall or bang her head as any type of internal bleeding would most likely be fatal.

That afternoon Beverly stopped by with a little gift for Annie and they had their first formal meeting. Beverly walked over to her bed, held her hand, and introduced herself. I could tell by the expression on Annie's face that she felt the love. She clung to Beverly's hand with both of hers as they talked for a while. Then out of nowhere, Beverly asked Annie if she'd mind if she prayed for her.

Annie was looking up at Beverly when she said, "I don't mind."

I watched Annie close her little eyes, and we all bowed our heads. We then heard a prayer, so wonderful, loving, and peaceful it was probably one of the defining moments in Annie's journey.

From that day on, anytime Annie knew Beverly was coming around, she'd get excited. Annie loved having Beverly in her presence, she made her feel safe.

The gift Beverly gave Annie was a little white box with a tiny mushroom bird and miniature cross inside.

I didn't speak to Annie about the difficulties she had the previous two days for a period of time. Then one day she was telling me about how connected she felt to Beverly. That's when I told her about the night an "angel" visited her bedside. She listened intently, absorbing everything I said. I'm sure she found the story very intriguing, as this was a conversation we'd never had before. I can only surmise that if she had asked me a question, it probably would have been, "What is this all about?"

August 18, 2008: Around 8:30 A.M. Dr. Moore Sr. came into the room. He examined Annie and spoke to her about her condition.

He then looked at me saying, "We have to somehow get her platelets up."

I remember him standing at the foot of her bed, scratching his head, and saying, "Ann, I think you're one of the most difficult cases I've ever had."

Dr. Moore Sr. was the first oncologist in Wichita, Kansas, going all the way back to 1969. He never told me that; I looked him up on the Internet when he became Annie's oncologist. We had one of the finest oncologists in the Midwest on our team, so the statement he just made worried me.

I knew his dilemma, as they had no idea, or thoughts that she was going to survive this long. But now that she had, she was starting to push the limits of science as they understood it.

By this time I knew the platelet issue was bad, however, I didn't really understand the true scope and depth of just how serious it was. Within the next thirty minutes or so, I would know everything I needed to know. We were in trouble!

I thought about what Dr. Moore Sr. said for a short period of time, then I decided to chase him down, knowing he'd still be on the ward somewhere. I found him standing outside a patient's room writing notes. I told him I didn't want to give Annie any more chemotherapy, as it was killing her, and aiding in the lowering of her blood counts. What a mistake that was! His reaction and words were swift and decisive. They made me feel like I'd just taken a left and right hook to the face. But I didn't fall down; I just listened.

He said, "Bob, we have to make our stand now. We are running out of time and if we don't get those platelets up soon, Ann is going to start bleeding. She will have a brain hemorrhage or start bleeding from her nose, eyes, ears, stomach, and anywhere else she can bleed. We will not be able to stop it." He explained that with her bone marrow being so compromised with the myeloma, her platelets were not going to come up. The only way to stop the myeloma was for the chemotherapy to start killing the cancer. Then, even with the chemotherapy, we should start seeing a slow gradual platelet rise.

It was hard for me to follow those instructions as I knew the chemotherapy was killing what platelets she had left, which was very few. I also understood how desperate Annie's situation was, and this event was going to be all or nothing. Dr. Moore Sr. was making his stand, and it was imperative that she got her chemotherapy on time. I was the only one allowed to give her the drug, even in the hospital. His honesty frightened me, but he taught me to be honest with Annie too. Not that graphic, but honest. He once told me, the folks that have cancer know a lot more about what's going on than we understand. It's best to tell them the truth.

Now I knew the answer to one of my questions. Why wasn't Annie in intensive care? I kept hearing the word critical, and yet she was on a ward. I was now of the understanding that if she started bleeding, the ICU couldn't help her either. It was all about the platelets. If they didn't start coming up soon, she wouldn't survive, no matter where she was.

In my mind, the reality was that Annie was living minute by minute and we needed a miracle. Of course, looking back a few days to when Beverly arrived on the scene, we had our miracle. When Beverly first walked into Annie's room, it was very spiritual, emotional, and I can't deny that. However, at that time it was very difficult for someone like me to fall on my knees and truly believe Annie was going to survive this event. I didn't fully understand or appreciate the significance of Beverly's presence in Annie's life.

Dr. Moore Sr. knew the platelets weren't going to come up until he started getting the cancer under control, and that we were in a race against time. He also gave me a total understanding of what to look for in terms of progress with Annie's illness.

From that day on, I was always at the nurses' station around 6:00 A.M. to get her laboratory results. Her blood was now being drawn at 4:00 A.M. daily. I was looking for that little consistent bump in the platelets.

At 4:08 P.M. Annie was given another unit of platelets. That same afternoon Annie's sister Lesley arrived from California. Annie needed her, as she was great company and willing to do anything for her sister. With her, she brought everything good; and the supporting role she'd play during these difficult times was very important to Annie.

Beverly was still stopping by every day and praying with Annie. Yes, I said praying with Annie. If you knew Annie the way I did, that was a small miracle in itself. A pattern was starting to flow as Annie listened intently and seemed to want to hear more. Annie knew she had a death sentence, and I think in the only way she could, she was exploring her options. Was there really something else going on out there that she needed to be aware of?

At some point, after Annie came out of her coma, Beverly got to have some quiet time with her.

Later, after her visit with Annie, Beverly told me Annie said, "I could feel my body coming back the night you were at my bedside."

I didn't know that! So I decided to speak with Annie about that night, seeking information on what it was like.

She was reluctant to talk at first, but finally opened up and told me it was very dark, she felt a deep sense of loneliness, and she was fearful. Annie had a sadness in her voice and made it obvious to me that she never wanted to go back there again. That was really all she said. But, it helped me understand why she was clinging to Beverly, as the message she was receiving from Beverly was the opposite of what she felt in the darkness.

August 19, 2008: I went to the nurses' station and got my printout of Annie's blood counts. I was excited to see that her platelets had moved to 4,000. The difference between 3,000 and 4,000 isn't significant, in that she's still critically low. The question was: Is this the little bump? At 2:01 P.M. that afternoon Annie received another unit of platelets. Her condition was still stable.

August 20, 2008: I once again took the early trip to the nurses' station to receive her printout. The platelets moved to 5,000, still very critical, with a slight upward trend. Her HGB dropped to 7, so she would have another blood transfusion today.

Early this morning Dr. Grant Rine, Annie's radiology/oncologist, stopped by to check on her, but she was sleeping at the time. He stood at the foot of her bed, and we had a chance to talk. He told me that if the platelets didn't start pulling up by the weekend, things could get very difficult for Annie. He told me that it was imperative that the bone marrow started producing more of them, and quickly.

I'd already got that message from Dr. Moore Sr., and hearing it again just made me realize even more how compromising the situation was to her. I couldn't help but wonder if the cancer would start regressing in time for the platelets in her bone marrow to start pushing out into the bloodstream. Annie was living on hope and a lot of Beverly's prayers.

Around lunch time, just after Annie received a unit of platelets, she was awake and started slurring her words. She didn't seem to know what she was talking about.

Melissa said to me quietly, "Momma is having a stroke Dad, look at the left side of her face, it's dropping down."

It was so typical of a stroke patient. Still, I thought it might just be the medications she was on, as that can often be the case. I called the nurse in and at the same time tried not to alarm Annie. The nurse came in, took one look at Annie, then immediately got in touch with Dr. Dang, the hospitalist on duty. When Dr. Dang arrived, Annie was asleep. I let Melissa talk to her about what she suspected.

She asked Dr. Dang if they would give Annie a brain scan.

Dr. Dang said "No, I suspect it was the medications she's on."

When Dr. Dang left the room, Melissa said, "I disagree with Dr. Dang. Momma has had a stroke."

If Dr. Moore Sr. had been there, he would've told us a scan would be irrelevant; even if she was having a stroke, there was nothing they could do as her platelets were too low.

Later in the afternoon Annie awoke from her sleep. Lesley and Melissa were trying to talk to her, but she didn't make any sense. Annie became very frustrated, so the nurse decided to give her some more anxiety medication, which immediately put her back to sleep. At this point, it was pretty obvious that she had a stroke.

This turned out to be a long day. At 4:03 P.M. and 7:00 P.M. Annie received more blood transfusions.

Annie was living on the edge, and I can't even imagine what she must have been thinking; or was she even aware of the seriousness of her condition? I honestly didn't know.

I was starting to get tired, and suffering from all the trauma surrounding her cancer. The days were long and the nights difficult. I tried to stay awake as long as I could and didn't get much rest. I've heard people say they had to sleep with one eye open; I understand now! If she moved or needed me, I seemed to always know. Annie couldn't wake up and press a button for a nurse, so she needed someone close by to help her.

August 21, 2008: Annie was still having problems with her speech, making it obvious she'd gone through some sort of changes yesterday. She knew what she wanted to say, but couldn't get it out properly. That wasn't a big problem, as we made a strong effort figuring out what she wanted. From this point on, Annie's speech and memory gradually returned, but were never the same.

(Annie had a brain scan about two months after the event. There was clear evidence she had a stroke. It's almost impossible to survive a stroke with the platelet count she had; but she did.)

The morning counts revealed that her platelets were still at 5,000. Her HGB was 8, which meant she would be getting another blood transfusion soon. At 3:51 P.M. she had another unit of platelets.

Dr. Moore Sr. was doing all he could to get Annie's platelets up, so he had decided to allow Lesley and Melissa to donate some of their platelets. The platelets she just received belonged to Lesley. The previous unit of platelets belonged to Melissa, and didn't work.

Another thing we had to watch carefully was her white cell count. A sign had been put on her door requiring all personnel that entered her room to wash their hands, and wear a mask, which was tightly controlled. Her white count was 2. At home, when her immunity was low, I could control germs and carriers. At the hospital, it's not that easy. The nurses have a job to do, and although they are very careful, they are around sick people all day long, providing a vehicle for transporting germs.

August 22, 2008: When I arrived at the nurses' station this morning I had a pleasant surprise. Her platelets were at 22,000, still critically low, but going in the right direction. Her white cell count was still 2, and her HGB was almost 9. For most folks that would be terrible numbers, but for Annie it was starting to look good.

As you can imagine, Lesley was riding Melissa quite hard today as her platelets seemed to have worked, and Melissa's didn't.

August 23, 2008: When I got the morning report, things were looking bad again. The platelet boost didn't hold; the count was back down to 8,000. Her white count dropped to 1.03, which again put her at high risk of infection. She was only a germ away from uncertain consequences. Her HGB was 8, so she'd be getting more blood.

Annie was starting to understand her circumstances and how bad they were. There were mornings when I'd come back to the room with my morning report, and she'd see the disappointment all over my face. I tried to hide it, but couldn't. It affected us all, further reinforcing how sad the times were.

I talk about the blood counts, but how must she have been feeling physically? Her potassium, sodium, protein, albumin, and calcium were all very low. Although low platelet and white cell counts are very dangerous, they don't make you feel ill. They're just symptoms of a much larger problem. Low HGB has a multitude of side effects, but usually can be managed through transfusions.

At 11:36 A.M. she was given another unit of transfused platelets. At 7:16 P.M., and later at 11:31 P.M., she received red blood cell transfusions. We were on a vicious cycle.

Although the day was sad, it was still a good day, and I started learning to be thankful for each day I have on this earth with her, not dwell so much on the negatives, just understand them, and help her keep climbing that mountain.

Melissa, Lesley, and I had a daily schedule. Each evening around 9:00 P.M. Melissa took Lesley to our home so she could rest. She'd be back up the next morning by 7:30 A.M., usually with Melissa. Sometimes Melissa couldn't get the time off and couldn't come up until the evening. As for me, I'd pull the recliner up near the bed facing Annie, and sleep as best as I could. It wasn't easy, but very important, as I would be aware of any problems. Her blood pressure and vitals were checked about every hour. I never left her on her own, especially at night. The nurses tried hard to get me to sleep on a portable bed they wanted to bring me, but as I did throughout our journey, I declined. I didn't want to get too comfortable; if she had a problem, I wanted to be there for her.

August 24, 2008: I had a pleasant surprise with this morning's report. Her platelets were 20,000, still critical, but we seemed to be making progress. Her white count was still too low, and her HGB was just under 11. As we were learning to live day by day, this was going to be a good one. Our moods were very elevated and just maybe, the chemotherapy was starting to work.

When Beverly arrived, she was able to share in our excitement. Beverly had been a nurse for about fifty years, of which thirty were on the cancer ward. In her mind, Annie was receiving intervention from a higher power, and she wasn't surprised at all.

August 25, 2008: Talk about depressing! When I got the morning report, we'd lost all the ground we gained from the day before. Her white count was very low at 1, and we needed masks to be around her. Her platelets were 6,000, which was critical. Her HGB dropped below 9. Those were all very significant drops for such a short period of time.

Looking back to a conversation I had with Dr. Moore Sr., I was learning to live with what he had told me. He mentioned that multiple myeloma is very difficult to control, full of highs and lows. I was getting the message loud and clear.

Around noon Annie had another unit of platelets. The rest of the day was as usual; doctors, lots of nurses, and many nurse aids. Seemed we were always busy, but Annie didn't mind as I think it calmed her knowing she was getting such good care.

I'd like to share a story as told to me by Melissa, that happened on the evening of the 24th, while Lesley and I were across the street getting a burger. It's about the little mushroom bird and cross that Beverly gave Annie.

At some point during this hospital stay, Melissa got a very tiny zip lock bag and put the bird and the little cross inside of it. She pinned the bag and contents to the wall beside Annie's hospital bed where she could see them when she was worried. The bird is significant, in that a song was written about it in the 1950s by a famous gospel singer. It goes like this; "I sing because I'm happy, I sing because I'm free, his eye is on the little ole sparrow, so I know he's watching me." Melissa said she walked over to the bed to check on her momma, whom she thought was sleeping. She noticed tears running down her face and said, "Momma, are you crying?"

Annie turned her head over to face Melissa and said, "Mel, I don't know how to pray."

Sad, but why would she know how to pray. Once the story was relayed to Beverly, she made a special trip up to the hospital and took care of Annie's spiritual need. I would like to have helped her but I wasn't sure if there was a right or wrong way to pray. Anyway, I felt the task at hand was too important to be handled by anyone other than Beverly.

August 26, 2008: The morning report didn't change much. The platelet and white blood counts remained the same. Her HGB dropped below 8 which led to another two units of blood and one unit of platelets.

Annie wanted to go home as Lesley was leaving tomorrow. I approached Dr. Moore Sr. with her request and he agreed. We hadn't gained much ground, but undoubtedly saved her life by quickly getting her in the hospital with immediate intervention. While at home, blood could be drawn from her by a home health agency, and I'd take Annie to the infusion center based on the results.

From this point on, I always knew what to do. It wasn't easy getting her in the car, but I knew I could. She could receive blood and platelets on an outpatient visit at the infusion center, and with the continued low white count she'd be around fewer germs. Sometimes the side effect of taking the patient home can be remarkable, in that, the patient starts getting better rather quickly. Even if they don't, they feel better as was the case with Annie. Remember, *there is no place like home.*

Before Annie could leave the hospital, Dr. Moore Sr. wanted a PICC line (peripherally inserted central catheter) placement. The line was inserted in a vein on the inside of her right arm just above the elbow. The line was fifty to sixty centimeters in length and runs through the vein, with the end located in a large vein near the heart. The purpose of the line is to stop the necessity of a patient from continually having IV placement. Plus, it had dual insertion points so more than one IV can be running at a time. When we left the hospital, Annie's right arm was black and blue from all the previous IV sites.

Dr. Moore Sr. knew that even though we were going to be home, she would need many more transfusions, as there wouldn't be much change in her needs for life-sustaining fluids, blood, and platelets.

The PICC line takes about thirty minutes for placement. It's done in a totally sterile environment by a specialist in that field. If germs were to get in, they'd go straight into the bloodstream. Anytime it's used for administration of fluids or anything else, it has to be handled carefully. Every seven days I had to replace the bandages around the entry point, with the date of replacement marked on the bandage in felt tip. Another of my duties was to keep a close watch on the area where the PICC line entered her arm, in case any hard little nodules formed under the skin. If that happens it's a sign of clotting and the line is removed immediately. If that happened at home, my instructions were to call Dr. Moore Sr. or the on duty oncologist for a consultation. I'd be advised on what I needed to do.

If you're curious, the procedure for putting in the PICC line is more frightening than painful. While in the hospital, the nurse puts an eight-by-twelve inch sign behind the head of the patient's bed on the wall. It reminds nurses that the arm is off limits to blood pressure checks, injections, and any medical procedure.

When I received the discharge paperwork there were instructions for me to take her to the infusion center for more platelets tomorrow.

When we got home that evening Annie was very happy and her spirits were very elevated. Lesley cooked us all dinner that evening and we had a good laugh up until it was Annie's bedtime.

August 27, 2008: This was another sad day for Annie and me as her sister Lesley had to get back home and go to work. Still, Annie was very glad to be home in her own hospital bed. Imagine that!

In case you're wondering, Dr. Moore Sr. didn't order a PICC line earlier on in her hospital stay as they carry a high risk of infection, and with white counts as low as Annie's he felt it was too dangerous. At home with my continued disinfecting about everything in sight, her risk factor was very low.

I'll admit, with Annie's threat of bleeding I was fearful of having her home at first. But I knew the drill; whether we we're home or in the hospital, if she started bleeding internally it couldn't be stopped. I knew what the outcome would be and what I'd have to do; hold her tight and love her through it. Just imagine how insecure that made Annie and me feel.

The main concern Dr. Moore Sr. had was simple. Don't let her fall or bang her head. From watching the one point bumps in the platelets, I knew Dr. Moore Sr. had an inkling that the chemotherapy might be starting to work. I knew he wasn't sure, but there was a possibility.

A normal person with low platelet counts will usually stay in bed for safety reasons. Annie wasn't about to do that, so I'd get the walker out and take her on walks in our home. From our dining room through the kitchen, then through the living room, across to the guest bathroom, and back to our dining room was eighty-one feet. That was good exercise for her and lowered the risk of pneumonia setting in. Either Melissa or I did that with her daily, when she was up to it.

At 3:51 P.M. Ann had one unit of platelets, and once again we were told to report to the infusion center in the morning for more. Also, they would do a CBC and check her blood counts.

As we continue along our journey, things slowly started calming down. That's the nature of multiple myeloma. But as you will see over time, what Annie just went through was like a walk in the park on a beautiful day.

Chapter 8

Surprise Birthday Party

As I suspected when we were discharged from the hospital, we'd be busy for awhile with Annie's blood counts. Over the next three months her platelets only climbed above the "critical low point" one time, and that was only for a couple of days. Her white count was usually low, and at times, it took extreme measures to keep her from getting infections. She had to have several blood and platelet transfusions too. In addition, she also had problems with her protein, calcium, magnesium, sodium, albumin, and more.

Dr. Moore Sr. mentioned in several of his progress notes that her aggressive multiple myeloma is causing many problems and side effects. Quite simply, Dr. Moore Sr. would see a problem and fix it with medications, which often led to other problems. That's the roller coaster effect. Fixing a problem that had to be fixed usually created several more. It was very frustrating at times, and kept pushing caregiving for Annie to a higher level of intensity.

Annie's appetite over this period of time was very poor, so Dr. Moore Sr. decided to prescribe her Megace, the only thing that seemed to work for her. The side effect of that medication was a substantial risk of blood clots, but Annie was losing ground with her weight and her weight loss had to be addressed.

From the 28th of August until December the 8th, 2008, we made over thirty trips to various different medical offices. It was a very busy time, but Annie was hanging in there. She was worn out from all the cancer treatments and the numerous transfusions of platelets and blood she had to have, but overall she did quite well.

The following is an overview of that period of time highlighting some of the events.

September 2, 2008: We went to the cancer center today to have Annie's blood drawn while fasting. The most troubling news we received today day was that her blood sugar was elevated to one hundred twenty-five. A blood sugar count over one hundred while fasting puts the patient at risk of becoming a diabetic. Anytime her blood sugar got over one hundred, Dr. Moore Sr. would recheck her medications to see which one was causing the problem. Annie had been using the drug Seroquel for quite some time as a sleeping aid. That medication can cause elevated blood sugar, so it was replaced and her levels dropped almost immediately.

Also during this visit, Dr. Moore Sr. started Annie on IV Zometa, which is a drug that has the opposite effect of multiple myeloma. It takes the calcium from your blood and puts it back into your bones. It would be given monthly at the cancer center laboratory, where she was also starting to get EPO (Epogen) injections in her tummy once weekly to help boost her red blood cell count.

September 3, 2008: Today Annie started cycle two of her chemotherapy and Decadron. Annie always looked forward to her Decadron as it made her feel good, gave her a bit more energy, and increased her appetite. The noticeable side effects that I saw were swollen feet and ankles. There is plenty more, but usually reversible when the drug is discontinued.

Now that I knew and understood Annie's treatment schedule, I looked on the internet to see how it lined up with the latest research and studies. Her regimen of drugs and chemotherapy was the new standard for treating her disease. There was a chance her life expectancy would increase by ten percent. Having already surpassed her life expectancy by a few months, I really didn't know what the ten percent meant. As far as I was concerned we were making this journey together, day by day.

September 6, 2008: Annie had a lovely weekend to look forward to. Her sister Shirley, and husband Dillard, arrived at our home this morning. Shirley's birthday was on September 5th, and as one of her birthday presents, her husband Dillard drove out here from Chesapeake Bay, Virginia. Annie had a lovely bag of English sweets waiting for her sister that we picked up from World Market. It turned out to be a very pleasant and relaxing weekend for us all. With the blood transfusions from the previous day, Annie was feeling better, and in reasonably good form. They left Monday morning to go back home, which made Annie very sad; but with our hectic schedule she'd be busy, and wouldn't have much time to think about it. I guess that was a good thing.

Shirley/Ann

September 8, 2008: Annie was seen today at Heartland Cardiology for swelling in her lower legs and shortness of breath. She saw Dr. Assem Farhat, her cardiologist of several years. He found no evidence of congestive heart failure and said the heart was functioning normally. He decided not to start diuretic therapy to remove the fluids, as she'd been struggling with dehydration.

Annie wasn't only suffering from multiple myeloma; she had severe coronary artery and vascular disease. In July 2006 Dr. Ammar, a vascular specialist, placed three stents in her aorta. Annie had two ninety percent blockages and one seventy-five percent blockage. Dr. Ammar stated after he placed the stents that Annie "was slowly checking out."

Annie also had two stents placed in her heart in October 2007. This was a problem for Dr. Moore Sr., as cancer and heart disease don't do well together. Some of the medications he had to use to fight the cancer didn't always set well with Annie's heart, but he did a wonderful balancing act, and her heart did well.

September 9, 2008: Today we went to the cancer center for lab work and to see Dr. Moore Sr. Her platelets dropped back down to 18,000, her WBC was 3, and her HGB was 11.01. Not good numbers, but better than they were. I could tell by the tone in his voice that Dr. Moore Sr. was a little optimistic that the tide was turning. However, until he did her next bone marrow aspiration in November, his optimism was guarded.

I'd been watching the numbers since day one and felt the same way as the doctor. I was learning to identify the difference between low platelets from the cancer versus the chemotherapy. Chemotherapy only stays in the body a couple of days or less. Of course Annie was taking chemotherapy 21 days on and seven days off; but during the down time from her last chemotherapy cycle, I noticed a small jump in her platelets, which led me to believe the chemotherapy was partly responsible for the loss of platelets and that her bone marrow was starting to produce life sustaining blood cells. If true, we were on the verge of something very special. The possibility left Annie and me with anxious anticipation, and a new sense of hope we hadn't had since the prognosis.

After we left the clinic I wheeled Annie to the elevator. We were waiting outside the elevator when I started smiling. She asked me what I was smiling about, and I told her from following all the progress notes and lab reports I felt she was definitely making progress with the cancer. She started smiling too, and at the same time the elevator doors were coming open. We immediately saw these two very tall and well dressed gentlemen, one standing on each side of the elevator door. As I pushed Annie in, and turned the wheelchair around so she would be facing outward, I said to her in a rather laughing voice, "Don't worry Annie, I got your purse."

Those two gentlemen started laughing and laughed all the way to the ground floor. As I pushed her out of the elevator one of the gentlemen said, "Thank you, I needed that." Annie was cracking up too.

Trying to navigate our way through the tangled web of cancer wasn't easy, and when we had an opportunity to have a good laugh, we embraced it.

September 20, 2008: This was going to be a special night. The Leukemia and Lymphoma Society sponsors a special event each year called Light the Night Walk. It's a group walk in honor of blood cancer survivors, patients in treatment, supporters, and for those who lost loved ones to a blood cancer.

It was very important for Annie to attend this event for many reasons, but knowing Annie the way I did, and seeing how supportive she was of others, I believe she simply wanted to show her support.

When Annie and I arrived, a group of Melissa's friends had made a large banner in Annie's honor which simply said "Annie's Angels." I took several pictures of her that night and of her new "Angels" holding the banner behind her, while she was seated comfortably in her wheelchair.

There were many different scheduled events, as well as the two mile walk. The news media was there, along with some guest speakers. There were colored balloons given out for the three different categories of the illness. The gold balloons represent the deceased, red were for supporters, and white were for the survivors. We tied Annie's white balloon to her wheelchair for the walk.

Not long after we started the walk, we encountered a flight of stairs that went up to a large bridge, which became a barrier for Annie and me. However, it was only temporary as two guys came over, grabbed the wheelchair, and carried her all the way up the grassy knoll, so our walk continued as if there never was a barrier.

As the night ended, Annie was very thankful that she got to meet such a wonderful group of people. She called them her family. When you have cancer, it doesn't take long to realize that you have just become a member of a much larger family. By the way, it's a family of compassion and love, and I can't help but think that if we could see the world through their eyes, without the disease, the world would be a much better place. That would be my wish.

This picture was taken before the walk started. Annie is sitting in her wheelchair with little Mykel, who was struggling with Myelodysplastic Syndrome, pre-leukemia. Annie and I were friends with Mykel's family. She was such a precious innocent child, but sadly, one year later she lost her battle due to complications of the disease. She was four and one-half years old.

Little Mykel and Annie

September 26, 2008: Today Annie was assigned a new home health agency. They would send out a nurse twice weekly to take Annie's vital signs and do a general well-being check. The nurse only stayed about an hour each visit; but that one-hour break for me twice a week was a blessing, as it gave me time to catch up on some of my chores without any interruption.

Physical and occupational therapy came over a couple of times a week for an hour as well. However, they couldn't do much as she wasn't very mobile and her bones were still very brittle.

They were with us for a couple of months and did what they could. Annie always enjoyed their company, and looked forward to their visits. They worked off her schedule as best they could.

Realistically, I was the only one that could meet Annie's needs. I knew what they were most of the time before she said anything. It was very difficult for me to keep up at times, but when I needed that additional boost, I simply did a reality check and did what I had to do.

Honestly, with her low platelets and white blood cell count, how did she survive? Many doctors and nurses asked that question. It was becoming apparent to many that something else was going on with Annie. It seemed to be more than a coincidence.

October 2, 2008: This was one of those days Annie always looked forward to. She was going to the cancer center to see Dr. Moore Sr. During our visit it was obvious he was feeling more optimistic than when he last saw her, so he decided to do a twenty-four-hour urine study today. Basically, what he would be looking for was the total protein and monoclonal peak, which is myeloma protein. They are measured in milligrams per total volume of urine over a twenty-four-hour period. The study of her urine would be matched with the study conducted on June 25th, 2008. Dr. Moore Sr. would get a good idea on the status of her cancer. Of course, the only real way to know was through a bone marrow aspiration.

Annie also received her IV Zometa today and I was advised by Dr. Moore Sr. to go ahead and start cycle three of her chemotherapy and Decadron. The dosages for both drugs remained the same.

Looking over Dr. Moore Sr.'s progress notes from this day, he noted that Annie is suffering from severe abdominal pain, most likely caused by the chemotherapy and Decadron. She was put on AcipHex, one tablet per day, to try and calm her stomach.

He also noted that he upped her MS Contin to 60 milligrams every twelve hours. What he did by increasing the MS Contin, which was extended release morphine over twelve hours, was allow me to cut back on the 15 milligram immediate release morphine tablets. So essentially, we had an increase of one medication, with the cause and effect of decreasing another. She still used the 25 milligram Fentanyl patch and the occasional Percocet. This was all in response to an MRI of her spine three days earlier. The MRI noted myeloma in the bone, but no destructive lesions. Pain control was still very important to her, and was in the forefront of her care.

October 4th, 2008: Later today we received the results of the twenty-four-hour urine study. The comparison rates from the two different types of proteins are from this date and June 25th, 2008, when she was first diagnosed. Total protein today was 318 milligrams, down from 12,976 milligrams. It was now within normal range. The monoclonal peak, which is the myeloma protein, was now 99 milligrams, down from 11,297 milligrams.

That was wonderful news, and was a clear indication that Annie had at least a partial remission. As the test conducted on the urine is very sensitive, it was noted in the laboratory report that there were still free kappa light chains detected. The light chains are the monoclonal peak I spoke of. This type of protein comes from the malignant plasma cells. On June 25th, 2008, the percentage of the protein as measured in the twenty-four-hour urine was 91 percent. The percentage today was 31 percent, which indicated a partial remission. Dr. Moore Sr. needed to get the percentage down to "0."

This was good news, however, I knew Dr. Moore Sr. would not let his guard down as multiple myeloma by nature was so unpredictable, hard to control, and if given the chance could come back with a vengeance. I also knew Dr. Moore Sr. was optimistic, but would never take anything for granted, and continue to keep a close watchful eye on Annie, while continuing with her aggressive treatment.

For many reasons, the past few months have been very tough on Annie, but while being a healthy woman, one of her favorite past times was shopping. When we were coming home from many appointments, she'd look at the department stores and say to me, "I wish I could go shopping." She hadn't been shopping since her diagnosis. Of course, she wasn't well enough and couldn't go. Now that we had a home health agency assigned to her, she was not allowed to leave the house except for medical appointments. Reason being, if you're well enough to shop, you don't need home health care. She'll get her chance in May 2009, a day that is sure to make you smile.

It was nice to see Annie moving toward remission, however, as her disease was symptomatic multiple myeloma, we never stopped fighting the symptoms. If it wasn't one thing it was always something else.

She still had Beverly coming over on a regular basis reading scripture to her. One evening, I was in the kitchen and heard Beverly having an intense conversation with Annie. I don't know a lot about the Bible, but after what I witnessed over the past few months, I was listening to the conversation while doing my chores. I was finding the conversation very confusing, as it seemed as if Beverly felt she had very little time due to Annie's condition, and was trying to get as much information to Annie as quickly as possible.

A while before Annie got sick I spent some time in California with my brother Tim, who was a senior pastor. During one of his sermons he asked the congregation if they knew what the word "kiss" meant. He made a couple funny jokes then got serious. He basically said, when you are talking about the Bible or religion in general, it can be very difficult for some folks to understand. So kiss meant, "Keep it simple silly."

I walked into the room, tapped Beverly on her shoulder, and said, "Kiss." She looked up at me with very curious eyes, and I simply said, "Keep it simple silly."

She smiled and looked back at Annie and said, "Ann, have you understood anything I've been saying?"

Annie replied, "Not much."

Beverly laughed and thanked me, and from that day on she slowly started breaking down the subject matter into small segments so Annie could understand the true meaning of the word. It worked well for them both, and I was learning a few things too. Annie highlighted verses in the Bible that she liked to read when she was alone. Almost every night Beverly called our home and said a prayer over the phone with Annie. Some nights Annie would fall asleep and miss the call. She'd say, "Oh, darn it. I missed Beverly's call last night."

I'd look at her with a smile and say, "You didn't miss it, you just don't remember it." I always held the phone to Annie's ear so even if she was asleep, she got her prayer. It was kind of strange really, witnessing Annie starting her spiritual journey, transforming from an atheist, and saying words that were so *not* Annie. I didn't mind, as it had a very calming effect on her, which helps one fight cancer.

There were nights when she was very restless and couldn't get to sleep, even on all the narcotics. I'd ask her if she wanted me to read to her from the Bible.

Her reply would always be, "Yes please."

It was awkward for both of us as I didn't know where to start, and she couldn't help me. I'd never read the Bible before and neither had Annie.

On one particular night I stumbled across the Book of Job. Immediately, I knew that was a good place to start. On a few occasions while in the hospital with Annie, I would be asked to leave the room as the nurse was going to perform a sterile procedure. I'd go to the hospital day room, and pick up literature on people suffering from cancer; I was looking for understanding. I found a few pamphlets discussing suffering and referencing the Book of Job in the Bible. Even though her suffering was on a whole different level from Job, it wasn't long after I started reading that I saw a parallel forming between the two. Job took a real beating, but his love for his creator never wavered. As I read her the story of Job, I couldn't help but wonder, would Annie be that strong, or would she get disillusioned and reverse her journey? Obviously I didn't have the answer to that question, knowing only that time would tell.

The Book of Job is a very good read for believers and non-believers; and I believe that's why there was so much literature on Job in the hospital day room. There is so much suffering in the world today, and on many levels it makes sense of what at times appears to be an insane world. The Book of Job is not about cancer, it's about faith and our ability to overcome suffering through faith.

At this point in Annie's journey, I was becoming a very angry man and searching for answers as to why a lady that was so kind to others, with a very healthy lifestyle, seemingly doing everything right, could be brought down in such a cruel way. It was starting to appear that Annie and I were both looking for answers outside the realm of science. Was it logical? At the time I didn't know, but I believed what was happening to us was probably being replicated all over the world. When you love deeply, you desperately seek answers, and your mind opens to different forms of logic.

October 27, 2008: Today Annie had her PICC line removed as it appeared the need for blood transfusions was now minimal, and the risk of infection from keeping the PICC line in her arm was high. Annie knew that getting the line out was a good sign, and it made her smile when she heard it was coming out. She also started cycle four of her chemotherapy and Decadron.

October 28, 2008: Today my sister Marcy arrived from California to spend a week with Annie and me. Marcy was a real blessing, and basically took over day to day care of Annie, to include fixing all the meals and keeping her occupied. I was able to do some much needed maintenance to our home and work in the yard. It was a good week, and Annie really enjoyed her company.

Marcy was a singer of songs, many of them being gospel. She would set on the couch and on many occasions sang Annie to sleep with songs like Amazing Grace. She was also a Christian, and much more able to help Annie than I. My mind was always full, trying to solve the problems of our chaotic lives. While she was here, I got a much needed break, and I think seeing an old familiar face of love was very good for Annie. When Marcy left, with the break from my daily caregiver duties, I was well rested and had a renewed sense of strength.

November 24, 2008: Today was one of those days that Annie hated. She was going to have a bone marrow aspiration. In Dr. Moore Sr.'s progress notes on this date, he wrote; "Ms. Harrison is here today for follow-up and management of her aggressive myeloma. She is here also to start cycle five of Revlimid and Decadron." He noted that "Her counts are still down, and we are trying to get out to a possible autologous stem-cell transplant," which means they would be using her own stem-cells. He further stated, "After today's bone marrow aspiration, we will know exactly where we are with the cancer."

This was not going to be a routine appointment in Annie's fragile condition with all the diseased bones. Knowing Annie would need Beverly by her side, I'd called her a few days earlier and made arrangements for her to meet us at the cancer center. During the aspiration process Beverly held her hand and said a continual whispered prayer, while I had my arm around her shoulder area and hugged her. Annie received great comfort having Beverly around when times were traumatic for her. Beverly was a special gift to Annie and this family.

December 6, 2008: Annie was still experiencing shortness of breath and generally feeling unwell, so I took her over to Family Medicine East to see Dr. Klein. After he checked her over, he ordered a chest X-ray which revealed a small infiltrate, which was pneumonia, in her lower left lung. Dr. Klein tried to get her to go to the hospital, but as the pneumonia was slight, she wanted to take the antibiotics over the weekend, with the promise that if her condition worsens, she'd let me take her to the hospital. Annie could be very stubborn at times, but she knew if she went in she'd be there for a while, she was so weary of hospital stays.

When a patient has multiple myeloma and develops pneumonia, it can be a medical emergency. She didn't want to go, and my power of attorney didn't allow me to make decisions for her when she was clearly aware of her circumstances. When one has a low white count, and very little immunity to germs, sometimes it's better to play the odds as germs are everywhere in a hospital. So I agreed with her decision not to be hospitalized, with the hope that the antibiotics would work.

December 8, 2008: Beverly came over at 7:30 A.M. to take care of Annie while I went to an appointment. About an hour after I left, I got a call from Beverly telling me she was taking Annie to the emergency room. Her breathing had become labored, and Beverly got the sense she needed some help. I was not surprised and told her to get going while I got in touch with Melissa to get her pre-admitted, which would avoid the long wait in the emergency room. I always networked Annie into the hospital when needed. If Beverly, with all her experience with cancer patients said she needed to be in the hospital, I didn't question her.

I arrived at the admissions desk about fifteen minutes after they got there and took care of Annie's admission needs. Annie didn't have to do anything other than sit back in her wheelchair and let me take care of the admission. About an hour later she was admitted and placed on the cancer ward, Wesley Medical Center.

The admitting physician or hospitalist doctor was Dr. Natvig. Annie was admitted with new onset of congestive heart failure, fluid retention, anemia, possible pneumonia, high blood pressure, chronic pain, and confusion. The doctor further stated that Annie was suffering from shortness of breath, even when resting, and was getting anxious, as she felt she could not get any air in. She noted, "The antibiotics are not helping." Dr. Natvig changed her antibiotics to an IV antibiotic, Rocephin.

Annie's cardiologist, Dr. Assem Farhat was consulted and came over to evaluate her. His diagnosis was congestive heart failure, secondary to volume fluid overload versus her chemotherapy, versus nephrotic syndrome. This syndrome involves the kidneys, and can cause swelling, high blood pressure, excess excretion of protein in the urine, and weight gain from fluid retention. An underlying disease such as diabetes and lupus can cause nephrotic syndrome in the kidneys. His recommendation was to start her on a diuretic to force diuresis. In other words, remove her fluid volume overload. I knew that fluid overload could cause congestive heart failure, and it was a side effect of her chemotherapy as we'd been here before.

Dr. Natvig ordered a blood chemistry, CBC, and a twenty-four-hour urine check. The urine, once again, was to check for protein; this time emitted by nephrotic syndrome.

Her blood chemistry and CBC were like they always were. WBC was 3, HGB was 9, and platelets were 23,000. Annie's blood chemistry demonstrated low protein, calcium, albumin, and magnesium. It was noted, "She was given IV magnesium to boost her count."

December 9, 2008: Annie was starting to feel better today. The diuretic had accomplished what it was supposed to do, her fluid retention had dissipated, and she was now breathing much easier. In addition, she was receiving respiratory treatments, which are essentially breathing treatments with medication several times a day. Her breathing was now starting to stabilize.

Later this evening her protein report came back and it was 405, well above normal. That was apparently due to the nephrotic syndrome and was being treated.

December 10, 2008: Annie was feeling much better today, so I got in touch with Melissa and Beverly, asking them to throw a surprise birthday party for Annie at the hospital. Beverly got busy and took care of all the red tape and the planning started. The party would be on December 12th, Friday evening, her actual birthday. That would be the first surprise birthday party I'd ever thrown for Annie, and I was going to make sure it was a special night for her.

December 11, 2008: Dr. Moore Sr. paid us a surprise visit today, and when he walked into Annie's room he was bubbling with excitement as he gave Annie some great news; her greatest birthday gift of all. He was stopping all chemotherapy as her bone marrow was compatible to remission status. She was so happy! We both had a good cry that evening, as Annie was surviving against terrible odds, and the thought of her getting a remission earlier on in the disease, when she first started treatment, was just a pipe dream. She gave Dr. Moore Sr. a heartfelt thank you, and as he left the room he didn't look back, just simply put his hand behind his back waving goodbye to her. He felt the emotion too.

With her compassionate kind ways, Annie was the type of patient that grew on the doctors and other medical professionals. It didn't matter if a medical professional was giving her ten pills, or sticking her with a three inch needle, she always knew they were trying to help her, and her response in a very soft, quiet voice, was always the same, "Thank you."

Later on that evening around 8:00 P.M. Annie and I were laying on her hospital bed, both very tired and overwhelmed from today's good news. Out of the corner of my eye, I saw this man come in the room wearing a track suit. He came over and introduced himself as Dr. Moore Jr., Dr. Moore Sr.'s son. We were very excited to see him and knew why he was there. Dr. Moore Jr. was going to start an intense evaluation on Annie to see if she qualified for a stem-cell transplant. He told us he was going to be her stem-cell transplant oncologist. He asked a few questions, told her he'd see her soon, and left.

After he departed the room, we were both kind of giddy with excitement. So far the road had been long, but one obstacle at a time was being knocked down. We were both very humble and thankful that if all went well she'd get the transplant she so desperately needed.

Annie was pleased knowing that Dr. Moore Jr. would be doing her stem-cells. However, he would have big shoes to fill, following in the footsteps of his father. Overtime that became a subject of much conversation and some good memories.

Annie needed the transplant and I believe that Dr. Moore Sr.'s goal all along was to keep her alive as best he could and get her in some sort of remission so she could have the transplant. You can be in a partial remission and still get the transplant, but as a rule of thumb, the stronger the remission, the better the response.

December 12, 2008: When Annie woke up this morning I was awake, sitting beside her bed in my recliner. I gave her a loving hug and wished her a happy birthday, on a day that was full of anticipation and excitement for me.

Before she woke up, I had been watching her sleep. I felt so fortunate to still have her on her birthday, which a few months earlier would have been difficult to imagine. Beyond a doubt, I knew now that every moment I had with Annie was a gift to me, one that just kept on giving.

Annie wasn't feeling very well today, which wasn't unusual. She looked anemic, and was feeling a bit breathless and tired, which I always associated with potential low HGB. The morning's CBC was showing an HGB of 8.03. It was not quite low enough to be transfused, so she was going to be tired today, and a bit breathless, but there was nothing I could do. The party must go on!

I sat with her, told her the status of her blood count, and for her not to worry as her counts would drop more tonight leading to a blood transfusion tomorrow, which would make her feel better. It was obvious there was a bit of confusion going on in Annie's head, as the evening before she was celebrating a remission and the next day she's looking at another blood transfusion. I'd already discovered the complexities of being a caregiver for a cancer patient, full of highs and lows. She was just looking for reassurance, and I gave her what she needed.

The thing about Annie was that she loved a good party and mingling with the crowd. Once the excitement started, I was sure she would rise to the occasion and her worries would filter to the back of her mind.

It was around 3:00 P.M. when I went out to the car and retrieved the new candy apple red walker I'd had Melissa pick up for me to give Annie as a present. It had a seat that opened up to reveal a little pouch that would hold her goodies. When I took it inside and showed her, she was so excited and really loved it. I sat beside her bed and put it together, knowing she would be using it tonight. It was a bit more complicated than I had thought as I had to install the brakes too. But, in typical womanly fashion, I could hear her words ringing in my ears, "Why don't you men use instructions?" So I picked up the instructions, and sure enough, it took about five minutes to put it together.

We had a surprise today too. Our daughter Victoria and her husband Gene drove here from Colorado for the party. It was going to be a good night.

Around 6:00 P.M. I told Annie they were getting ready to turn the Christmas tree lights on in the lobby, so we needed to go there and participate in the event. She got so excited—her first walk with her new walker and the magic of a Christmas tree lighting. She had no idea what was waiting for her.

Beverly had a very decorative ten foot wide table sitting in the lobby, surrounded by comfortable chairs. The table was filled with refreshments, cakes, and a sundry of goodies. There was a spot reserved for the birthday girl at the center of the table.

Vicky, Melissa, and Beverly came to the door and told me the staff was getting ready to light the tree. I got Annie out of her bed and helped her stand with her new walker. As we slowly left the room, I walked in front of her, moving backwards, in case she started rolling too fast. We were going to go west down the hallway about ten yards, making a left turn, to enter the south hallway where the Christmas Tree would come into view. As we moved slowly toward the tree, and started seeing the people close-up, she started recognizing some of the people but didn't catch on. Finally, people started yelling out "Happy Birthday" to her and singing "Happy Birthday to You." It was truly a beautiful, precious moment, and Annie lost it emotionally, while sobbing vocally. I grabbed her, put my arms around her, and just held her. What a moment! Annie felt so honored. There was probably twenty people there, which was good due to the short notice. Everyone was giving her hugs and kisses; and it was simply *beautiful*. I guided her to the birthday girl spot, which was a few feet across from the tree. She sat there, visited with everyone, eventually opened some presents, and played with the grandkids. "It's a night I shall never forget." Many good memories were made that night for many people. It was truly a "Hallmark" moment.

Birthday Party

December 13, 2008: Her blood was drawn at 4:35 A.M. When I received the results, I was a little shocked. Her WBC was low, and her HGB was 7, much lower than I expected. Her platelets had improved to 34,000, which was an indication of her remission status. She received two units of blood that morning and eventually had a good day. Annie's low HGB was most likely due to the chemotherapy she'd been taking, and along with the cancer can damage the bone marrow, making the production of new blood cells a slow process.

December 14, 2008: Today was a good day as we were told we could go home. Annie and I loved going home to all our comforts and familiar surroundings.

Dr. Netvig stated, "She is doing quite well and is stable enough to go home."

It always took me an hour or so to get the car packed, as when Annie was in the hospital, we sort of moved in. We tried to keep her in her own colorful nightdresses as much as possible. We had her colorful bedding, pillows, and even some Christmas decorations.

When you walked into her room for the first time, you knew it was someone special. Actually, she was no more special than anyone else, but to her loved ones she was everything. We always tried to make her feel special and the doctors and nurses always enjoyed entering her room. They all knew, and never questioned our unwavering dedication to Annie, to include how we always tried to keep the room atmosphere in an upbeat mode through spontaneous laughter. If we could find something to laugh about while living in the sick world of cancer, regardless of how Annie was feeling, we didn't hold back. Sometimes it seemed as though she was totally unconscious, then I or Melissa would make someone laugh and you could see her lips crack a gentle smile. Annie could have laid there and died, of that I am sure. But she chose life, and with life there is always a little laughter, even during the worst of times, lingering in the shadows. *You just have to find it and pull it to the forefront.*

The hospital was my second home too. I took my showers and did all our laundry at the hospital. The laundry room was not far from Annie's room on the ward. It wasn't easy being there twenty-four hours a day as Annie slept a lot. The majority of my time was spent sitting in my hospital recliner just watching her. I didn't turn the TV on as it was too distracting. Wesley Medical Center was good to me, and if I wanted, they'd bring a tray of food up for me when Annie was receiving her meal. I didn't take advantage of them, as breakfast, lunch, and dinner was served downstairs at the cafeteria. I'd usually get my food there, bring it up to Annie's room and eat while watching her. I'd often bring up some calorie-filled snack for her as well. She never acquired a taste for hospital food, but when I shared hers, I found it quite good.

Chapter 9

Stem-Cell Transplant

Decomber 25, 2008: This was probably the most beautiful and special Christmas Annie and I ever observed. Annie was not supposed to make it this far. Looking back over the past six months, how did she? When I write, I don't have the words to describe just how ill she was. Yes, she received her remission. So things are good, right? Not really. She will always be basically confined to a wheelchair, in a hospital bed, and on lots of pain medications. I used to say to her, "Annie, I am so thankful I still have you to love and care for. I just wish your remission was like all the other folks we know." They are able to get in their cars, drive to town, live their lives, and able to get out and enjoy themselves in the process. Annie couldn't do that and knew the difference too. I wanted so much for her to get her self-confidence and independence back. However, greed is a bad thing, and I knew Annie received a reprieve from her imminent death sentence, and we knew we should be thankful. We were! Yes, there was the occasional moment, but no pity parties.

What made this Christmas so special was Annie. It was around this timeframe in her illness that I started noticing subtle changes in her, where her mannerisms at times were like that of a child. She didn't want a big Christmas tree, she wanted to put up a small four-foot white Christmas tree we had stored in the basement that she purchased from a garage sale. So I retrieved the tree from the basement, put a Christmas tree skirt over an antique spool cabinet in front of our west facing window, then sat the tree on it. You probably know what I mean when I ask the question, "Have you ever seen a Christmas tree decorated by a young child?" Well, we have one. We had four plastic containers of Christmas ornaments, garland, and a sundry of other things for decorating, and I think she tried to put most of it on that little tree. How about this? The Christmas balls with those little wire hooks on them—we had them hanging all over the living room, even off of the cloth furniture. She thought the tree and our home looked so beautiful. The young grandchildren would come in and say, "Nanny, what were you thinking about?" She'd just let loose with one of her rapid belly laughs, which in turn made us all laugh. We all loved it, and left things pretty much as they were, with the exception of some of the ornaments on our cloth furniture. It truly looked like a magical scene out of a child's dream. It was a wonderful Christmas, filled with joy and so much love.

After Christmas Day was over, we decided to leave the tree up for an extended period of time, as a reminder that there truly is a "Reason for the Season."

Christmas Tree

Just after Christmas, Annie had a general blood chemistry analysis. Out of twenty-nine items checked, she was low in eleven. Her platelets, white count, and HGB were all low. So as you can see, although she was in remission, she was still battling some of the same old adversaries.

December 29, 2008: We saw Dr. Moore Sr. today, and was told we had an appointment to see Dr. Moore Jr. on December 31st. Apparently it was time to start moving forward with all the testing to see if she was a good candidate for a stem-cell transplant. He also noted he would be sending her to see Dr. Farhat, her cardiologist, about the fluid buildup in her legs, and saving the best news for last he noted that her last bone marrow aspiration was negative for cancer! That was great news as we knew Annie was in remission, but had no idea that the bone marrow was clear of cancer.

December 30, 2008: Annie went to see Dr. Farhat today to check on the fluid buildup in her legs. After examination, his impression was that the fluid buildup was due to congestive heart failure. This wasn't a serious event, but needed to be watched carefully. He started Annie on Bumex, which is a diuretic, to remove some of the pressure off her heart by removing the excess fluid. She was also started on potassium tablets for a deficiency that had been troubling her for quite a while. We were to call him back next week so he could check on her response to the new therapy.

December 31, 2008: We went over to see Dr. Moore Jr. today to visit with him about the possibility of getting an autologous peripheral blood stem-cell transplant. That essentially means that they will be harvesting her stem-cells from the bloodstream, rather than the bone marrow. Until recently, the procedure Annie was having was called a bone marrow transplant. The stem-cells were taken from the bone marrow by multiple aspirations of the hip bone with the patient under general anesthetic in the operating room. However, through studies and research, the scientists found that peripheral stem-cells were easier to collect and usually produced a more rapid recovery of white blood cells and platelets. Dr. Moore Jr. discussed the risks versus the benefits to the procedure. Due to the high-dose chemotherapy

Annie will receive, the blood counts will drop down to the critical low area in just a few days. It can be very dangerous, but 97 percent of all patients survive, and can significantly increase their chances of survival for a longer period of time; meaning they will have a longer remission period. At the time of Annie's illness, the gold standard was two stem-cell transplants, several months apart. Although Annie was technically showing no signs of cancer in her bone marrow, she could only have one transplant due to her chronically ill health.

He noted in his progress notes, "She appears chronically ill and was recently hospitalized because of pneumonia. She is currently fighting a new pneumonia with antibiotics." He further noted, "I contacted Dr. Farhat and received cardiac clearance to proceed with Annie's stem-cell transplant." Dr. Moore Jr. would do a bone marrow aspiration today to get a current status on her bone marrow.

January 5, 2009: Dr. Moore Jr. requested a CBC today to check the status of her blood counts. Her white count was 7, which was very good. Her platelets were 63,000, low, but not critical. Her HGB was 11; low. He noted that "She was slowly recovering from her recently diagnosed pneumonia."

January 9, 2009: Annie got some bad news today. No, the cancer wasn't back, but the bone marrow aspiration she had December 31st was non-diagnostic. She will have a repeat bone marrow aspiration today. Some folks don't have much pain with the aspiration, but in Annie's case, Dr. Moore Jr. noted in his December 31st progress notes that when Annie was diagnosed back in June 2008, she had a very heavy tumor burden in her bones and a lot of bone destruction. When a bone marrow aspiration is done, a sharp object is pushed through the skin to the bone and from that point on it takes a lot of pressure to break through the bone to the marrow. That's why the procedure was so painful for Annie. Her damaged hips were a mess, and putting a lot of pressure on them was very painful.

I've got to say this, because it is true. Dr. Moore Sr. was Annie's favorite oncologist, beyond a doubt. But she now had a comparison, between father and son, on bone marrow aspirations. She told me she preferred the way Dr. Moore Jr. did the procedure. I thought that was cute, and it made me laugh. I was not allowed to comment on that back then, but I can now!

January 15, 2009: We went back and saw Dr. Moore Jr. for the results of Annie's bone marrow aspiration, and a family conference. He noted that her bone marrow was compatible with remission status, and that her pneumonia had completely cleared. The family conference was about the things I spoke of earlier on December 31st, 2008. The main reason he wanted the family there was to make sure we had a good support system in place for Annie and me. A stem-cell transplant would put pressure on me as Annie's caregiver in a way I could never have imagined. There was a possibility I might need backup, and he wanted to know who that was going to be.

When Annie had her transplant, it would be done on an outpatient basis, which is how it's done these days. If the patient lived too far from the hospital, they were encouraged to find a place closer. The only way I can say this is, "It's like an emergency waiting to happen." The odds are that about eighty percent of the patients will be hospitalized with some sort of emergency after the transplant. Getting to the hospital quickly is important. Also, after the transplant for the first thirty days or so, you are required to go to the treatment center for a CBC seven days a week. We also got to meet the transplant team today; they were wonderful, compassionate medical professionals.

January 19, 2009: Annie was once again admitted to the hospital for vomiting, dehydration, and persistent nausea, most likely due to the narcotics as well as underlying stage three multiple myeloma. She was given various laxatives and was placed on IV fluids, with a Doppler study of her heart being ordered. It was also noted on admission, "The patient is thin, cachectic, and appears ill." *Cachectic* means "A profound state of constitutional disorder, general ill health, and malnutrition."

Looking back, this is once again my point about Annie's remission. It didn't matter how hard she fought or how hard I worked and cared for her; the cancer had already left its mark on her.

January 20, 2009: From today, and on January 21st through 23rd her platelets fell back down to critically low. Her red and white cells were low as well. Apparently, her bone marrow had somewhat backed off on producing platelets, white and red blood cells. At times, I would get so frustrated with the numbers that I just wanted to scream. Annie and I were doing everything right, but it didn't seem to matter.

The doctor also ordered a scan of her lower extremities today and found blood clots in both her legs and hips. With Annie, if it was not one thing, it was the other. Blood clots are very dangerous and if one broke away, it could hit the heart with catastrophic results in a very short time. Dr. Moore Jr. came over to see Annie today, and placed her on Heparin, and later changed her to Coumadin. Those were blood thinners and being used to try dispersing the clots.

Earlier on in the story, I spoke of the only drug Dr. Moore Sr. had prescribed that helped Annie's appetite was Megace. I spoke about the side effects of that medication as having the potential for blood clots. Today, the Megace was stopped.

Not long after the Megace was discontinued Annie started having appetite problems again, and was prescribed the medication Marinol. My understanding is that it has some of the same ingredients as marijuana. It worked well; her appetite picked up sharply as she always had the munchies. After a couple of months on the medication, I was informed by the pharmacy that Annie was being switched to the generic form, called Dronabinol. Within a week or so, she started losing her appetite. I spoke to Melissa, who in turn spoke to Dr. Klein, Annie's family doctor. He sent the drug company a letter trying to get her changed back to Marinol. The company said the drugs are basically the same and have the same effects. I did some research and took my results over to our local pharmacy for analysis. There was one key ingredient missing, which made the generic drug much cheaper, and was the key to her low appetite. I wrote to the drug distribution company, telling them what I discovered, but it didn't matter. They were going to follow company policy and keep pushing the generic medications as they were more profitable. However, it made me very curious; Annie could get the best medical care and the best chemotherapy available, and was never denied anything. All of a sudden, I'm having problems getting a bottle of pills.

January 21, 2009: Annie was starting to feel better as the doctors were starting to gain control back over her many deficiencies. Dr. Farhat had a Doppler study of her heart conducted today. It turned out to be a normal study and appeared her heart was still doing okay.

January 23, 2009: Annie was making progress and improving every day. They were still watching her blood clots, and were going to let her go home when they felt she was safe.

January 24, 2009: Annie was doing much better and we were told she could go home today. She would be on the blood thinner Coumadin, and hopefully wouldn't get any more clots. Coumadin is a good medication, but requires many blood checks. Your blood has to be watched closely, as the doctor can't afford to let the blood get too thin or too thick. They monitored her blood through what is called an INR test of the blood. The INR basically gives the doctors a high and low number. His job is to keep adjusting the medication so the blood count stays near the center of the high and low numbers. It's tricky, and can be difficult to do. I was given a booklet on Coumadin so I would know what foods to feed her and what to stay away from. Her diet became extremely important. For example, you can't eat cranberries while on Coumadin as they make your blood thinner, and aspirin is out of the question. We had some problems at times, but managed okay.

Going home was always a good day and this day was no different. Annie was feeling reasonably well, as defined by the history of her illness. Her biggest problem was spinal pain from the damage to her spinal cord and nervous system. But there was nothing they could do other than keep administering the pain medications; surgery was not an option.

As far as her narcotics went, I never overmedicated her. I was always fearful of her being sedated and not able to move around. Pneumonia loves a person like that. Obviously, there were times when she was out of it for a couple of days or more due to the narcotics, which was beyond my control when she was experiencing severe pain. At times like now, when she was feeling reasonably well, I'd cut back on the pain medications just a bit. Yes, she was in a little more pain, but sometimes going an extra couple of hours, keeping her mind busy, gave her that little edge and kept her from being sedated. I loved her, and paid close attention to her needs versus her wants.

January 27, 2009: Today, I received a phone call from Veronica Hart, RN, TriWest case management services. She introduced herself and told me she was replacing Carol as Annie's case manager. Veronica was a stem-cell transplant case manager, and we would be needing her soon. She would make sure Annie received everything she needed. Annie was really blessed with good health care, and it always lifted her spirits knowing folks were looking after her needs.

February 9, 2009: A CBC was conducted at the cancer center today, and we received some good news. Her WBC and HGB were both within the normal range which was a milestone, and the first time her HGB had been normal since her diagnosis. Her platelets were 77,000, still low, but the highest they'd been since July 2008. When considering that this is an incurable blood cancer, what a blessing for Annie and me. You would have loved to have been in our home with us, as many times we'd look at each other and either smile or laugh. Her bone marrow was actually working.

February 12, 2009: Today, we met with Dr. Moore Jr. again. He also had a second family meeting that lasted fifteen minutes. Once again, he went over the risks, benefits, and common side effects associated with high-dose chemotherapy and autologous peripheral blood stem-cell rescue, as well as the rational for doing so. He also noted his discussion included, but was not limited to, morbidity or mortality from the drugs themselves, the transplant procedure, failure of engraftment, dependence on transfusion of blood products, serious infection, or death from infection or organ toxicity.

For those of you that don't know, *engraftment* is the return of the stem-cells to the bloodstream from the bone marrow, after the high-dose chemotherapy and stem-cell transplant. When Annie received her high-dose chemotherapy, I called that, "The walk of death." The idea behind the high-dose chemotherapy is to kill all the cancerous cells in the body and bone marrow. However, it doesn't have the ability to recognize normal healthy cells, so it kills them too. Essentially Dr. Moore Jr. was going to take Annie to death's door, and then bring her back slowly and hopefully with a population of noncancerous cells. Dr. Moore Jr. was a lot like his father, in that he'd tell you things that you might need to know, but rather not hear. We all know the old saying, "The truth will set you free." It will, but might scare the heck out of you in the process.

He further noted, "We discussed the stem-cell harvesting dates." I'll speak about harvesting as we get closer to the date. The actual harvesting and transplant are done on separate dates, and both are uniquely interesting. I was very fascinated by all the unique scientific technology I was being exposed to.

On this day, Melissa cut about four inches of her momma's hair off. We knew for sure that Annie would be going forward with the transplant and lose all her hair. So every week or so Melissa would cut a bit more off. Annie looked really cute with short hair, and we all approved. Eventually, on the date of high-dose chemotherapy, she was bald. Even then, we could see how beautiful she was.

February 20, 2009: Today we went over for a follow-up cardiology appointment with Dr. Farhat. He said Annie was doing well from a cardiac standpoint, and he was very pleased with her progress. He said he would see her in three months or earlier if the need arises. This was a nice day!

From this point on, until April 17th, Annie usually had a CBC weekly and sometimes twice a week. During that period her white and red blood cell counts stayed relatively stable; a little low at times, then normal at other times. Her platelets bounced all over the place. Her low point was 25,000, critically low, on March 13th, 2009. Her high point was 126,000, low, on April 13th, 2009. That was the day she would be receiving her first bag of high-dose chemotherapy.

The next several paragraphs are a good depiction of how a stem-cell harvest works. It's tiring on the patient but reasonably pain free. To me, it was a very fascinating experience. I was getting to watch a procedure that probably over 95 percent of all nurses haven't seen, but many had on their bucket list.

March 5, 2009: Today, we started the stem-cell mobilization process at the cancer center. Annie was given a G-CSF injection, just under the skin, in her tummy. Its purpose is to stimulate the bone marrow to make so many stem-cells that they overflow out into the blood stream, and are able to be harvested. After the high-dose chemotherapy, her white blood cell count would drop down to "0," leaving her with an extremely high risk of infection with potentially fatal results. Her white cells need to engraft quickly.

March 9, 2009: Today we went to Via Christi-St. Francis Hospital on an outpatient basis, so Annie could have a triple lumen catheter placed, to be used in her stem-cell harvest. The catheter is similar to a PICC line, but it has three ports, instead of two. The catheter is a tube that is placed in a large vein in your upper chest with the internal tip extending as far down as your heart. It's usually inserted by a surgeon or radiologist with local anesthetic. It's basically used the same way as the PICC line, and during stem-cell harvest two ports are used, which leaves one open for liquid or other uses.

After checking in at the stem-cell transplant ward, Annie was wheeled down to a radiology room for placement of her catheter by a radiologist. She returned about forty-five minutes later with her new Triple Lumen Catheter, and was placed in a large private room on the ward.

The first thing I saw when she was wheeled into her room was the catheter sitting rather awkwardly on her chest. I was used to seeing the PICC line in her arm, and now seeing a catheter on her chest seemed rather odd. I asked her if the procedure was painful and she said "No." It didn't seem to bother her one way or the other.

She really needed and wanted this transplant. It would not provide a cure, but by design, it should give her a longer remission period thus extending her life. Her thought process was so natural and normal; she was trying to stay alive as long as possible in hopes that a cure for this cancer would be found. I'm sure that is the dream of most cancer patients. One day, some fortunate person with Annie's disease, is going to be in the same circumstances she is now, when the announcement comes out that they have found a cure. What a glorious day that will be for many families around the world whose loved one is dealing with this dreadful disease.

It was now time to harvest her stem-cells. Each harvesting session would take from three to four hours. After today, each harvest would start at 7:00 A.M.

A specially trained nurse, wearing a long yellow sanitized gown, pulled this very large machine into the room, which I called the "harvester." Two lines were hooked from the harvester to ports in Annie's catheter. What this machine does is essentially draw blood out of Annie, separating and collecting white blood cells, including the stem-cells, along with a few red blood cells and platelets. The remaining blood cells were returned to Annie through her catheter. It looked to be a reasonably simple and painless procedure; but I knew it was very high tech. In case you're wondering, through the process only a few cups of her blood are in the harvester at any one time.

Our results this day from the harvest weren't very good. Only 270,000 stem-cells were collected and she needed a minimum of two million stem-cells over the four day harvest to do one transplant. Annie had another G-CSF injection.

March 10, 2009: Today's harvest was very poor, and Annie and I were very disappointed. The results were much worse than yesterday.

March 11, 2009: No attempt was made today, as they were giving her body a rest. She did have another G-CSF injection.

March 12, 2009: They made another attempt today, but harvesting was stopped due to poor yield. They only collected 50,000 stem-cells. Annie was heartbroken; she really needed and wanted this transplant. The stem-cell transplant coordinator throughout this process was Stephanie Rader, RN, BSN, Oncology. She was the one that broke the bad news to Annie. She told us to stay put for a while, and Dr. Moore Jr. would come over to visit us.

Without being there, it's probably difficult to understand the disappointment, or maybe I should say sadness, that Annie was experiencing from her poor harvest results. Multiple myeloma can come back with a vengeance, and is very unforgiving. But for now, it was a waiting game to see what Dr. Moore Jr. had to say.

Dr. Moore Jr. came over this afternoon and spoke to Annie. He told her he could try to harvest her stem-cells the old way, by aspirating the stem-cells from the bone marrow, but was reluctant to do that. He told her that her bones were in a badly diseased condition from the myeloma, and it'd be very difficult for her. As he started to walk away, he said to Annie, "I guess some things aren't meant to be."

As Dr. Moore Jr. was leaving the room, Stephanie said to him, "Dr. Moore, what about trying Mozobil?"

He looked at her and said, "I doubt that her insurance will pay for it."

I spoke up and told him it pays for everything else, why wouldn't it pay for the Mozobil. I didn't know what that drug was used for, but from Stephanie's voice I had a feeling it was something useful.

He instructed Stephanie to go over to the office and have the girls run it through our insurance.

About an hour or so later when they walked back into the room, Dr. Moore Jr. was smiling, and Stephanie was making some type of vocal noise. There was absolutely no problem with the insurance.

Dr. Moore Jr. explained to us that Mozobil just recently came out of clinical trials and had only been on the market a couple of months, and was very expensive.

Stephanie said they'd used it on six patients so far, and it worked on five. The drug works with the G-CSF injections to enhance the creation of stem-cells.

We were very excited and hopeful when Dr. Moore Jr. told Stephanie to give Annie a couple of weeks break, and set up a new schedule so we could start over. The cells they already collected would be saved and added to the new collection.

Earlier, I mentioned that Annie was getting great medical care, to include the latest cancer drugs. Mozobil was administered through an injection in Annie's tummy. Annie had the first injection the day before her next harvest started, and three during the harvest. Those injections were $13,700 each; yet I couldn't get a prescription drug she so badly needed for her appetite. It didn't make any sense to me; but it clearly showed a disconnect between a patient being able to get the best chemotherapy, verses having to take a lower standard appetite increasing drug that was also instrumental to her well-being, and it didn't work.

March 23, 2009: We saw Dr. Moore Jr. today, and he had her infectious disease tests redrawn for the next harvest. If she had an infection, they would've put things on hold. He noted, "I am proceeding with the Mozobil plan."

March 27–30, 2009: On those four days Annie had G-CSF injections. She had her first Mozobil injection on March 30th at 5:00 P.M.

March 31, 2009: We went back to Via Christi-St. Francis for another attempt at harvesting Annie's stem-cells. Annie had a G-CSF injection prior to the harvest. Today we had some good news; with the new Mozobil injection, they were able to harvest 770,000 stem-cells. It was noted, "At 5:00 P.M. Annie went back to the cancer center for another Mozobil injection."

April 1, 2009: Today they harvested 510,000 stem-cells. Annie was given another G-CSF injection, and then went over to the cancer center at 5:00 PM for another Mozobil injection.

April 2, 2009: Today the harvest was low; they only collected 170,000 stem-cells. Annie had another G-CSF injection and her Mozobil injection at the cancer center.

April 3, 2009: On this day they collected 240,000 stem-cells. The grand total from both harvests was just over 2,000,000, and was just enough for one transplant.

Dr. Moore Jr. would have like to have harvested four million stem-cells. Reason being, high dose chemotherapy was going to kill off all her blood cells, so the more stem-cells he can put back into the blood stream the greater chance of success and survival.

It took Annie eight days to complete the harvest and get the needed stem-cells. Some people take only two days to harvest their stem-cells and most are completed within four days. Annie was obviously unhealthy, and I felt she probably fell in the 3 percent category of not surviving the transplant. But Annie had a tenacious fighting spirit, and I knew this was a risk worth taking. She was fighting for her life and wanted more time. A stem-cell transplant, if successful, would likely give her extra time, so we pushed forward without hesitation.

Annie was given ten days off to regain her strength before starting the high-dose chemotherapy.

April 10, 2009: I called Beverly this morning with a few concerns. I asked her if she thought Annie might be ready to accept Jesus as her savior. I knew Annie was at high risk of some serious issues when the high-dose chemotherapy was induced into her bloodstream. Annie wasn't strong like most of the folks we met getting stem-cell transplants, and I knew it was going to be a real challenge for her. Beverly told me she'd come over this evening and speak with Annie about being saved. It was always going to be Annie's decision, but with all the appointments lately, and the high risk procedure looming, I wanted Annie to have that choice. I didn't tell Annie about the call I made to Beverly, or the request I'd made on her behalf; and quite frankly I didn't know what her answer would be.

It was around 7:00 PM when Beverly arrived. She was sitting in the wheelchair at Annie's bedside. I was standing beside Beverly up near the head of her bed. Beverly chatted with Annie for awhile, then simply asked the question, "Ann, are you willing to accept Jesus Christ as your savior and Lord?"

Annie just shook her head, meaning yes.

Beverly held her hand and said a beautiful prayer, and when she was finished, Annie had accepted Jesus as her savior. It brought tears to my eyes, and I was very proud of her. In the face of such adversity and the unknown she chose what she believed to be her salvation, offering her a better alternative, if things went dreadfully wrong.

For those who believe, faith is a wonderful thing. It takes hope to a higher level, which is not possible without faith. I understand that people without faith still hope their loved ones will somehow survive their own unique illness, but what happens when they don't survive?

Annie was always going to die, and we all knew that. Having faith set her free. I didn't want Annie to die, but I knew when the time came, the thought that she might be going to a better place was very personal. It seemed as though Annie was unlocking many mysteries through her continued survival and spiritual journey. As for me, I was an observer, and not on the same level as her. However, as I understood it, her salvation was making her feel safe; there would be no more darkness, and as her faith grew, her fear of death would subside. To a person of faith, it's a win-win situation. She believed she was going to a better place if she doesn't survive the transplant; for Annie, it doesn't get any better than that. And that's what faith is all about.

Annie would now start her new journey with the knowledge and security that if anything went wrong, she would meet her creator. Whatever happened from this point on could always be put into perspective. Every hour, every day, every month that we had Annie was truly a blessing. I must admit, the term coined for her by the nurses in the early days of her cancer, "Their little miracle girl," seemed to have some credibility. Apparently Annie's journey was never about living, it has always been about dying and unlocking some of life's mysteries along the way. She's certainly doing that. As I said earlier, Annie was an atheist all her life. The theory she aspired to throughout her life has now been flipped upside down in eight months and she's excited about it.

After Annie fell asleep that evening, I had a chance to think about what had transpired on this night. I was happy for Annie, but I found it rather sad that it took cancer and Beverly to take Annie on her spiritual journey. There was a couple of occasions during our marriage, before she got cancer, that I brought up the possibility of taking her and the kids to church. Her words to me were very crushing; she was not interested in a man called God. So I guess I feel a bit cheated, as now she's a person of faith and in many ways has left me behind. Over the past few months she's seen and felt things that I don't even understand. Yes, I'm thrilled that she got rescued during the storm; and I wanted that for her. Perhaps its wishful thinking, but I would have loved to have been able to play a bigger role in that part of her journey. But for now, and hopefully for a long time, I will remain her closest confident and caregiver. I'm going to take her on a journey too; I will love her every minute of every day without prejudice. I'm going to give her every ounce of effort I have in me, and when that isn't enough, I will find the strength to give her more. That will be my promise to her. Beverly will take care of her spiritual needs.

Over the next several days, Annie started the most dangerous part of the process. You know how a harvest works, now I will give you an up to date and accurate accounting of how the stem-cell transplant process works, and the difficulties Annie had. If you go through the process, or know someone that will, this is actually how it works.

April 13, 2009: Today Annie will start "The walk of death" and receive her first IV bag of high-dose melphalan. Once the high-dose chemotherapy gets in her system, it can't be removed and all her blood cells will start to die. This event was a struggle for me as we'd battled low platelets since the beginning, and I knew if her platelets didn't engraft quickly, the outlook for her would be poor.

I knew the difficulties and challenges ahead, but felt Annie was emotionally and spiritually prepared. Before we left the hospital today I was given a black leather bag that looked like an airplane carry-on bag. Inside the bag was two battery-operated pumps: one for continuous IV fluids and one for continuous nausea medicine. There was a button on the anti-nausea pump that could be pushed for an extra boost of medicine if she needed it. Also in the bag was two, 1,000 cc bags of hydration fluids and a small bag of nausea medicine. This would be my responsibility at all times when we were away from medical care. High-dose chemotherapy is some serious stuff with extremely dangerous side effects. Annie had to be hydrated at all times, and hopefully there would be no vomiting. With her platelets and blood counts falling, as they'd soon be, vomiting is not a good thing. Too much internal pressure could cause her to bleed.

Some patients are strong enough, for the most part, to take care of themselves, although throughout the transplant process they will have a caregiver. Annie was not that patient. She was too broken up, weak, and chronically ill.

As her caregiver, her life in part depended on how well I cared for her at home. She had to live in as germ free of an environment as possible, and for the most part not be around kids or unhealthy people. I was good at that, as I already had plenty of experience. That didn't trouble me so much. I was more concerned about the potentially lethal side effects of the chemotherapy. I had to keep reminding myself that the survival rate from a transplant is 97 percent, and that was good odds.

April 14, 2009: Today Annie had her second IV bag of melphalan. She was very tired, but so far no nausea or hydration problems. The pumps were working fine.

April 15, 2009: We spent a good part of today at the cancer center doing laboratory work and hydrating Annie. She was still okay with the nausea and vomiting.

April 16th 2009: Early this morning, around 2:00 A.M., one of the hydration bags started getting low. I turned off the pump and hooked up a new bag of fluids. When I went to restart the pump, it wouldn't start. I followed the directions carefully, but had no luck. I then called the emergency pump repairman and spoke to him for a while. He took me through a few steps on starting the pump, with no positive results. He said he would be over with a new pump in less than an hour. It took him about thirty-five minutes to get here. The new pump was set up and running in just a few minutes. Stem-cell transplants are taken very seriously, and it only takes one thing to go wrong, and the consequences can be very bad.

After the pump maintenance technician and I visited for a while, he left, and I started preparing Annie to go get her stem-cell transplant. Being a caregiver for a person as sick as Annie was never easy, and sometimes getting rest was not an option. Without sleep this was going to be a long day and I didn't know when I would get my next chance to rest. We had to be at Via Christi-St. Francis at 6:00 A.M., with the transplant starting at 7:00 A.M. Beverly was going to meet us there. In all her years as a nurse she'd never seen a transplant before and was very excited.

The process started at 7:00 A.M. when the nurse gave her pre-medications for the transplant. There were two nurses and a person from the stem-cell laboratory in the transplant room. They all wore long yellow sanitized gowns. Annie was lying on a bed near the table with the warm water where the stem-cells were thawed. The person from the laboratory removed a container of stem-cells from the liquid nitrogen container and handed them off to another nurse who thawed the stem-cells in warm water. Once thawed, the nurse attached IV tubing to the bag of stem-cells and connected the tubing to Annie's catheter. It takes about fifteen minutes to infuse each bag of stem-cells, and she would receive eight bags today. Each bag of stem-cells has a certain amount of preservative called DMSO that helps protect the stem-cells during the freezing process. There is a limit on how much preservative a patient can receive in a day, so Annie would have a two-day transplant. The DMSO can make the patient smell like garlic, canned tomatoes, or sometimes a bloody Mary. The smell usually goes away in a couple of days.

April 17, 2009: We arrived at Via Christi-St. Francis for Annie's second batch of stem-cells. The start time was once again 7:00 A.M. Annie had eight bags again today. Once the transplant process was completed she had a G-CSF injection.

April 18, 2009: This being a Saturday, you would have thought we would have an easy day. We had to get up at 6:00 A.M., get ready, and drive the twenty miles over to the cancer center auxiliary branch and be there by 8:30 A.M. It's located across the street from Via Christi-St Francis and open on weekends. Stem-cell-transplant patients are seen seven days a week. When we got there, they'd do a CBC and check out the pumps I was using at home. The blood counts were steadily in decline, and although not critical yet, they were getting there. She received a G-CSF injection.

April 19, 2009: We went back to the auxiliary branch for her checkup. Her white count was starting to struggle; her platelets were now critically low, but not enough to transfuse. She had a G-CSF injection to boost her white cell count.

April 20, 2009: Today we went to the cancer center for laboratory work and a CBC. We also saw Dr. Moore Jr., who told us her counts were still falling, but didn't require transfusions. She received another G-CSF injection.

April 21, 2009: We went to the cancer center again today, and received basically the same report as yesterday. The counts were still falling, and Annie received a G-CSF injection.

April 22, 2009: This was the day I was talking about when I used the term "The walk of death." Annie's white count was 0.03; she had essentially no immunity. Her platelets were 1,000; critically low. Her HGB was 8; low. Remember, on April 13th her platelets were 126,000, and her white cell count and HGB were basically normal. Today, she received two units of platelets and a G-CSF injection.

On this same day, Annie saw Dr. Reddy who was standing in for Dr. Moore Jr. Melissa and I were standing beside Annie when he looked at her saying, "Mrs. Harrison, I'm so sorry, but it's time for you to be hospitalized." His words made Annie sad, she just wanted to go home.

Annie was hospitalized for diarrhea, dehydration, and low white cell count. She'd been getting her fluids around the clock, but high-dose chemotherapy doesn't care. It destroys anything and everything it can in the body; and can cause major side effects that don't show up for a year or more. It can damage any organ in the body.

We took her across the street to Via Christi-St. Francis Hospital where she was given a room on the stem-cell transplant ward. Once Annie was comfortable inside her room, and hooked up to IV fluids, I was relieved of my pump duties. The nurses up there are all specialists to stem-cell transplants. They really keep an eye on their patients, and are limited to the number of patients they're responsible for. It was more like an intensive care unit, and really interesting watching them hustling around. Everything and every procedure was always on schedule.

This is where the word engraftment comes in; and it's now a waiting game. If the platelets or white cells don't engraft in a reasonable amount of time, the patient has a poor outlook and it can be fatal. Dr. Moore Jr. told me he likes to see an upward trend within five to seven days. Her HGB would not be a problem, as her red blood cell transfusions always worked for her. It did get down to the 7 range a few times, but once transfused, they came right back up.

April 23, 2009: Annie's WBC remained the same; and she still had no immunity to germs. Her platelets were at 1,000; and still critically low. Her platelet transfusion hadn't worked, and she'd receive another transfusion of platelets today. If Annie had a normal response to transfused platelets, her platelets would have risen, and her dangerous condition would have subsided somewhat.

April 24, 2009: Annie's WBC had dropped to 0.02. It wasn't unexpected, but left us all feeling a little uneasy. Her platelets were 6,000; and still critically low. She would receive more platelets today. Annie was obviously in a precarious situation and couldn't afford an infection or to start bleeding. In her weakened state, most likely she wouldn't survive an infection. I will say this, her diarrhea was under control, she was weak, but generally feeling better. What I just said probably sounds like a conflict in terms, but it really isn't. The process of harvesting her cells, followed by the transplant and high-dose chemotherapy, put her body in a naturally weakened state. More so then it would for healthier transplant patients. Her numbers were bad, but she was actually feeling better.

April 25, 2009: Annie's WBC had moved to 0.07, still dangerously low, but trending up. Her platelets were back down to 1,000, and still critically low. Annie received another unit of platelets today.

Her WBC was the doctor's main worry, as infections from a low white count are very dangerous and cause the patients most of their problems. That was now compounded by the fact that they had not anticipated that her platelet transfusions would not work.

April 26, 2009: Annie's WBC was trending up, and was now 1.03. Good news! Her platelets were still at 1,000, and still critically low. Annie received more platelets again today.

April 27, 2009: Annie's WBC was 3.01, looking better, and significantly reducing her risk of infection. Her platelets were still stuck on 1,000, and still critically low. Dr. Moore Jr. decided not to give her any more platelets, as they weren't working. When most people get platelets their count shoots up, and they get out of danger almost immediately. It's rare for patients with low platelets to die. In Annie's case they couldn't say that with certainty. I knew her platelets needed to start engrafting soon.

I asked Dr. Moore Jr. about giving Annie Amicar, a drug that Dr. Moore Sr. gave her when her platelets were low. I was noticing red spots all over her body called petechia. When your platelets are very low, over an extended period of time, the small blood vessels under the skin start to bleed in places.

Rather than start Annie on the medication, he told me with a big smile on his face that he'd put in a consultation for Dr. Moore Sr. to come over tomorrow and visit with Annie. He did that for Annie! He knew how much she cared for his father, Dr. Moore Sr., so I believe he gave her a very gracious gift. She'd be seeing Dr. Moore Sr. in the morning. That ranks among the top of all gestures she received during the thirty months.

April 28, 2009: That morning, when Dr. Moore Sr. came in, Annie was lying on her bed with her pink NY Yankee cap on.

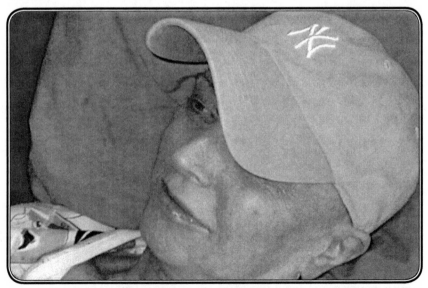

NY Yankee Pink Hat

I didn't know this, but he was a Yankee fan. His first words were, "Ann, where did you get that hat? I love it."

She explained to him that I was a Yankee fan, and Melissa had picked it up for her at a sports shop.

We laughed a lot, had a great visit, and then he examined her, acknowledging that she looked good, but did have a problem with the petechia. He left with a pleasant goodbye, and went to the nurses' station to prescribe her the Amicar.

Her platelets were still at 1,000, and still critically low. We knew she didn't have a lot of time before she'd started bleeding. Her skin already looked like it had rashes all over it from bleeding under the skin.

But, she was feeling good and happy and it was just a waiting game that would be resolved one way or the other in a few days. It wasn't time to panic, but looking at her, regardless of how good she was feeling, was troubling.

April 29, 2009: Dr. Moore Jr. came in with a bit of good news. His strategy of stopping the platelet transfusions was working. Her platelets were 3,000; critically low. That might be the upward trend we desperately needed. Annie was still feeling upbeat, seemingly oblivious to her circumstances with the platelets. I think Annie was feeling so good that, as far as she was concerned, everything was going to be okay.

April 30, 2009: Her WBC was now normal. Her HGB was up and down, but transfused red blood cells kept them in check. Her platelets climbed to 4,000; still critically low. It seemed we were on a small roll.

May 1, 2009: Today her platelets were at 5,000; however, it was apparent the engraftment was starting to work. We were not out of the woods by a long shot, but we were starting to see the upward trend. Annie just needed to ride out this storm until it passed.

I started hearing the news that Annie would probably be dismissed from the hospital tomorrow afternoon, so I planned a big surprise for her today. Via Christi-St. Francis has a nice gift shop on the ground floor that includes some clothing. I was going to take her shopping for the first time since her diagnosis. I got permission from the charge nurse, who said it would be okay, but too make sure she didn't fall or bang her head.

It was during the morning hours when I approached Annie with a question. I told her there was a lovely little gift shop downstairs, and asked her if she would like to go shopping. Talk about winning the lottery! Her reaction was priceless! I had to get her little makeup bag out, then sit with her for over an hour watching her get ready. Normally I would get a bit impatient with her over taking so long to get ready, but not this time. I sat in amazement, watching this lady I loved so much, fighting so hard for something most of us simply take for granted, *her life.*

I got her in the wheelchair and we took off. On the way down she was so excited. It appeared she wanted to stop and tell everyone along the way, "I'm going shopping." If you're a woman who loves to shop, which most women do, you know how she must have been feeling after being off the playing field for so long; simply wonderful!

The gift shop was probably twenty by thirty-five feet and on every shelf there was beautiful colorful items. There was literally "stuff stacked on stuff." They even had a nice jewelry rack. Outside the gift shop they had a dozen or so clothes racks filled with colorful clothes of all sorts.

When we got close to the gift shop and she started seeing the clothes racks outside the shop, she zoned out on me. She was locked onto the clothing, and before I knew it I was holding a pink and a blue nightdress. They were really cute, made of cotton, and had ice cream designs all over them. She also picked out a couple of beautiful colorful tops that were made in India. Once we made it inside the shop, she was having trouble containing herself. Her eyes seemed to light up like a couple of large Christmas bulbs. I could see rather quickly that my effort to keep her sitting in the wheelchair wasn't working too well. She'd say to me, "Can you hold the wheelchair while I stand up and look at the items on the shelf?" That was a bit of a problem as she was still weak from the treatment. However, we made it work. I put one of my feet under a front wheelchair wheel so it couldn't roll, and then just sort of spread my arms out around her so if she wobbled a bit I could steady her. Annie was having a blast. She purchased a couple of purses, all sorts of knick-knacks, and things that I'll simply call stuff. She was trying to buy a little memento for everybody she loved. When we got through, she'd spent almost four-hundred dollars. She was so happy, and her spirit was elevated to a high I hadn't seen since she got ill. I left her in the gift shop sitting in her wheelchair, while the attendants kept an eye on her. I carried the "stuff" up to her room and she played with it all afternoon.

On our way back to her room, she was sitting in the wheelchair smiling from ear to ear. Most of the nurses knew she was shopping, and when she entered the ward greeted her with smiles and many comments on her shopping spree. The conversations seemed to go on forever. If her nurse or anyone entered her room she'd offer them a "Pressie," as she called it. It was a precious day and will linger on in the ole memory bank forever.

This picture was taken by Melissa the evening of her first shopping trip in a long while.

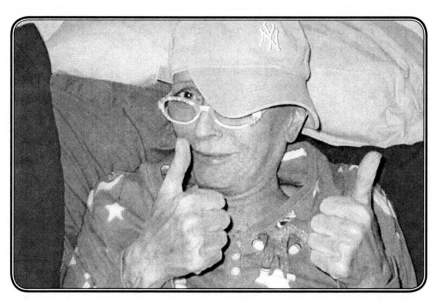

Thumbs Up

May 2, 2009: This morning, Dr. Moore Jr. came into the room and told Annie that her platelets were still at 5,000, a critically low count. However, he was going to let her go home this afternoon. He spoke to us about how dangerously low her platelets were. He said he felt that she was well enough to go home, but once there, we needed to take all the necessary precautions to keep her safe until the platelets came up. We'd been there and done that many times before, so we weren't worried, as long as she didn't bleed. Also, he stated that the Amicar was working, as all the petechia was gone.

I don't want to underemphasize the importance of a good platelet count. Annie sitting on 5,000 platelets is very dangerous. Platelets of that level are like a ticking time bomb. We knew a gentleman who had a platelet count of 28,000, and from the pushing of a bowel movement had a brain hemorrhage and died. His room was next to Annie's when we were at Wesley Medical Center. But keep in mind what I said earlier; transfused platelets usually work and keep folks out of a life threatening situation. They just wouldn't work for Annie, which always left her in danger. If an old ulcer started bleeding, she wouldn't have enough platelets to stop the bleeding and would simply bleed to death. Surgery wouldn't be an option with her low platelets.

It was about noon when Annie looked at me with her little sparkling eyes and said, "I'm a bit bored."

I asked her what she'd like to do. Big mistake!

"I fancy a bit more shopping."

How could I say no? I went to the nurses' station and had a word with the nurse.

With a smile on her face, the nurse replied, "Take her shopping while I get the doctor to draw up her dismissal paperwork."

When I walked back into Annie's room and gave her the good news, she was all smiles.

Once again I helped her get cleaned up while listening to a conversation about all the things she meant to buy yesterday, but forgot to.

This time, when we departed in the wheelchair, she was wearing her comfortable track pants, one of her new tops, and her pink Yankee hat. She looked beautiful.

Annie was always known for the unique way she dressed. She took fashion trends to a whole new level by mixing and matching the different trends, and creating her own unique look. But today, her attire was so out of character for her, and she didn't even notice; she was going shopping again. And that's what the world of cancer does to a person. It's easy to forget who you were, who you are, and what you were all about; you simply change.

When we got to the gift shop, she got into the "zone" again, and bought more "stuff" that she was thrilled about.

This time she only spent three-hundred dollars. I didn't mind her spending the money, but in my mind, I was certainly questioning some of the "stuff" she purchased. It was quite simply "Frou Frou."

When we got outside the gift shop, I spoke to her about all the money she spent on "stuff."

"I don't think about the money I spent Bobby. I think about all the money you've saved. This is the first time I've been shopping since I got ill." Priceless! I couldn't argue that point with her. Annie loved to shop, and it was good for her spirit. When we got back to the room we sorted her new treasures, and I started putting the things into bags to take down to our vehicle.

On my way down, as I walked by the gift shop, I remembered this pretty little red alligator skin-type clutch bag that she wanted. I walked into the gift shop, looked it over and decided to buy it for her.

When I got back to the room, she saw the purse and got excited all over again.

She remarked, "See, you're as bad as me. You like to shop too."

I just laughed and said, "Secretly, I've always wanted a red purse Annie."

She loved it, and laughed so hard, saying, "You're crazy!"

We were living in the insane world of cancer, and anything I could do or say to make her laugh was so important to her emotional stability. She was my bright and shining star, and I loved her more every day. She was so helpless, defenseless, and precious. In my mind, she was a gift, and I was beginning to understand love in a way that many people never will. As I was starting to find, true love penetrates deep into your soul. There is no anger and no resentment. It isn't conflicting and I found it very spiritual. It seemed my goal in life was to keep Annie safe, and to share every minute I could with her in happiness. I always loved Annie, however, I have to realize and accept that I never really knew the true meaning of spousal love until now. As chaotic and sad as our lives were, we were always taking the time to "smell the roses." Sometimes, we would look at each other and laugh for no reason. We'd both found true love, but what a price we were paying.

Taking care of the one you love can be very tough, tragic, and yet very beautiful. Sometimes we'd be sitting in her hospital room and get caught up in uncontrollable laughter. The nurses would stand outside the door, looking in, trying to figure out what was so funny. Then I would see their bellies jumping up and down and they were laughing too. I'd tell Annie and she'd start laughing harder, and the cycle continued. The funny thing is, we were often laughing at ourselves and our circumstances. We didn't know what else to do. It's not as strange as you might think, when all you have left is sorrow or laughter. All our plans, hopes, and dreams of our upcoming retirement together were gone. So we learned to laugh at ourselves and make every moment we had left together special. We both knew Annie's journey would not end on a good note. So we accepted our fate, and just got on with our lives as best we could.

On our way home today we had a joyful trip full of conversation and anticipation over her stem-cell transplant, and the opportunity for a longer remission it could provide. Of course, the car was stacked with bags of stuff that she invariably had to look through to make sure she hadn't left anything behind.

May 3, 2009: From this day on until June 3rd, we went to the cancer center every day, sometimes for hydration, but usually for a CBC, and a get-well check. By May 26th her platelets had slowly climbed to 36,000, a critically low count, but trending up. Her

WBC and HGB were always near normal. Dr. Moore Jr. would be following Annie's illness as long as she was alive. That's how stem-cell transplants work. Annie had volunteered for a program that allowed Dr. Moore Jr. to put all her information into a database for research scientists to follow. They were always looking for answers to this dreadful disease.

May 21, 2009: Today Dr. Farhat did a thorough examination of her heart. From a cardiac standpoint she was doing well; and we were to come back in three months for a follow-up, or sooner if needed.

May 26th, 2009: We saw Dr. Moore Jr. today, which was a day plus forty status, post stem-cell transplant. She was doing okay, but he noted, "Next week I will be doing a bone marrow biopsy and aspiration." He was checking to make sure her bone marrow was still clear.

Here's an interesting fact I would like to share. The day a person has a stem-cell transplant and gets new stem-cells, it becomes their birth date. Think about it—all her old cells were killed off. It's sort of like being reborn. One-year post stem-cell transplant is a "Happy first birthday." You are now one year old.

June 3, 2009: Today was a dreaded day, but a happy one. Annie had a bone marrow aspiration and was slowly producing new blood cells, and so far, the transplant was a success. Annie really needed another transplant, but with the difficulties she had, they wouldn't even attempt it. I was okay with that, as I knew Annie was blessed to have survived.

Writing this story is not the same as being there. I can never convey just how tough that process was on her. It was minute by minute, day by day, touch and go, all the time. It was a very stressful time, as each time we received her platelet report, and it wasn't good, we had to wait twenty-four hours until the next one. When you really love someone, it's not a good place to be.

Also today, Dr. Moore Jr. turned Annie back over to Dr. Moore Sr. for her oncology needs. The two doctors would be in consultation at all times on the status and progress of her health care.

June 6th, 2009: I took Annie over to see Dr. Moore Sr. today. He noted, "She is coming down off morphine and starting to feel more pain." He was going to send her over to see Dr. Berger and see if he could provide her any further help with vertebroplasty. She'd also be going over to see her surgeon, Dr. Pence. He wanted to know if there was anything they could do to help her. He further stated, "She no longer has any blood clotting and can come off the Coumadin."

The next scheduled appointment with Dr. Moore Sr. was July 27th, 2009. I can tell you that between June 6th and July 27th Annie was doing reasonably well. During that period her platelets stayed critical, but they can take up to a year to come back. We still went to the cancer center for blood tests, but no official appointments. I was able to take her out in her wheelchair shopping, and over to visit friends and family. Considering everything she had been through, life was good.

July 27th, 2009: We went to the cancer center today to see Dr. Moore Sr. He noted, "She is to continue her IV Zometa once a month, to put the calcium back in her bones," and, "She is scheduled to see a neurosurgeon about her back." Dr. Moore Sr. further noted, "She needs help! Her painful spine is the main reason she has to take morphine." This was her one-hundred-day post stem-cell transplant. A report would be filled out and sent to Dr. Moore Jr. for dissemination.

This afternoon Annie and I went to see Dr. Grundmeyer, a neurosurgeon, for the results of her recent MRI. He told Annie he could certainly fix her back and she'd be 85 percent pain free. The problem was, at the moment she was too weak. The surgery would take approximately ten hours; eight hours on the back, and then he'd come in from the front, and that could take another two hours. Annie really wanted the surgery, and was doing everything she could to get stronger.

To this day, my heart still aches for her and her courageous fight. Every time she started getting up, she always got knocked back down again. When that happened, it really hurt me. I couldn't fight what I couldn't see, only what I felt. It was a constant struggle emotionally for Annie and me, most of the time. Even on a good day, the doom and gloom was always there, lingering in the shadows. Avoiding it wasn't all that hard, but Annie never had much time between events. There was always something just around the corner, waiting, watching, for the right moment to strike.

Chapter 10

Near Death Experience

August 10, 2009: Annie received a call today from her sister Lesley in California. While they were talking, Annie held the phone away from her mouth, and asked me if she could go to California for ten days.

I told her that with her immunity problems, it probably wouldn't be a good idea. It upset Annie, as she wanted to go. She felt it could be the last time she'd ever be able to make the trip. She was in remission, but had limited mobility and was very frail.

Over the years of traveling to Los Angeles, Annie made many friends. There would be lots of hugs and direct contact with germs. Every fiber in my body told me the trip could easily end up in a disaster.

Lesley got on the phone and told me that she and some friends were hiring a large hall and having a big surprise party in Annie's honor. That made me even more apprehensive. As it was a surprise party, I wasn't allowed to speak to Annie about my concerns, knowing the last thing she needed was being around bunch of people contagious with who knows what.

I stood my ground for a few days, but the pressure was building from Melissa and a couple of the doctors. They felt Annie had been living on the edge long enough, and deserved a short vacation. I was told I couldn't protect her forever. Their thoughts were, when the cancer came back, she wouldn't survive again. I knew they were probably right, but I still disagreed.

August 14, 2009: This morning Annie and I were sitting at the dining room table having some breakfast.

Without much warning she started crying, saying "Please, let me go."

I told her the risk of infection was just too great. I said, "Annie, I love you and don't want to lose you."

She countered by saying, "I know you love me, so be happy for me. This could be my last chance."

She manipulated me into saying okay. She promised me she wouldn't let people get too close to her, which I knew wasn't true. When Annie's white count was down to one, if someone got near her, she'd hold her little arms out for a hug. She never really understood the risks she was taking, or maybe in her own way knew her survival was limited and just didn't care. I could have gone with her, but knew if I was there I'd spend my whole time pushing people away from her and make her "special event" miserable. Annie was still not aware of the party.

Later on in the day I called her sister Lesley, and told her I was going to let Annie come out. I told her about my concerns and I got the same promise Annie made me. I didn't believe her either. I guess in some way it made me feel better by at least discussing the issues.

Annie was on several different medications, so I had to make a detailed list with instructions and put in her bag of pills. I knew Lesley would make sure Annie got her medication on time.

This was one of the toughest and most difficult decisions I'd made so far. I think what influenced me the most was reflecting back on all the difficulties Annie had with the cancer, and knowing it would be back. I had to stop being selfish and thinking of myself. She deserved a chance to have some fun and get out of this world of cancer she'd been living in. I knew the trip would be good for her, if she didn't catch some sort of germ.

Annie usually flew with US Airways. It always flew out of Wichita, made a stop at Phoenix, and then to Ontario, California where her sister met her.

I got in touch with US Airways and started working on the logistics of getting Annie there and back safely. I discussed my concerns in detail, and they assured me they would take good care of her.

August 20, 2009: Annie and I went to see Dr. Farhat today for an EKG. He wanted to make sure her heart was still functioning properly after the high-dose chemotherapy. Some of the effects from the chemotherapy don't show up for quite awhile after the patient receives it. Her heart was functioning normally, with no signs of swelling. Her weight was 106.8 pounds, and from a cardiac standpoint she was doing reasonably well.

August 24, 2009: I took Annie to the airport and parked in front of the US Airways terminal. The baggage handler came over to the car to assist us. Annie knew him well, as she traveled often. I got her in the wheelchair and wheeled her inside, while the baggage hander brought the bags in. He gave me his word he'd stay with her until I got back from parking the car. When we checked in, I was given a pass so I could push her through security to her gate.

When we got to the gate, the US Airways agent came over and discussed her trip with me. She told me what their plans were, and reassured me that her trip would be smooth. I was still very anxious, but went with the flow, as I could see the excitement building in Annie's eyes. We transferred her into one of their wheelchairs, and they took her to the plane before anyone else was allowed to board.

Lesley had contacted some of her friends, and had a beautiful hospital bed delivered and waiting for Annie at her home. Lesley also had a nice wheelchair with comfortable pillows waiting at the airport. In addition to all that, there was a new portable potty sitting near the hospital bed. Lesley loved her sister and it really showed in the effort she made to ensure Annie was comfortable while at her home.

Annie called me from her cell phone after the airline agents got her comfortable in her seat. She said she loved me and thanked me for letting her go visit her family and friends. At that moment Annie's spirit was very elevated. I was still at the gate and not going to move until the plane was flying safely in the air. I was really sad and knew

I'd be a nervous wreck while she was gone, and miss her terribly. I couldn't wait for her to get back so I could get my hands on her, and she hadn't even left yet. For the past fourteen months we were almost always together; this was going to be a long ten days.

Eventually the US Airways flight took off, filling my mind with so many emotions. I knew I needed to let her go, but at the moment it was very hard for me. One of the thoughts that troubled me was what if they had an in-flight emergency, or worse? Who would care for her? It was starting to feel like my mind was playing head games with me. Eventually I turned my focus to the sky and watched her airplane until it disappeared from sight. Now all I could do was wait until I received the call telling me she was safe.

Within five hours of departure, I received that long-awaited phone call from Annie. She said the flight was marvelous, and that US Airways flight attendants took great care of her. She seemed really happy, and I was happy for her. While she was in Los Angeles, I spoke to her every morning, for at least an hour.

August 31, 2009: I called Annie this morning as usual. As soon as she started talking, I knew we were in trouble. She couldn't say more than a couple of words without taking in more air.

I said, "Annie, you're getting sick."

She replied in a soft voice, "I know it."

My first concern was that she had a buildup of fluid in her lungs, possible pneumonia, or fluid retention from possible congestive heart failure. I'd seen it many times before, and felt so helpless! Over the period of the illness, I became exceptionally good at seeing potential problems in their early stages and taking the appropriate action. This was my biggest fear, slapping me in the face.

I asked Annie to put Lesley on the phone. I told Lesley to have a close look at Annie's legs, check for any swelling, and to take her temperature. While Lesley checked Annie out, I held the phone to my ear listening for any sounds or conversation between them, and as I did I could feel my heart pounding in my chest as I waited with anxious anticipation.

Lesley got back on the phone and said her legs looked okay, and her temperature was normal.

I gave Lesley the following instructions: check her temperature and legs for swelling every hour or so, and if it starts to elevate or her legs swell, take her to the hospital emergency room immediately. Lesley was to tell them she has symptomatic multiple myeloma, and may be experiencing a fluid overload or have pneumonia.

The nearest hospital, Loma Linda, was very close to Lesley's home. On this issue, I knew I could trust her. Lesley and I usually spoke daily over the phone, and she knew how quickly Annie's condition could deteriorate when she gets ill.

Annie didn't progress any further with her illness, but my suspicions were that she was ill, and it just hadn't reared its ugly head yet.

September 2, 2009: Annie arrived home this afternoon and she seemed well, but I was still worried. The symptoms Annie had in California were typical of the way an illness starts when you have multiple myeloma. My instincts told me there was something else going on.

September 3rd, 2009: When we woke up this morning, Annie seemed okay. As I gave her morning medications to her, she told me how Lesley made her take her medications on time, every time. That pleased me, but I wasn't surprised.

To be on the safe side, I contacted Melissa at Family Medicine East and set up an appointment for Annie to have a complete checkup tomorrow afternoon.

September 4, 2009: I took Annie over for her appointment at 2:00 PM. Her blood work was basically okay, with low platelets, which was nothing new. She had a chest X-ray, which was within normal range for her, so we went home and decided to have a good weekend together.

September 5, 2009: Today was a good day as we relaxed, and for the third time I got to listen to Annie's stories again. She was so proud of herself for making that trip, and I was very proud of her too. She said she had a wonderful time and made lots of good memories.

She told me around fifty to sixty people attended the surprise party in her honor. Annie said she didn't know many of the people, but made many new friends and had many pictures taken with them. I loved the picture of her with short blonde hair, which was still growing after her treatment with high-dose chemotherapy. She was holding a glass of purple juice, saluting the camera. I loved the picture even more after I told her it's not a good idea to have a glass of wine when on morphine. That was one of the things I warned her and Lesley about when she went there.

Her reply was, "I didn't have very much, and unless you have cancer with a death sentence, you'll never understand."

She was right! Physically, I usually had an accurate impression of how she was feeling, but mentally, I didn't have a clue. Annie was on "death row," but hadn't done anything wrong.

Annie Making a Toast

September 6, 2009: This day started out as most, and she seemed to be feeling pretty good throughout the day. Melissa came over in the afternoon and we played around and made Annie laugh. Around 6:00 P.M. when Melissa checked Annie's temperature, it had spiked to 102 degrees Fahrenheit. We both told her she needed to be transported to the hospital, and I was going to call 911. She begged me to give her something for the temperature and give it a little time. Annie could be a handful at times, but I respected her wishes, and gave her two Percocet tablets which contained 500 milligrams of Tylenol each. I told her I'd wait until 8:00 P.M. for a response, and not a minute longer.

At 8 P.M. her fever was gone, so I got her out of bed, wheeled her to the dining room table, and fixed her some macaroni and cheese. She seemed fine, so Melissa left for home. Around 10:00 P.M. I helped her into the hospital bed, checked her over, and all was still well. At 12:30 A.M. I gave her nighttime medications to her, checked her over thoroughly, and she still seemed okay.

When I laid down, it was around 2:00 A.M. My mind was focused on the two events that happened over the past week of Annie feeling unwell. This time we added a high fever and I knew something was wrong, but for whatever reason, the underlying cause of the two events hadn't revealed itself. I'd been through this sort of event several times; it always took some sort of intervention to get it under control. It never just faded away!

September 7, 2009: We got up this morning, did our usual routine of getting her washed, her medications, and breakfast. She had a snack for lunch, and laid down on her hospital bed around 2:00 P.M. for a nap. I did my usual chores, the dishes, cleaning, and sanitizing while she was resting.

Around 5:00 P.M. I walked over to her bed and put my hand on the back of her neck to make sure it wasn't radiating heat, which I'd been doing throughout the afternoon. As soon as my hand got close to the back of her neck, I could feel the heat. I hustled to the medicine cabinet, grabbed the thermometer and took her temperature. It was 102.5 degrees, but the heat from the back of her neck was so intense I knew it would be getting higher. I ran next door, and luckily Sarah and Janet were home. They were both nurses with 70 years experience between them. They ran over to our house with a kit to check Annie's oxygen saturation. Essentially, the oxygen saturation measures the level of concentrated oxygen in your blood. Annie was very low at 84 percent. Her breathing was labored and she was in obvious distress. Normal oxygen saturation for Annie was 95 to 96 percent on room air. When Sarah got the reading, she didn't say anything to me, just simply showed me the number. I saw the number and said, "I'm moving," meaning I was calling 911.

The fire department and paramedics arrived about fifteen minutes later. By that time her temperature was approaching 104 degrees. She was in respiratory distress, and I knew it. They took her vitals and noted that her fever was still around 104 degrees, and her oxygen saturation was unchanged. They put her on oxygen and transported her to Wesley Medical Center. When we arrived, they didn't waste any time getting her in the hospital.

Once we got her inside, and into a bed, they hooked her up to an IV for aggressive administration of fluids. Her temperature was 102.9 degrees, and her blood pressure was 120/76.

Dr. Womack was the attending physician in the emergency room. After they drew her blood and did all the things they needed to do, he probably made a decision that saved her life.

He walked over to me and said he'd be treating her with broad-spectrum antibiotics with Vancomycin and Zosyn for probable sepsis, which is blood poisoning.

When a person is in Annie's condition, with her underlying immunity compromised gets sepsis, there can be as little as a three-hour turnaround period. Anything outside that window usually results in death. The vital organs are poisoned, and simply stop functioning. It can be a very painful death, and does happen, although rarely, with multiple myeloma patients.

By this time, my tears were flowing. I didn't cry; they just ran down my face. I'd been so traumatized from all the pain and suffering I'd witnessed to this point in her journey, and it was getting more and more difficult with each event. The only thing I had going for me at the moment was the strong sense that Annie had a higher power on her side. I understood the desperate situation she was in and that she was going to need some help.

Annie's chest X-ray came back positive to left upper lobe pneumonia. Once they saw the X-ray, Annie was immediately taken up to the Cardiac Intensive Care Unit and put in isolation. Annie was now relatively safe from getting germs or transferring germs to others. She was placed in a room, off of a smaller entry room. Being a military retiree, I called the entry room her first line of defense, which is essentially what it was, as the rooms were separated by glass sliding doors.

Annie was experiencing major breathing problems, and struggling to get enough air. She had two tubes, one in each nostril, pushing air into the passageway. About every thirty minutes they turned the volume up a bit, but it didn't seem to help. I was starting to get anxious, as I'd been through some traumatic events, but seeing Annie struggling for air took things to a whole new level. Thankfully, Annie was sedated at the moment. When she knew the paramedics were coming she started getting anxious, so I gave her a Xanax to keep her calm. But, I suspected her anxiety was more due to her labored breathing than the paramedics.

September 8, 2009: In an effort to administer aggressive fluids, antibiotics, and other medications a PICC line was installed this morning. Annie was approaching the maximum amount of oxygen she could receive from the wall-mounted device. I could feel panic creeping through me, as I knew if the lungs are not taking in the appropriate amount of air, over time the vital organs and tissue will be affected. There was urgency in her care; and they still didn't know what was causing this event.

By the afternoon it became apparent she had reached the maximum amount of oxygen the apparatus could provide. It stated in one of the progress reports, "Even with the antibiotics and aggressive treatment, her condition is deteriorating rapidly."

Dr. Troung, a pulmonologist, was called in to evaluate Annie. He realized quickly that Annie was in respiratory failure and needed immediate intervention. He decided to try her on the BiPAP, which is basically a mask connected by tubing to a BiPAP ventilator. It delivers noninvasive positive pressure for impending respiratory failure. After several long-agonizing minutes, Annie's rapid breathing was quickly turning into an emergency. Her breathing was so rapid it seemed as if she was exhaling and inhaling at the same time. I was standing beside her, with my eyes locked to hers, while she was sitting up on the bed struggling for air. I could see the fear in her eyes, questioning me, looking for some sort of reassurance or telling her everything was going to be okay. All I could say was, "Hang in there, Annie."

Melissa had the Bible out and was reading Psalms 23 to her momma. As soon as she read it, she'd say to her momma, "Do you want me to read it again?"

Annie would nod her head yes.

The situation was very intense, and Melissa kept reading until Dr. Troung recognized that the BiPAP was failing.

He walked over into the first line of defense room and motioned for us to come in. We quickly started walking his way and while in mid stride he looked at us and said, "We need to put your wife on the ventilator now, or she is going to code."

I asked him if he needed our permission, and he said, "No." Then I asked him if it would help her.

He replied that it will breathe for her, provide life-supporting care and maybe give us time to find out what's going on. He said her illness is progressing very rapidly and we still don't know what the underlying cause is.

Melissa told him her mom was a DNR, and he acknowledged her by saying, "If her heart stops beating, we will not resuscitate." As he was moving back to Annie, he told Melissa and me to go to the waiting room.

Melissa and I went out into the hallway and just started hugging each other and crying. We were both very fearful, and knew life-supporting measures were a good thing, but the outlook for Annie was obviously in question or she wouldn't be on the ventilator.

Another problem was that her platelets were low and, unless it was an emergency, they would never push a large tube down her throat as the risk of bleeding was too great. There were a few times in her illness, previous to this event, where the doctors wanted to scope her stomach but didn't as the risk of bleeding was high.

We waited for a good hour or maybe a little more. The first person that came to the waiting room was Dr. Dang. When I walked out into the hallway she told me that Annie was critically ill, and that Dr. Troung would be out in a few minutes to speak to us. I asked her if Annie was going to be okay, and she didn't say a word. She simply put her two index fingers together pointing straight into the air. She was telling me in her own way that Annie's chances were fifty-fifty. We had been there before, but never as traumatic as this. It was obvious that Annie was going to need all the help she could get with this event.

A little while later, Dr. Troung came out with a couple of pictures he wanted to show me of the inside of Annie's lungs. He had taken them with some sort of scope. They were before and after pictures of the suctioning of the inside of her lungs. The before picture showed many of the tiny, thin-walled air sacs, called alveoli, which were all full of what looked to be pus. What they actually do is complicated, but it's to do with the exchanging of gases. In the second picture they were beautifully pink and free of pus. I don't know how many he cleared of pus, but he seemed pleased. It wouldn't change her infection, but would help her breathe. He said the ventilator was now breathing for her, and she seemed to be comfortable. He then gave us permission to go back to her room.

When Melissa and I walked in the room, we weren't ready for what we saw. Annie was lying in her bed, unconscious, and now on the ventilator. Her arms were down by her side, tied at the wrists to the bed rails with some sort of soft cloth. We could see her chest rise and fall; it was apparent the ventilator was simply giving the doctors more time to try to resolve what had become a very complicated illness. They administered her IV Propofol, an anesthetic, to help her rest.

I knew there were a lot of issues surrounding the ventilator and diseases such as Annie's. The ventilator is used to support a single failing organ, which in Annie's case was her lungs. When a person is terminally ill, it's a difficult decision whether to ventilate the person or not. Reason being, the ventilator will not fix any of the problems related to the illness, and this is where the controversy comes in. If Annie's illness didn't start to turn around in a week or so, when would they shut the ventilator down? And who would make that decision?

This was my first experience with the ventilator, but I'd heard from other caregivers that it can be a frightening experience, as sometimes one is left with more questions than answers. That seemed to be the case with Annie at the moment.

September 9, 2009: Dr. Tom Moore, infectious diseases, was consulted by Dr. Dang and came over today. In his physical examination notes he writes, "Critically ill and acutely ill, frail older lady."

Annie had been a very young looking, attractive woman when diagnosed at age 58. Fifteen months into her illness, the doctor's notes just about said it all.

He spoke with me extensively about her history the past few weeks, to include where she had been, right down to the local area. He indicated she might have contacted a virus from the soil. He also stated, "Given the history of travel and the incubation period, I can't completely exclude swine flu (H1N1 influenza A)."

He had Annie immediately started on Tamiflu, 75 milligrams twice a day, and ran many tests and cultures.

September 10, 2009: Dr. Tom Moore came back over today and examined Annie. He stated, "There is increased pulmonary vascularity suggestive of mild congestive heart failure." Respiratory swabs were obtained, and he checked her for *Legionella*, which is Legionnaires' disease. He wasn't ruling anything out, and equated the event that was taking place in Annie's lungs to an "Explosion."

Annie had an X-ray later today, which showed she had an extensive bilateral pneumonia, with the greatest concentration in the upper left lobe, but with no abscess. That was terrible news. She had it in both lungs, and with her immunity being so compromised by the cancer, she didn't have many soldiers to fight this battle with.

Later in the afternoon, Annie was feeling poorly and very agitated. Propofol wasn't helping her rest or sleep. A contributing factor may have been the steroid she was on which can, and often does, promote sleeplessness.

She kept jerking her little skinny arms toward her as forcefully as she could. She was trying to get loose, and I was afraid she was going to hurt herself. I said "Hang on a minute Annie, I will loosen the restraints a bit so you can move your arms." I guess I loosened them a little bit too much. I turned my head for a second or two and when I looked at her she had both hands on the ventilator trying to pull it out. I managed to get her hands away from the ventilator just as a nurse walked in. The nurse gave me a stern look, then helped me secure them back in place. Apparently the nurse went back to the nurses' station and called Dr. Farhat, and told him what I had done.

When Dr. Farhat came over while making his rounds, he leaned over the bed and gave her a big hug, and in a very nice way told her why she needed the restraints. He was looking at her, but I had no doubt he was talking to me.

It was my fault, and it almost caused a problem, as some folks have been known to pull the ventilator out and injure themselves. There is a balloon-type device at the bottom of the ventilator holding it in place, and if pulled out before the balloon is deflated, it can cause injuries. Watching Annie fight so hard to free herself made me sad. I'd never given any thought to the consequences of releasing her hands; but I guess common sense would dictate that the patient was going to try to pull the ventilator out of their throat if given the chance.

September 11, 2009: Dr. Farhat came over this morning on a consultation request from Dr. Dang to check on her possible congestive heart failure. His impression as written in his notes was, "Respiratory failure requiring ventilator with severe pneumonia and evidence of fluid overload." Further, "Congestive heart failure (diastolic and systolic) with an ejection fraction decreased to 44 percent." That was more bad news; moreover, her heart was getting weak and starting to struggle.

Dr. Farhat treated her for the fluid overload with Lasix, which worked well for Annie in the past, and with the reduced fluid volume her heart wouldn't continually be on overload. He also started her on low-dose Lisinopril, a medication which can be used alone or in combination with other medications to treat heart failure. It would also decrease certain chemicals that tighten blood vessels, allowing the blood to flow more smoothly while helping the heart pump the blood more efficiently.

Dr. Troung came over around noon to check the ventilator to see if her breathing had improved or not. I was watching him as he bent over and just seemed to be staring at the machine. He raised his head up and called me over to the machine, and in an elevated voice said, "Look, look, look!"

I looked, and all I saw was some sort of meter and a bunch of numbers.

He remarked in an excitable voice, "She is starting to breathe on her own." He stated that her lungs were breathing at about 15 percent of their capacity.

That was good news and meant something was happening inside her lungs, and hopefully she would gradually improve. Most likely, her pneumonia was starting to retreat. What a blessing and miracle that would be. Annie was literally knocking on death's door a day ago.

Dr. Tom Moore came over this afternoon and was pleasantly surprised too. He ordered another X-ray, and indeed the pneumonia had retreated a little. The question was, would that continue?

He said he was still looking for answers, and that the illness she was suffering from was almost totally associated with the lungs.

What was still bothering him was, "What was the underlying cause?"

He said there was such a rapid onset of pneumonia, there had to be something else going on.

September 12, 2009: Dr. Troung came over again this morning and checked on her breathing status. He was very pleased and said Annie was making remarkable progress. He said he'd get a call from the nurse later today on her status and start weaning her off the ventilator if she continued to improve.

Around 4:00 P.M. one of the nurses checked the ventilator and called Dr. Troung, giving him the status of her breathing. I'm not sure of the percentage, but the decision was made to start the weaning process. The nurse slowly started turning down the ventilator a little at a time over a two hour period, and Annie seemed to be tolerating it well.

He received a call from the nurse again around 6:00 P.M., under pressure from me. The ventilator was turned down to the point it was almost off. Annie was essentially breathing by herself.

He indicated that he would come over after he completed his rounds and remove the ventilator if he could. When Dr. Troung arrived, he was pleased with the results and took the ventilator out. He was very happy for us, and had a beautiful smile on his face.

I must admit, I did push a little to get the ventilator out for several reasons, of which most were probably not justified. Despite the Propofol, Annie was hardly ever asleep. I told them on one occasion to give her more, as she was not resting and too aware of everything that was going on. It was obvious that it's a very uncomfortable feeling having a ventilator stuck down your throat. The doctor said they couldn't increase the medication as it might put her to sleep for good, which was not an option. Being restrained in a bed is necessary, but must be a horrible feeling over five days.

The justifiable reason was quite simple; Dr. Troung told me he likes to work off a seven-day window. Sometimes when a patient is on a ventilator, and every case is different, the ventilator is eventually taken out and they can't breathe on their own. They quickly panic, go into respiratory distress, and some folks actually die. Obviously, the brain is part of the reason we breathe. Being on a ventilator too long can disrupt the signals that the brain sends. The results can quickly become an emergency. Of course, that's not normally the case, but it does happen. So I was pushing to make sure she got off the ventilator within that window, especially as she was already starting to breathe over the ventilator.

When they took the ventilator out and untied her wrists, she was so happy, and tried desperately to talk. But she was so hoarse, it was very difficult understanding an excited, rapid speaking, hoarse lady. Her voice started coming back clear the next day.

She still felt ill, and would be in the ICU for a few more days; but she had received a miracle and she knew it.

September 13, 2009: Dr. Tom Moore came in today, as did Dr. Farhat. They were both very pleased as her pneumonia was in retreat and her heart was getting stronger.

Earlier in the story you met Dr. Moore Sr. and his son Dr. Moore Jr. Well you've now been introduced to his other son, Dr. Tom Moore. He was nominated to become the assistant director of the CDC just before he started caring for Annie. She was always in good hands with him, as her infectious disease doctor.

September 14th and 15th, 2009 turned out to be reasonably routine days. Annie was still receiving IV antibiotics along with her other medications, still saw her doctors, and had some X-rays. They were making sure she was not in danger of any sort of relapse.

September 16, 2009: Annie was moved out of ICU to general population on Eight Tower, cancer ward. Annie was placed in a private room in an effort to isolate her from as many germs as possible.

September 17, 2009: This morning Annie started putting the bug in my ear; she wanted to go home.

Dr. Tom Moore came over and spoke to us for a while. He was observing Annie, making an assessment on whether she could go home or not. He knew I would take good care of her, but that wasn't the point. He needed to know that she was well enough to leave the hospital. In the end, he agreed!

He told us even though he never got a positive test result for swine flu, he was convinced, due to her very rapid deterioration, she probably had it. He couldn't find any other reason, and swine flu doesn't always test positive. He told Annie, even though she was in remission, with her compromised immunity, she could still catch any germ out there. So, we needed to be careful and keep her as germ free as possible.

September 17, 2009: Based on Dr. Tom Moore's and Dr. Farhat's recommendation, Annie was stable and could go home. Dr. Dang got the discharge papers together and we were 'out of there' later that day.

Before I close out this chapter, I would like to mention a few items of interest.

When Annie entered the hospital, from that moment on her treatment was intense and ongoing throughout the day and night.

We literally didn't go more than twenty minutes or so without having a nurse or doctor in the room; hence the name Intensive Care. Her doctors and nurses were wonderful and played a critical role in helping Annie survive this event.

I certainly wasn't sure she was going to get through this event, but when she did I wasn't surprised. I had already witnessed Annie survive events that many in her condition wouldn't have. She was always fighting the odds.

If we put this event in perspective, what were the odds of a multiple myeloma patient with little immunity surviving sepsis, double pneumonia, and most likely swine flu? According to Dr. Tom Moore, the odds of Annie surviving this event would be hard to calculate. His inference was, "A catastrophic event like this would prove to be very difficult for the healthiest of patients to survive." I was beginning to see that her survivability of such bad situations baffled many people. I certainly didn't have any answers, other than her tenacious will to live, brilliant doctors, and her faith.

When Melissa and I made Annie laugh, the ventilator made a loud honking sound that could be heard throughout the ward. If you knew Annie's laugh, you'd understand the noise it made. Annie loved to laugh and when she started, it was usually from deep within and rapid. The nurses weren't happy with her laughter and said we were stimulating her too much. I respected their thoughts, but didn't agree. At this point in her journey, I knew that laughter was good medicine and good for her soul. Laughter helped make sense of the insane world we were living in.

One day Melissa walked in the room and said, "Momma, aren't you ever going to die? You keep putting us through this over and over again." That was Melissa's and my sick sense of humor.

Annie started howling with laughter, the horn was going crazy, and we got in trouble.

The nurse came running in, giving us a piece of her mind. She had every right to do that; but it happened not long before Annie got off the ventilator, and things were looking good. I told Melissa she had better go home before we lost all our privileges. She was annoyed, but left. That's just how we were as a family. We found laughter during some troubling times.

Dr. Troung was a very reserved individual, and very proper. After one visit to our room, you could always tell he loved coming in. We always made him laugh.

He once said to me, "Is your daughter here today?" Melissa really got him going, even during the bad times. We as a family never allowed Annie to get too down; we kept giving her reasons to fight. Annie was always so much fun and loveable, and even when she was too ill to laugh, she appreciated the fact that we didn't act like she was dying all the time.

Yes, at times our stimulation of Annie aggravated the nurses. However, their exceptional care for her and our aggravating stimulating ways, with the help of exceptional doctors, and I believe a higher power, helped Annie survive a very serious event. As I said once before, she could've lain down and died, of that, I have no doubt. However, as long as she was willing to fight, her family was going to fight just as hard for her, and so was everyone in the medical field.

The verse that Melissa was reading to her momma, Psalms 23, many of you have probably heard before. Here are two partial sentences from the verse. "The Lord is my shepherd I shall not want; and yea though I walk through the valley of the shadow of death I shall fear no evil." That was a very powerful message for Annie. I was surprised that Melissa picked up the Bible and started reading to her momma, and chose that verse. It was as if Melissa saw this coming and already prepared herself for what she was going to do. I couldn't have found that verse in time to start reading it. I guess Melissa was doing her bit to help reassure her momma, just in case things went dreadfully wrong. Those were comforting words whether one believes them or not. This went on for several minutes and you can imagine the intensity in the room. I'm trying to comfort Annie who's in obvious respiratory failure; and Melissa is loudly reading a bible verse to her, while Dr. Troung and the nurses are just trying to make meaningful decisions as quickly as possible.

I'm going to close this chapter with one very precious moment; a moment that will stay with me until my memory fades.

On day four of being on the ventilator, Annie was moving her hands around motioning to me. I had to use all my mental capabilities to figure out what she needed. It went on for a few minutes before I asked her if she wanted to write something.

She nodded her head yes.

I was getting ready to break the rules for the second time. I went to the nurses' station and got her a piece of paper and pen. Remembering the last time I loosened her hands, this time I loosened them just enough so she could put pen to paper.

The first few words I couldn't understand. She got frustrated, but hung in there. She then wrote, "Am I going to be ok?"

I reached down and put my hand on hers and said in a tender voice, "It looks like you're going to be just fine, Annie."

The next note she wrote I will keep forever. It simply said, "Bobby, I love you."

I still have that note inside the Bible that Beverly gave her, which is in front of a large picture of her. Every time I look at the note, it takes me back to that tearfully beautiful day.

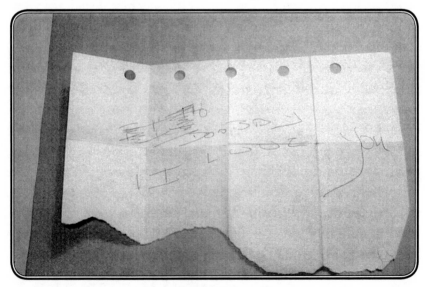

Note; Bobby, I Love You

Chapter 11

Hospice

When we arrived home from the hospital, we had the usual celebration. Beverly came over, we shared the highs and lows of the event and impact it had on us all. It was becoming apparent that Annie was on a spiritual journey, one that neither we nor anyone else had control over. Annie seemed to have a protector, and for reasons that still weren't clear, was surviving against the odds.

With terminally ill patients there's certainly the luck factor, and coincidence. At some point, such as the case with Annie, there just seemed to be something greater going on. Annie's survival on a daily basis was difficult for most to understand. So what was her survival all about? Maybe she was being spared so I could tell you about my little 'atheist' wife's incredible journey and the choices she made without prejudice. I don't want to sound like a saint; and it confused me too at times. But it is what it is, as the odds were overwhelming against her taking a spiritual journey; and surviving cancer this long.

We sat with Annie and discussed her hospital stay and how difficult things were. Even though her sedation medication didn't work that well, she really didn't remember much about anything that happened. To her, it was like being in a heavy fog and not being able to get a clear view of the road ahead.

Things went okay for a few days, then during the beginning of October 2009, she started having problems with nausea and terrible constipation. We eventually got her constipation somewhat under control, but the nausea persisted despite her nausea medications.

Her appetite started to diminish, so we tried her on a liquid diet. Even then, if she drank too much, she got nauseated and sometimes vomited the contents of her stomach up. Her bowel movements became very inconsistent and moved about every three days, if we were lucky. Times were starting to get tough again, and no one seemed to have a clue as to what was going on.

Melissa came over on her lunch break at least once a week and drew her momma's blood for a CBC. She'd take it back to the lab for the results. Annie's platelets were always critically low, but not enough for treatment. Her WBC held steady at the normal range; and her HGB was low, but not enough to have a transfusion.

When November 2009 rolled around, things were not getting any better and Annie was starting to get very upset. Not only was she dealing with the nausea and constipation, she was in a lot of pain, and was generally miserable. It was becoming a frustrating burden for me too, as there was so many questions, and no answers. Sadly, she was having to learn to cope with her new reality.

Sometimes Annie would sit with the back of her bed raised, staring out the window for three to four hours. She would not say a word—just sit and focus on her bowels.

It was very difficult for me too, as I didn't know how to help her, and nothing the doctors did seemed to work. We were seeing her family doctor on a regular basis since her last hospital stay. They took some X-rays, and we could see the stool in her bowels, which we tried to address with laxatives. The laxatives didn't work all that well so we started giving her enemas. They helped her a bit, and removed some of the stool from her bowels, but nowhere near enough. The doctors were at a loss over her constipation and the cause of her nausea.

It is easy looking back on the past few chapters and seeing how difficult her life was. Yes, she was blessed, but she suffered torment and pain on a daily basis that most of us can't begin to comprehend. As her husband and caregiver, it provoked so many emotions. I guess the word "despair" would be the most appropriate. I never knew what to expect on a daily basis. It was difficult at times, just trying to keep her spirits up; but I still believed in my heart, if you love someone enough, you will always find a way to cope with your emotions and keep theirs at the forefront. As I was learning, cancer takes on a life of its own and tries to swallow up everything and everyone around it.

Dec 3, 2009: This morning I was away from the house for a while on personal business. I didn't have anyone to watch Annie; but as I was only going to be gone for a short time, she said she would sit in her wheelchair and watch television.

I'd only been gone about thirty minutes when I received a call from Annie saying she fell, and was on the floor in pain. I told her not to move as I was on my way home and would be there in less than five minutes. I didn't call EMS as Annie and I had a protocol, and I knew her well. From the phone call, I knew she was hurting, but not in immediate danger. Her verbalization told me that. When I arrived home, I found her on the floor beside our dining room table. She had wheeled herself over to answer the phone. When she sat back down, she missed the wheelchair and landed on her bottom. She was experiencing moderate pain in her pelvic area, so I went to her bed, picked out one of her soft pillows to put on top of her wheelchair cushion, and then helped her back into the wheelchair. Annie told me she didn't want to go see Dr. Klein today, she wanted to wait and see if her pain level would decrease overnight.

December 4, 2009: When Annie woke up this morning, I went over to her hospital bed to help her get into her wheelchair so I could take her to our dining room table, where she liked to sit and watch her morning shows. As I started to move her, it was obvious she was in more pain than yesterday, and it was coming from her pelvic area. As this was a Friday, I told her we'd go over to Dr. Klein's office today and get an X-ray. She agreed! She didn't want to go through the weekend without a checkup.

We drove over that afternoon and had the X-ray of her pelvic area; however, the X-ray was negative, which in my mind didn't speak to the pain. My thoughts were that Annie was on a lot of morphine, and shouldn't be feeling heavy pain. Instinctively, I knew there had to be a problem in her pelvic area somewhere. They just couldn't see it, as is often the case with standard X-rays.

Dr. Moore Jr. and Dr. Moore Sr. had been trying to wean Annie off some of her morphine for quite some time, and were making good progress. She was now on less than half the amount of her peak dosage. She would now need extra morphine to control the pain, which was probably going to make her bowel issues worse. High dosages of morphine over an extended period of time can put your bowels to sleep. They simply stop working, and sometimes the area of damaged intestine can die and has to be surgically removed. She had that problem prior to and through her last hospital stay two months ago; by cutting back on the morphine the bowels often start working again. Regardless, she had to have more pain medications as she was hurting. There would be consequences; however, the consequences had already been in place for awhile, we just didn't know it.

December 7, 2009: Today Annie was very nauseated, vomiting and couldn't keep anything down. I called Melissa and had her visit with Dr. Klein about her momma's condition.

Annie was set up with an appointment with Endoscopic Services for December 10th. They wanted her to be fasting over night prior to having her stomach scoped. It would require sedation, but is a very noninvasive procedure and takes about ten to twenty minutes. That would hopefully give us some answers on the vomiting.

December 10, 2009: Today we went over to Endoscopic Services to get Annie's stomach scoped. Dr. Tom Klein scoped Annie's stomach at 9:00 A.M., and was very surprised with his findings. After fasting, Annie's stomach was still full of fluid; so he used a stomach pump to drain 1,000 cc of fluid from her stomach. His instructions when we left his office were to take her straight to her general practitioner's office for IV fluids, as she was dehydrated. As for the stomach, he said her bowels were moving, "way too slow," thus the fluid buildup and vomiting. He sent a tissue sample of a suspicious looking area in her stomach to surgical pathology.

In layman's terms, vomiting was caused by overfilling the stomach. When you put too much liquid in a glass, it spills out.

CAUSE OF ANNIE | 139

Annie was suffering from the same principle. We now knew why she was vomiting, but not the underlying cause.

We went over to Dr. Terry Klein's office where Annie received 1,000 cc of fluid. As this was an IV, the fluid would bypass her stomach and not cause vomiting. After receiving the fluids and having an empty stomach, she felt a bit better. There was now an urgency of getting a CT scan of her abdominal area to try and isolate the source of her problem, as her nutritional levels were lowering rapidly. Melissa called Open MRI of Wichita and set her mom up to get a CT scan of her abdomen on December 17th.

December 12, 2009: Today was Annie's 60th birthday, but there'd be no celebration. I had started a tradition a few years earlier for Annie when her two sisters died from cancer. I always picked up a dozen roses in their favorite colors. The four amberina roses were for Annie, the yellow roses were for Wendy, and the pink roses were for Tracy. Annie also received a couple of telephone birthday wishes today and some cards. It wasn't a very good or festive day as Annie wasn't feeling well. My main goal was to keep her as comfortable as possible.

December 14, 2009: Pathology results came back from Annie's tissue sample. The suspicious area of the stomach that Dr. Tom Klein took the sample from was most likely caused by an old peptic ulcer or drug induced. No malignancy was noted by pathology.

December 16, 2009: This morning when Annie woke up, she was complaining of a burning sensation in her chest, which usually meant she had a chest infection. I called Melissa and set up an appointment for the afternoon, and a little later took Annie over to get a chest X-ray. The X-ray revealed an infiltrate in her lower left lung, which was diagnosed as pneumonia. Anything to do with pneumonia and Annie was always serious. As the pneumonia was isolated to a small area of the lung, Annie was put on a ten-day antibiotic, high-dose Levaquin. It usually worked well for her, and once again, Annie didn't want go to the hospital. She'd rather wait and see if her body would respond to the antibiotics.

December 17, 2009: Today we went to Open MRI of Wichita for a CT scan of her abdomen, with and without contrast. Contrast is a liquid dye used to illuminate the area being scanned. The results of the CT scan didn't show any bowel obstruction, but did show a large amount of stool or fecal material in the colon where she was constipated.

The CT scan also revealed two fractures in her pelvic area that couldn't be seen on normal X-ray. The fractures were not there in a September 2009 CT scan. They were obviously from her fall on December 3rd, and were the source and reason for all the pain in her pelvic area. When Annie was told of the fractures, she wasn't surprised, and seemed to take the news in stride. Annie knew her bones were still brittle and could break easy.

I wasn't surprised either, as I knew the pelvic area is one of the areas prone to fractures with multiple myeloma patients.

Annie was taking her antibiotics every day, but feeling so miserable it was difficult to tell if she was making progress with the pneumonia or not. But for the moment, that was being over shadowed by her continued vomiting whenever she ate or drank. Once she vomited and her stomach cleared, she'd eat more. Soon as she reached a certain level, it would all come back out again. Annie was hungry but couldn't keep anything down, and for both Annie and me this was becoming a source of great frustration and turning into another nightmare. It was getting increasingly difficult for me to control our lives, when Annie's illness was certainly out of control and modern technology wasn't giving us any answers. I really was at wits end, and knew we needed some help, sooner rather than later. If you can't eat or drink, it doesn't take long for serious problems to start rearing their ugly heads from malnutrition.

On Christmas Eve, Melissa and the grandkids stayed with us, and we tried to make Christmas Day pleasant for the little ones, but it wasn't easy. Melissa and I cooked a large dinner to include one of Annie's favorite foods, homemade sausage rolls with flakey pastry. Annie was feeling rough that evening, and although hungry she only had a small bite of one sausage roll.

December 26th, 2009: At 1:00 A.M. Annie was feeling worse and I'd seen enough. I knew she didn't want to go into the hospital, but my gut feeling was that her pneumonia was worse, and whatever was causing her to vomit had to be resolved or she was going to become nutritionally insufficient to the point it might be hard to re-stabilize her.

Sometimes, the bowels and vomiting problems do resolve on their own; and I'd hoped they would, but I was starting to realize she must have a bowel obstruction of some sort. It was time to get her in the hospital and try to resolve the issue causing the problem. As her caregiver and husband, I knew this situation needed to be turned around as soon as possible. The "let's wait and see approach" was not working. No one suggested she needed to be admitted to the hospital, so I decided to take the matter in my own hands, call 911, and get started on the intervention.

December 26, 2009: The paramedics and fire department personnel arrived around 1:30 A.M. Her oxygen saturation was in the middle 80's, she was going into respiratory distress or failure. Annie was immediately put on oxygen and transported to Wesley Medical Center.

Once inside the emergency room, we were greeted by Dr. Liepins, who would be her attending physician.

In his admission notes, he states, "Annie is a cachectic, ill-looking, sixty-year-old female who is alert and orientated." I mentioned this word earlier, but this time I will elaborate. Keyword is *cachectic*. It's derived from the word cachexia, which means "a profound state of constitutional disorder, general ill health, and malnutrition." The pictures shown on the Internet to match the word cachexia, are the pictures we've all seen of the POWs at the concentration camps during WW2.

At home, we did everything we could to avoid this problem. This new event she was experiencing was just another major side effect of her cancer. When I looked at Annie lying in her hospital bed, I always felt like I could have done more to help her. Melissa always reminded me that I did everything I could, and that the doctors were doing all they could too, but the CT scans or X-rays weren't giving them a definitive answer.

Melissa said, "Dad, the only way they may be able to get to the bottom of this is exploratory surgery."

Melissa's statement concerned me, and my response to her wasn't all that positive; "Momma's platelets are holding steady at 15,000, critically low. Exploratory surgery is not an option. Beyond that, she is probably too weak to survive the surgery."

During admission, Dr. Liepins ordered a CT angiogram of the chest. He was looking for PE, or pulmonary embolism, which is a blockage of the main artery in the lung, or one of its branches, by a substance that has traveled from elsewhere in the body. In his admission notes Dr. Liepins stated that he didn't think she had pneumonia.

The angiogram didn't identify any pulmonary embolism, but what he found was rather shocking—Annie had developed pneumonia in multiple lobes of the lower part of both lungs. Apparently during some of her vomiting events, some of her stomach contents were being aspirated into the lungs, which led to the pneumonia. This was terrible news, and I knew we were now dealing with a double edged sword, and for the moment, the pneumonia would be the doctors' priority. Annie's weight loss and inability to keep food down would have to be set aside for now. Annie was immediately started on IV antibiotics for the pneumonia.

After Dr. Liepins completed all the preliminary testing, he had Annie moved up to Eight Tower, cancer ward, into a private room.

One of the first things they had to do was bring in a pump and completely empty the contents of her stomach. Annie also received a PICC line so she could receive TPN, total parenteral nutrition, as well as life-sustaining fluids she needed. She wouldn't be allowed to eat or drink for several days. Most of her medications would be given through the IV. The exception to her fluid intake orally would be when she had to take an oral medication. The objective of this treatment was to see if her stomach problems would resolve without high risk surgical intervention.

TPN was a white substance full of nutrients, vitamins, and minerals. Its only purpose was to sustain her while keeping her stable.

It was unlikely she'd gain weight while on TPN. Sadly, in cancer patients it doesn't work all that well. Weight loss in advanced cases of cancer such as Annie's is simply more complicated than adding more calories to the diet. The studies on TPN indicate that many cancer patients started on TPN will usually die within six months after its induction. Reason being, cancer produces a multitude of chemicals that also lead to excessive weight loss. This situation was all part of the cancer "roller coaster effect."

Once again, Annie was in a monumental battle for her life. Personally, Melissa and I thought this was possibly the end of all our hopes and dreams. Every event was starting to promote a more weakened state in Annie. It was hard watching the effects of the cancer beat Annie down, but that's what it does best. Looking back and having the advantage of an understanding of this cancer, this event, like many of the others, was most likely due to lack of an early detection.

December 27, 2009: As this was a Sunday, things in Annie's room were very quiet. She remained seriously ill, but stable. I was waiting in anticipation for tomorrow, when hopefully Dr. Moore Sr. would come over and check on Annie.

Today Annie's platelets were at 12,000, a critical low count, and she needed a blood transfusion as her HGB was 7. She received two units of red blood cells today.

This was a difficult time for Melissa and me, but Annie didn't really have the ability to understand what was taking place, as she was just too sick. However, for Melissa and me, it was just another sad reality of Annie's remission. Annie is still struggling with blood counts that are much more reflective of a person on chemotherapy and fighting cancer. Our emotions were very conflicting on this matter. Why was this happening again?

December 28, 2009: Around 9:00 A.M. Dr. Moore Sr. showed up outside Annie's room, and started reading her chart, to include notes from her admission. He'd been consulted by Dr. Liepins over the weekend. He knelt down by Annie and said, "What's going on Ann?"

Annie had a sad look on her face when she looked at Dr. Moore Sr. and just shrugged her shoulders.

He examined her thoroughly, looked at me with a wrinkled forehead, and just shook his head.

As he started to leave the room, I called out his name.

He turned and looked back at me.

In a quiet voice I asked him if he could help her.

"I don't know Bob, but when I leave this room I'm going to get the ball rolling."

I swear, whether it was through Dr. Moore Sr.'s efforts, or just a coincidence, within the hour Annie's room was full of activity. She had X-rays that day to check the status of the pneumonia, respiratory was in to help her with breathing treatments, and her blood was drawn. She received a total blood chemistry, as well as her blood counts. Her platelets were still 12,000, critically low.

December 29, 2009: After checking the previous days' notes, Dr. Moore Sr. came in this morning, talked to Annie for a few minutes, then left the room.

I was starting to realize the seriousness of the situation as Annie was on 6 liters of oxygen to maintain normal saturation. When we got to 10 liters, what were they going to do? Would she be taken to the ICU and put on the ventilator again? I followed him out of the room and asked him the big question. "Dr. Moore, are they going to put Annie on the ventilator again?"

He gently said, "No."

I said in a soft voice, "Well then what's going to happen to her?"

He simply said, "She will code Bob." He explained to me that Annie is way too frail, sick, and diseased to be going on the ventilator.

He then indicated, at the moment everything is on hold as they have to stop the pneumonia.

After talking with Dr. Moore Sr. I called Melissa at her work. I explained the situation to her. After we got off the phone, Melissa apparently called her sister, Victoria, and told her she might want to get out here to see her momma. Coincidentally, I called Victoria too, just after Melissa spoke to her, and she was already packing her car.

I told her to hang on, I'd get in touch with Dr. Moore Sr., and see if that was necessary for her to come out right away.

After chatting with Victoria, I paged Dr. Moore Sr., and spoke with him on the phone.

"Give me three more days Bob, we'll know by then."

So I passed on the word to Victoria and put her on hold. It was a long drive from Georgia to Kansas.

At some point in this day, Dr. Moore Sr. called Dr. Troung, Annie's pulmonologist, and asked him to come over and evaluate Annie's abnormal X-ray and check her for hypoxemia. This is a term used when the lungs aren't functioning properly, or the heart isn't pumping enough blood to the lungs. This can lead to hypoxia, which can actually lead to vital organs shutting down due to lack of oxygen. Dr. Troung's impression on evaluation of Annie was that she did have hypoxemia, secondary to her pneumonia, and diffuse pneumonitis. When a person is on pure oxygen over an extended amount of time, it needs to be between 25 and 40 percent. Anything greater can lead to oxygen toxicity and permanent lung damage that can cause the lungs not to work properly. Apparently, diffuse pneumonitis was damaging Annie's lungs. It became one of those issues where Annie had to have the oxygen, but it was causing other difficulties. It's that old roller coaster effect again. With cancer, some of the life-sustaining strategies had side effects, and this was a perfect example.

Dr. Tom Moore of the infectious disease department also came in today. His impression and evaluation were pretty much the same as those of Dr. Troung's. He recommended a CT scan of the abdomen be scheduled for later today, looking for some sort of intestinal blockages.

Annie had her CT scan in the late afternoon, and there were still no definitive answers to her bowel obstruction.

Dr. Tom Moore told me he'd be following Annie throughout this event for infectious disease control, maintaining her with an appropriate antibiotic strategy.

January 2, 2010: Dr. Moore Sr. came in that morning with some good news. With the respiratory therapy she was getting a few times a day, and continuation of strong IV antibiotics, the pneumonia was starting to subside. This wasn't an expected result, but I'm not sure it was unexpected either; moreover, with Annie it seemed anything was possible, and we were all learning that when it came to her, to expect the unexpected.

The ventilator question was actually answered that day. If a patient is terminally ill, very sick, as in Annie's case, there'd be no ventilator. Annie was too weak, and seemed to be giving in to her fate. On Sept 8th, 2009, she was placed on the ventilator under different circumstances. She was much stronger, with more ability to fight the disease. This time, it was the 4th or 5th antibiotic that actually worked and started turning the pneumonia. The doctors at the hospital had a whole arsenal of good antibiotics at their disposal, but it can be difficult at times to figure out which one is going to work, if any. They go one day at a time.

Patients with multiple myeloma and pneumonia, in her cachetic condition, don't usually survive this sort of event. Each time Annie survived one of her traumatic events, my faith in her survival just got stronger. I wasn't sure what was going on, but Annie was obviously being looked after by a higher power. I was at the point where I could no longer deny what I was seeing. Some doctors and many nurses were always surprised at how she was surviving such traumatic events. Nicole, a nurse that attended to Annie often when she was in the hospital would at times say to me, "Bob, how does she do it?"

My response was always a muted, "I don't know."

With multiple myeloma and little immunity to fight pneumonia the outlook is usually poor, but somehow Annie just seemed to push it aside. At the time, during this event, I didn't know or understand that her pneumonia was the least of our worries.

This was Annie's eighth day in the hospital, and to this point she's had 5 chest X-rays, 6 KUBs (X-rays of the abdomen), and 4 CT scans. They were getting clear evidence that the pneumonia was starting to retreat, but there was still no definitive answer on what was going on with her intestines. The suspicions were that there was a blockage somewhere, but the CT scans weren't picking it up.

January 3rd, 2010: Annie started getting a yellow skin color, so blood was drawn to check her liver. When the test results came back they indicated that the liver was not functioning properly, and she was getting jaundice.

Dr. Tom Moore came over and told me not to worry; it was probably the TPN, and he would stop it for now. I think I panicked a bit, knowing Annie wouldn't have any nutrition. He saw the panic in my eyes, and explained to me that this often happens as TPN is a complex formula, and sometimes has to be adjusted to the patient's needs. He was right as usual, and the problem was resolved within thirty-six hours.

January 6, 2010: Dr. Farhat was consulted by Dr. Liepins and came over to visit Annie today. After his examination he noted, "Her heart is stable, platelets are 18,000, and she has lost a lot of weight."

When Annie was initially admitted to the hospital, I asked for Dr. Moore Sr. and Dr. Assem Farhat to be consulted. I was told no, as this was a pneumonia and abdomen problem, and they wouldn't be needed. I disagreed! With one of the leading causes of death with multiple myeloma patients being pneumonia and further complications from the pneumonia, I felt it was imperative to have Dr. Moore Sr. on board. Annie had three stents in her aorta and two in her heart; and this illness would place substantial stress on her heart, so why not consult her cardiologist. Additionally, Annie loved those two doctors and they made her feel safe. In Annie's mind they were two of the best doctors in their specific fields, and they treated her very well. Annie had very kind ways, and in the worst of times a beautiful smile. Their presence, and participation in her care, always seemed to give her a psychological advantage and lifted her spirits. After I expressed my feelings as her husband and caregiver to the doctor, he said he'd take care of the matter and he kept his word.

January 7, 2010: Today they decided to start trying Annie on a soft diet: a small amount of juice, Jell-O, and things like that. They were hoping that the problem with her digestive system had reversed itself, and she'd be able to start eating again. She certainly needed it!

It worked for a few hours, then the vomiting returned. She couldn't keep food or liquid down. They kept trying over several days, but I knew it wasn't going to work until they could figure out why it was happening.

On January 12th, 2010, I got in touch with the appropriate folks at Wesley Medical Center and informed them that I wanted a second opinion from a different gastrointestinal doctor, whose name I haven't mentioned. I asked Beverly who she'd suggest, and I was told she liked Dr. Lievens. I put in the request, and it was approved the same day.

The reason for my request was simple. Her other gastrointestinal doctor hadn't been over to see her once while she was in the hospital. I was told by other doctors that he was treating her from his office. I'd already figured that out, as his name kept being referenced but he was never there. When I reached out for the second opinion, I told one of Annie's doctors and he said with a smile, "Took you long enough."

I felt very foolish as I was such an attentive caregiver. Logically I did the right thing, as a second opinion in this case where we'd been bogged down for so long with her digestive problems, was overdue. In the world of cancer, second opinions are quite common, and in most the literature I had at the time on Annie's cancer, and its side effects, second opinions are actually encouraged.

January 14, 2010: Dr. Lievens came in that evening and introduced himself to Annie and me. He said he'd gone over all her medical notes, X-rays and CT scans, and that he basically came up with the same conclusion as everyone else. There was no definitive answer to her intestinal problem. However, he did become very proactive in her care, which was something she didn't have with her previous gastrointestinal doctor. He was very kind, compassionate, and very involved in Annie's care on a day to day basis.

By this time, the fecal matter in Annie's bowels was starting to back up into her stomach. She was vomiting out fecal matter mixed with fluid from her stomach. I was beginning to think I was going to need two pails for the vomit, which would include one for me too. It was a disgustingly bad smell, and really upset me! How could someone be allowed to lie around, losing ground every day, and then start vomiting up fecal matter? It didn't make any sense to me.

The next day when I spoke to Dr. Lievens about my feelings, he gave me the cold hard facts. He told me that Annie was probably too weak to have exploratory surgery, but even if she could, no doctor will touch her with her critical low platelets. Annie's platelets have been critical low throughout this whole visit; and that's why everyone has taken the wait-and-see approach; hoping the problem might resolve itself, as it sometimes does.

Dr. Lievens was telling me that they were doing the best they could under very difficult circumstances, and modern technology wasn't giving up any answers; but there had to be one. There was no doubt in my mind, Annie had a blockage somewhere.

That evening around 8:00 P.M., Dr. Lievens placed an NG tube into her nostril down into her stomach. The tube was attached to a pump, which would keep her stomach pumped out at all times and there would be no more vomiting or drinking of fluids or soft diet. He told me her stomach will keep filling with fluids, even if she doesn't drink. Apparently, that is a natural process, and the pump would take care of it.

The NG tube was not too comfortable for Annie, but she tolerated it pretty well. Where it goes into the nostril, it takes quite a bit of tape to hold it in place. Where the tube protrudes out from the nose it takes on the form of an Elephant's trunk; thus, Annie named her tube an Elephant's trunk. It was just another one of those cute moments in an otherwise chaotic world of cancer.

Jan 21, 2010: I was laying back in my recliner early this morning, when I heard the sound of multiple footsteps coming down the hallway in a hastily manner. It reminded me of two soldiers marching. As they reached Annie's doorway they turned into her room and walked straight over to me. Startled, I jumped up and shook the reached out hand of a surgeon, named Dr. Nold, who then introduce his assistant to me as Dr. O'Conner. I didn't have a clue who consulted him, but he was there in Annie's room with his partner, and I got the immediate impression he was all about taking care of business.

He was young, and spoke with a confidence I hadn't seen in awhile. The first thing he wanted to do was get the NG tube out and follow her for a few days and see if there was any resolution to her bowel problem.

Dr. Nold had the NG tube pulled that day and the results were predictable. As soon as Annie's stomach was full from eating or drinking, it all came back up, nothing would stay down. That went on for several more days, as he really didn't want to do surgery unless it was the last resort.

February 1, 2010: Dr. Nold and his assistant Dr. O'Conner came into the room this morning. Dr. Nold said they would be doing exploratory surgery tomorrow morning. Dr. Nold explained to Melissa and I the challenges Annie would be facing, but felt we were running out of time, and he needed to act now. He was going to make an eight-inch incision in her abdomen and try to locate the problem. Her platelets were very low, and there was no guarantee she wouldn't have unstoppable bleeding, which would be worst case. There was also the possibility that she might not recover from the surgery as she was so weak.

Dr. Nold had a presence and a certain confidence about him that was unmistakable. Melissa asked him if her momma could die from this surgery.

He said she could, "But not on my watch!" He gave us confidence in the outcome, but we still knew the odds were stacked against her.

Annie had surgery in the past with low platelets, however, this time was different. She was very weak, and tired of being ill. I wasn't sure that if there was a problem, even if it were resolved, she'd have the willpower to fight back or even want to.

A different doctor came in that day, and noted that he warned the family of the dangers of the surgery, and her chances of survival but the family, Melissa and I, insisted on going forward. Various doctors had been telling me for days she was slowly dying, and of that, I had no doubt. However, Melissa and I weren't going to let Annie die without giving her a fighting chance. I knew, if she didn't bleed, he would locate the problem and hopefully be able to fix it. Keep in mind, I was following Annie's wishes to the letter. She wanted to fight and live as long as she could and I was not going to deny her that opportunity.

As her caregiver and loving husband, I had an emotional conflict going on here. Yes, she agreed to the surgery and wanted it, but if I flipped the coin over, she was saying she was very tired of all the pain and suffering, seemingly wanting to give up the battle. Maybe this was her plan; if anything went wrong during the surgery she wouldn't know about it, and it would all be over.

February 2, 2010: Annie was wheeled down for surgery at approximately 7:00 A.M., with Melissa and I right behind her. Once they got her into the staging area and hooked up to the monitors, we were able to come in and sit by her side for a while. They gave her two units of platelets hoping for a boost, even if it was a short one. While sitting by Annie's bedside, we didn't express our fear or anxiety, we just played with her. Melissa made some funny remarks about Annie sunbathing with her new battle scar, and generally we kept it very light hearted. It seemed to relax the nurses too. While we were still in the staging area, Annie received a phone call via my cell phone from Wendy's other son Jason in England, giving her his love and wishing her the best.

In the past, Melissa and I watched Annie survive events that most thought were not possible. Would this be any different? I wasn't sure, but I had confidence that if anyone on this earth could survive this surgery, she could. She certainly seemed to have a friend in a higher place that seemed to be watching over her. We'd know soon enough.

Melissa and I were in the waiting room for what seemed like eternity. Eventually Dr. Nold came out, with a big smile on his face, and said. "She has some of the strongest platelets I've ever seen. She only lost 10 cc of blood."

I found that hard to believe, but amazing.

He further stated that he had to remove eighteen inches of her small intestine, as she had a blockage about one half inch above her colon that left the opening, about the size of a pen's head. That's what was causing all the problems, and was undetectable.

Speaking with Annie prior to having surgery, she told me her worst fear other than death was the possibility of having to wear an ostomy bag for the rest of her life.

Dr. Nold had explained to her that he'd do what he could to preclude that from happening; but once he opened her up, saw the damage and how much intestine he was going to remove, he had no choice. His fear was that when the intestine was sewn back together, a small percentage of them leak or have seepage. In any case, they'd have to go right back to surgery. He said Annie couldn't survive a second surgery, so he had to give her an ileostomy. She would now be wearing a pouch for her bowel movements.

An ostomy is a surgically created opening in the body for the discharge of body waste. The stoma, or end of the bowel that protrudes out through the ostomy, is where the waste comes from. To solve that problem and catch the waste, you wear an ostomy pouch. There are many different types of ostomies, but they are basically for the same purpose.

Due to Annie's nutritional needs, Dr. Nold had a G-Tube inserted into her stomach. It came out her left side, with the visual part being about eighteen inches long. The TPN was discontinued and we'd now be tube feeding her with a pump. She was supposed to receive five eight-ounce cans of Osmolite a day, which would meet her full nutritional needs, but would not adequately address her need for a 2,000 calorie intake daily. They couldn't quite get four cans in her as she became very nauseated. Obviously her body was having some sort of issues with the Osmolite.

A little later on in the day, Dr. Nold came up to check on Annie and speak to Melissa and me.

I asked him, "Are we out of the woods now?"

"Not yet," was his reply.

He told me the portion of the small intestine he removed looked very suspicious. He said it looked a bit like lymphoma, another form of blood cancer. The intestine was sent to pathology for a quick look over, then dissected into slices. When we got the results a few days later, the report from pathology said it was basically dead tissue. Dr.

Nold was pleased with the results, but said from previous experience it looked pretty bad.

I didn't ask the question of what caused the intestine to die, as I was sure I already knew the answer. As I said earlier, excessive morphine use can put the intestines to sleep and sometimes they die. Annie could not have lived without her pain medications while suffering from broken and diseased bones the way she was. In my opinion this is the result of the excessive morphine she had to be on, and just another example of the roller coaster effect, caused by cancer.

February 3, 2010: The surgery went well, but Annie was pretty much unable to move, being sedated, and in a weakened state from the surgery.

Today I got my first experience with the ostomy pouch and what it represented. It had only been on Annie for one day, and started leaking body waste all around the seal attached to the abdominal wall. The wound care nurse was called up to change the bag, which only lasted a few hours and had to be changed again.

Annie's body was putting out so much waste, that it seemed to be overpowering the seal. The bag had to be changed many times the next several days. On one particular night, Annie's nurse Nicole changed the bag three times. Annie was allowed to eat most foods as long as they weren't too solid. However, she was very weak and her appetite was virtually nonexistent.

Sadly, Melissa and I were beginning to think she was giving up the fight, and we needed to start preparing ourselves for the worst.

It was starting to look like a real tragedy in the making. Dr. Nold resolved her problem and did a wonderful job. However, her weakened state at surgery was now becoming a serious issue. Annie became totally sedentary after the surgery, had to lie flat on her back, and with severe malnutrition, she was a prime candidate for bed sores, which she had for a few days now.

February 11, 2010: Annie was lying in bed that morning in agony with her back. She had three large bed sores on her spine, through to the bone, and one on her coccyx (tailbone). The wound care team came in and dressed them, but that was all they could do. Since the day Annie entered the hospital she was on IV narcotics, which helped with the pain but kept her sedentary. The hospital didn't have a lot of choices, as they couldn't leave her in pain.

Today Annie apparently heard some bedside talk about putting her on hospice. I must have been out of the room, as I wasn't aware of that.

That afternoon, while I was standing by her bedside looking down at her, our eyes locked onto each other and she abruptly started crying. We had a very sad, difficult, but gentle conversation.

She said to me very softly, "Bobby, please take me home. I don't want to die in the hospital."

I said, "Annie, I can't take care of you at home. I don't have all this equipment you need."

She replied in a very tearful voice, "You can buy it at the shops."

By that time we were both crying, and I didn't know what to do; but I made her a promise, whatever it takes, I will get you out of here.

I knew I was going to meet with strong resistance; however, my love for Annie and honoring her wishes were driving my thought process.

I got in touch with our nurse and had her call the hospitalist doctor on duty, Dr. Dang, and tell her I needed to see her as soon as possible. I knew her well, and assumed her feelings were that Annie needed to be on hospice.

About two hours later, Dr. Dang arrived at the nurses' station. I was contacted by Annie's nurse and asked to come to the nurses' station to visit with her. When I walked up to her, she was sitting at a desk watching me as I approached. I just looked at her and softly said, "Annie wants to go home."

Dr. Dang told me she couldn't go home, she was too sick.

So I asked the question, "Is she getting any better?"

Dr. Dang closed her eyes, leaned her head forward and nodded her head no, while saying, "She's losing ground every day. She needs hospice now."

I simply said, "Dr. Dang, if she is going to die, she can die at home."

I asked her to get in touch with hospice and get them up here as soon as possible. I wanted to hear what kind of service they provided, and go from there.

The tenth floor at the hospital is where they take patients for hospice care while in the hospital. I wasn't going to let Annie go up there, as that's usually a one way trip. And I had a plan.

Approximately two hours later, two very pleasant ladies from Amedisys Hospice entered Annie's room. We sat and visited for a while, and everything seemed okay, until we got to the comfort care part.

I asked them what happened if Annie needed IV fluids, blood transfusion, or platelets.

They told me they can't administer any life-sustaining fluids.

That was the deal breaker! I had no intention of taking Annie home and just let her die without a fight. My gut instincts and previous events told me that if I could somehow get the equipment to my home, we still had a fighting chance. Annie wasn't dying of cancer or pneumonia at the moment; it was malnutrition.

Dr. Nold had fixed her intestine problem, and yes, she was very ill and weak; but getting her home in her familiar environment might help.

I discussed the equipment issue with the Hospice nurses, asking if there was any way they could help me get the equipment Annie needed. To my surprise and delight, one of the ladies said they had a home health agency that would work with Annie and take all the necessary equipment to our home. The lady then made a phone call, and arrangements were made for the company representative to meet me first thing in the morning so they could make an assessment of what Annie needed.

A few people didn't agree with my decision, but I didn't care. I didn't base my decision on what other folks thought. I was supporting my wife, and if it turned out to be a disaster, so be it. Seriously, what was the worst that could happen? She'd die at home, surrounded by love; and this is what she would want.

I felt that Annie might be receiving some sort of intervention with her care that had helped us through some tough times. It gave me a strong sense that it wasn't Annie's time to die. Her situation was bad, and Annie appeared to be dying, but we'd been here before.

This quickly became an ethical event with me. I had the power on a piece of paper to put her to sleep that day, under doctors' advice. It just seemed to me, after all the traumatic events I'd seen over the course of her illness, somehow, some way, I knew I had to take her home. I can't explain the feeling, but when I made that decision not to do hospice or put her on comfort care, I felt a strong burden was taken off my shoulders, as I was putting this whole decision-making process back in the hands of a higher power, and in my opinion, I believe in some way I was being guided.

February 12, 2010: Total Home Care showed up this morning, and after speaking to some of the medical staff, they were able to identify everything they needed. They gave me a phone number and asked me to call them tomorrow and give them an approximate time we would be home. They'd be waiting at our front door with the equipment.

Taking Annie home, as frail as she was and understanding things could quickly go very wrong, was a challenging thought for me. But I did everything I could do to keep the negative impulses away, and for now, focus on the fact that Annie would be going home tomorrow. We'd been in the hospital for fifty-one days, and while there, she had ten chest X-rays, twenty abdominal X-rays, ten CT scans, approximately seventy-five blood draws and countless other tests. It was time to go home.

February 13, 2010: The first thing we did this morning was check her weight. It was seventy-nine pounds, and apparent she had lost considerable weight over the past few months, despite all the effort that went into her care.

Annie couldn't walk or stand, so I knew it would take me a couple of hours to sort the room, gather up all our belongings, and get the vehicle loaded. Once I got things organized, I called Total Home Care and told them they could expect us around 3:00 P.M., and that my daughter Melissa would be there waiting for them. A nurse helped me get her into the wheelchair, and wheeled her down to the car for me. It wasn't all that difficult getting her in the car as she'd lost so much weight.

On our slow ride home, Annie was very quiet and just sat and stared out the window of our car. We did have one very important conversation where I made her a promise that I would be relentless in her caregiving, but she had to agree to help me by fighting as hard as she could, as I knew no matter what I did, if she didn't have the will to live, she'd lose this battle.

When we arrived home, as I got her out of the car and into the wheelchair, I could see she was trying to smile, and I knew she was happy to be home. As promised, Melissa was there with the home health personnel and all the equipment. About an hour and a half later, after receiving my training on the equipment, they were gone, and Melissa and I had Annie all to ourselves.

As Melissa worked to make her momma comfortable in her bed, I went into the dining room, sat down, and tried to come to terms with what happened over the past couple of days. It occurred to me that after our narrow escape from hospice and death, we now had nothing to lose and everything to gain. There was no longer any doubt in my mind that we would fight this continuing epic battle as a team, with all the grace and love her creator promised her.

That was a very long fifty-one day stay in the hospital, and it was very tough at times; but with Annie there never seemed to be a dull moment. There was always something going on. Here's one of those priceless moments that happened around January 20th, 2010.

It was in the early afternoon, and I was sitting in my recliner reading the sports page while Annie was resting. It was not long before I heard the voice that only a husband can recognize. I knew I was in trouble, but had no idea why.

In her quiet stern little voice she said, "Bob, would you come over here for a moment?"

I said, "Yes dear, what do you need?"

She asked, "Are you stupid?"

I just stared at her and said, "I don't think so."

"How much are we paying for this apartment?"

I tried to explain to her that this was not an apartment by telling her to look around at all the equipment and the IVs in her arms. After pointing a few things out to her, I started recognizing the confusion in her eyes and changed my thought process. When she got confused, I'd learned over the course of the illness to go with the flow, as I didn't want her to feel that way.

So I replied, "Probably two thousand dollars or more a day."

"Well then you must be stupid." She asked me to walk over and look outside our windows, and tell her what I see.

As I scanned the area I wasn't really paying attention, as after several weeks in the hospital I knew what was out there, so I told her. "I see tall buildings, cars, and many people."

Her reply was, "Exactly. For that kind of money there should be a beach, or at least a swimming pool!"

I really couldn't argue that point! So I decided to let her take charge, by asking her what she'd like for me to do.

She indicated that she wanted an apartment across the hallway. She told me that she kept hearing people over there and they were having fun. (That was the nurses' station)

I asked her if she wanted me to go to the office and get our apartment changed.

She was shaking her head up and down, meaning yes I do.

She weighed about eighty-five pounds, could barely move, but she wanted to take charge of her life. I admired her for that.

I went to the nurses' station and found her nurse. I explained the situation to her and she started laughing. I said "It's not funny, you're not living with her."

She said, "Okay, go back to the room and I'll be down in a minute with her anxiety meds."

I told her I wasn't going anywhere until Annie had her medication, which seemed to make her laugh even more.

She then went to the closet, got the medication and went down and gave it to Annie.

When I went back to the room she was asleep. Thank heaven! I knew when she woke, she wouldn't remember the conversation.

This type of event happened often, and sometimes the situation could become very unstable as Annie would get very delusional and difficult to deal with. One morning around 3:00 A.M. I woke to some noise, and as I looked over towards her bed, I saw her standing by the bed dusting a table. She had climbed over the bed rail, IV tubes and all.

I said, "Annie! What are you doing?"

She replied, "I'm just having a little tidy up."

I got up, stood by her, and in a couple of minutes she was satisfied that the table with all the medical stuff on it was clean. So I lowered the bed rail and helped her back in bed. It got a little crazy at times, and she definitely kept me on my toes. But, that's the way it was.

On a different occasion, a few days later, she was getting ready for the high risk surgery that we spoke of earlier in this chapter. I was worried, so I asked her if I could sleep beside her tonight in her hospital bed.

She said, "I'd like that."

It was around 2:00A.M. when I heard her screams.

She was yelling, "Bob, Bob!"

I started saying, "Annie it's okay, I'm right here!"

She started yelling and flailing herself around saying, "You're not Bob!"

From that point on things got really bad! She started hitting me on the head in rapid motion, with her little hands and toothpick arms. I found myself trying to figure out what to do, without hurting her. She had two IV's going and was slowly working herself off the bed, despite my best efforts to control her. I couldn't do much of anything, as this event developed very quickly and was progressing in intensity, very rapidly.

Fortunately, a nurse heard her yelling and came running in, took one look at us and said, "I'm going to get help!"

What seemed like an eternity was getting ready to settle down, as I heard the footsteps of the only nurse that ever intimidated me.

She was on her way, and going to take control of the situation. She walked in, put her hands under Annie's arms, picked her up, and laid her on the bed. She held her there while the other nurse administered her anxiety medication. Annie fell asleep immediately.

The next morning when the nurse came in and checked on her, she was fine, in that she didn't get hurt during her delusional event.

The morning after that event I called my sister-in-law Lesley, and she figured out what the problem was. Annie had many stays in the hospital prior to this period, and was always on Dilaudid, which is several times stronger than morphine. Apparently on Annie's side of the family there was a history with problems when taking that drug. I didn't know that, but once I found out, I spoke to the doctors and she was switched to morphine.

She was in a bit more pain, but instead of the agitation, she just told fibs, made stuff up, and made us all laugh. She'd start talking, we'd start laughing, and she'd say, "Am I telling fibs again?" It always made her laugh too.

One day I was standing by the bed and she said to me, "Dr. Moore just called me on the phone, told me I was doing better, and could go home soon."

I just stared at her, and she said, "He didn't call me did he."

I said, nope!

She just started laughing saying "I'm fibbing again."

I'd just say yep, you are. Those moments, as bad or as good as they were, are precious to me.

Always remember, strong narcotics can mess with a patient's mind over a period of time. If you can, just go with the flow. It's not about being right, it's about caring for the patient or your loved one.

It was now becoming apparent that Annie's struggle was nearing its end. I knew this as each event was increasing in intensity, and were also draining her of her much needed strength.

This picture was taken shortly after Annie left the hospital. I'd like to note that she'd been in remission at this point for over a year, and as far as we knew was cancer free. It really pulled at my heart strings as most, if not all of the people we knew in the world of cancer in remission, were getting on with their lives, and living with a sense of normality. Once again, I will stress the importance of early detection and being pro-active in your healthcare. However, that alone is not enough. One must know the warning signs of blood cancer, and take immediate action by asking the tough questions to your doctor, and getting the necessary help. If you don't feel well for no apparent reason, bruising easily, your blood is too thick, your CBC or blood chemistry is not normal, and you're overly tired, start looking for answers. Perhaps you don't have a blood cancer, as those are symptoms of other illnesses too; but then again, you might. I sincerely hope that as you continue reading this story, the information you continue to glean will guide you in the right direction. No one should have to suffer Annie's fate in this day and age. It's very inhumane! *This was her remission.*

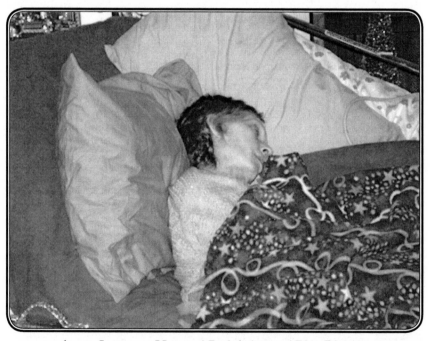

Annie Lying on Hospital Bed Asleep w/ Blue Blanket

Chapter 12

Last Summer

Feb 14, 2010: Bringing a seriously ill patient home from a hospital environment is a daunting task at best, and I was sure of only one thing; if Annie was going to survive we needed the perfect storm. I had no plan other than dealing with one event at a time, as they happened. I knew it was going to be difficult, but I also knew it was the right thing to do.

The first night we were home, I sat on the sofa watching her sleep and seemed to fall deeper in love with her. Although she looked to be very ill and frail, she looked so precious and relaxed lying on her hospital bed. I had a tremendous respect for her tenacious will to live; but it was now up to me to follow through on my promise. I wasn't sure if I could bring her back from the clutches of death or not. However, if I could be as relentless in my caregiving as she was in fighting the disease, we would be in with a chance.

Annie's feeding schedule was going to be treacherous. She needed five eight ounce cans of Osmolite daily. Each can contained much of her nutritional needs, but only 250 calories. Before we left the hospital Dr. Lievens told me she must have a calorie intake of at least 2,000 calories per day minimum, otherwise, we were probably fighting a losing battle.

The discharge instructions from the hospital had me starting the tube feeding at 6:00 A.M., and continuing on until 10:00 P.M. daily, using the Kangaroo Pump. The Kangaroo Pump is simply a small electrical pump that hooks to the IV pole and pumps the liquid at different speeds into the patient through a long clear tube. The bag hooks to the top of the pole, with a tube protruding down that fit into the peg tube in Annie's side. One can of Osmolite at a time was poured into the bag. Prior to hooking the tube up to the peg tube, I had a syringe that held 8 cc. of liquid. I'd fill that with water, insert it into the peg tube, and flushed it. The liquid food was very sticky, and the water usually kept the peg tube from clogging and gave her additional liquid for hydration. I did that before I started feeding Annie, after a couple of cans, and again when I was through. If the buzzer went off on the pump while feeding, I'd unplug the two tubes from each other and re-flush the peg tube. If the peg tube flushed okay, then I knew it was the tube from the bag. Rather than wasting time trying to find the blockage, I'd throw the food bag away and start over. It didn't take me long to realize their schedule would not work for us, so I started the daily feeding at 8:00 A.M., finishing at midnight. Reason being, I usually stayed up until 2:30 A.M. making sure she had taken all her medications, and was settled in before I allowed myself to relax. Plus, five cans of Osmolite only equaled 1,250 calories, so I had to find a way to get the other calories in her. By starting the tube feeding at 8:00 A.M., I could add some sort of calorie component with it. I'd make sure she had at least two bottles of Boost each day, which added about 400 calories to the count. She loved Breyers Ice Cream with raspberries sprinkled over the top, but her favorite was one thin, deep fried pancake with syrup and mandarin oranges. Sometimes she'd eat a pancake with syrup and mandarin oranges twice a day. Each serving was approximately 500 calories. The first week I basically fed her, and all she had to do was open her mouth, chew, then swallow.

Here's some important information if you ever have to tube feed a patient. Before Annie left the hospital, Mike, one of the nurses at Wesley Medical Center, Eight Tower, showed me a neat and a very quick way to feed her. He actually let me feed her for a couple of days under his guidance and supervision while she was in the hospital. He taught me how to bolus feed her through the tube. Once she started digesting her food okay, I changed over to the bolus feeding. It's very simple, safe, and saves hours of feeding time.

The first thing I had to do was discontinue the bag and pump. I took a new syringe that held eight cc, inserted the syringe tip into her peg tube, poured a portion of the contents of a can into the large open end of the syringe and gravity fed her. I held the tube as high up as it would go without making Annie uncomfortable. It takes ten minutes maximum for a can, and you don't have to keep listening to that annoying pump. It took an average of two and a half hours per can using the pump. As I slowly weaned Annie down to three cans a day, I gave her a can every four hours. I didn't stop giving her the cans of food until the doctor told me to. In Annie's case, I was feeding her a lot of junk food to get the calories up and show progress with weight gain. The three cans of Osmolite were basically making sure all her nutritional needs were met. My point is, once the patient is stable and starting to eat, bolus feeding will make your life much easier; and the patient's too. It is an acceptable way to feed your patient and you're not breaking any rules. One caution! Make sure when handling the peg tube you wear sterile gloves. Wipe the peg tube ending with alcohol before opening it up to insert the syringe. Make sure the syringe is wiped out too. A peg tube provides easy access for germs to enter the body, so keep the opening area as clean as possible. After use, I always soaked the syringe in white vinegar, a great germ killer. Even if you are using the pump, you still need to do this to keep germs out. That was always my first priority before feeding. Also, the area where the peg tube enters the body must be cleaned daily. I'd remove the old gauze, clean the area with wound cleaner, then reapply new sterile gauze. At night while she wasn't being fed, I'd tape the peg tube to the top of her leg so she didn't roll over on it, potentially pulling the tube out of position and having to be reinserted by a surgeon.

Total Homecare came over and gave me instructions on what to do and watch for. I listened patiently, however, I always knew what I had to do. What I needed the nurse to do was check her blood pressure, all vitals, and do wound care for her bed sores as they were severe and very painful. I moved Annie around in her bed every two hours or so to keep her from lying in any one position for too long, and promote healing. I used pillows behind her back for support when switching her from side to side. The pillows kept her from lying flat on her back.

As I said earlier, Annie had an ileostomy. Don't confuse that with any of the other ostomies, such as colostomy. An ileostomy is almost always wet. In other words, there is usually a continuous flow of fluid and waste into the bag. It may be a tiny amount, but it makes no difference when you are changing the bag. The area around the stoma has to be totally clean and dry before putting the bag on. If not, the adhesive on the bag will not stick properly, and the seal won't hold. Even the continuous emptying of the contents of the bag was challenging the first three weeks. As she was too weak to stand or sit, I had to empty the bag while she was lying down. I had to make sure all her skin was covered to protect her from any waste, and then empty the bag with a large syringe. It seemed everything I was doing with Annie at the moment was challenging. It didn't matter though, I knew one way or the other this situation would resolve itself in a few weeks. I was worried and had many anxious moments, but confident I could help her turn this event around.

When the nurse tried to train me on how to put the ostomy bag on, I'd say to her, "How can you train someone to do something when you can't do it yourself?" The first bag she put on Annie was leaking down her side fifteen minutes after she left. I called her company and told them I needed some help. I was told as the caregiver it was my responsibility to do the bag, and that the nurse was only allowed to come out twice a week. In all fairness to the homecare nurses, the nurses at the hospital couldn't get it to stay on either. Some days I'd have to change the bag six or seven times, and it was becoming a totally frustrating nightmare. Beyond a doubt, at least twelve nurses, including wound care personnel, couldn't get that bag to stay on her; so basically I was on my own with the bag.

Imagine, you're very tired and the time is 1:00 A.M., and you're getting ready to relax. One of the last things you do before laying down is check and empty the bag. Visually, you see a yellow stain around the outside seal, which means the bag has to be changed. The yellow stain is consistent with acid from her stomach, and if not removed quickly, it will fry the skin in that area.

Sometimes I could get the bag to stay on for five hours before it started leaking. I'd think I was making progress, until I pulled the bag off and saw bright red raw skin around the stoma with seeping blood, which was very painful for Annie. She often had tears flowing down her face when it was bleeding, as the acid from her stomach would run out onto the open wound.

One night Melissa called me at midnight to check on her momma. I told her she was okay but I couldn't talk as I was changing her bag. She called me back at 7:30 A.M. on her way to work and I was just finishing up the bag. Annie was experiencing diarrhea, so I had to lay pads out as far as one foot from the direction of her stoma opening, as the waste would shoot out six or eight inches at a time. I still managed to keep her clean and dry, and she was able to sleep through the night as I waited patiently for the wetness to stop. It took me a maximum of four minutes to put the bag on, once the running stopped. That was my window of opportunity, and if I missed it, it could go on for hours. It truly had to be that fast. I learned rather quickly when dealing with the ostomy that I had to always be prepared, and expect the unexpected. Some of the long nights were tough, as I still had to wake her up at 8:00 A.M. to start the feeding. I had many sleepless nights, but I survived and was keeping my promise to her. It was very challenging at times, but the rewards of having Annie for another day was special. Sometimes when I was changing the bag, when I got through, Annie would lean over and give me baby kisses on my shirt to show her affection and appreciation for the long, tiring, and miserable job I was doing. I did get great satisfaction out of the fact that I was doing something all the nurses I'd seen couldn't do. I got really good at changing the bag, and around the third month all the bags were staying on from twenty-four to thirty-six hours. At that point I usually changed the bag and put a fresh one on.

Sadly, I told Melissa one day, from the looks of Mom she'll be on the low end of the two to five-year life expectancy with multiple myeloma. I felt she'd recover from this event but overall she'd be in a more weakened state. Melissa knew her momma wasn't going to be around much longer too.

About three weeks after I brought her home, one morning I was in the kitchen area and heard her moving around, so I walked into the room. She was trying to get up and set on the edge of the bed. I looked at her with a smile on my face and asked her what she thought she was doing. She said something to the effect she wanted to come out and sit with me in the dining room. Her words gave me a rush of emotion that's hard to explain, but it gave me a strong sense that she wasn't ready to give up just yet. So I unplugged the pump from the wall, helped her into the wheelchair, and pushed her into the dining room pulling the IV pole. That was a glorious moment, as the odds of her getting better weren't very good. At that moment, I knew if I could keep her from getting an infection we were going to make it through this. I was starting to witness another event, which too many folks defied logic. Just think about it! In three weeks we were turning an event around that I was told would likely end in tragedy, yet we were now full of hope and promise once again.

Just imagine, if I'd made the wrong choice back in February on Hospice/comfort care, I'd be grieving her loss now rather than enjoying the beautiful woman I loved so much.

A short time later, Total Homecare was able to start Annie on occupational therapy, physical therapy, and eventually speech therapy. Angie, Allen, and Sarah came out twice a week at different times. Annie looked forward to their visits as they were extremely kind to her and helped her immensely. She always had lovely chit-chats with them, and they did their job professionally and with compassion. I enjoyed their visits too. They helped me understand how I could help Annie physically through gentle exercise, and help her work on her memory.

One morning Annie was sitting at the table putting her make up on, as I watched and chatted with her.

I said to her, "You know Allen is coming over this morning."

She said, "Oh, is he?"

As if she didn't know!

It made me laugh, as she was so skinny and frail looking, yet she wanted to feel pretty. I admired her for that, and often think it was her spirit at times that allowed her to keep moving forward.

March 15, 2010: I Received a call this morning from Veronica Hart, Case Management Program—TriWest. She was our case manager throughout the stem-cell process. It was now coming up to the one-year post stem-cell transplant. She would be transferring Annie's case management over to Paula Horineck, RN. Dealing with Annie's cancer, without their oversight, would've been much more difficult. Annie's medical records, including appointments and procedures, always crossed their desks. If they detected anything they were uncomfortable with, I always got a call. They were all about accountability, with not only the medical professionals, but me as well. They tried hard to make sure Annie got the best care possible; and I loved their business card logo, "Whatever it takes." That's about as good as it gets.

March 20, 2010: Today was going to be a special day for Annie. Her sister Shirley and husband Dillard were driving out from Chesapeake Bay, in Virginia, and would arrive this morning. They were going to spend the weekend with us. It was their second trip, and I think all we did for the two days was love, talk, laugh, and eat. It was a really fun weekend, and Annie got to spend some more quality time with her sister. Dillard and I, both being retired military, spent much of our time talking war stories. I'd known Dillard since the early 1970s, when he was dating Shirley.

They left Monday morning, unsuspecting that this would be the last time they'd ever see Annie. I remember giving Shirley a hug, and promising her I'd take good care of her sister. It was sad, but Annie and I had plenty of work to do trying to get her healthy.

March 29, 2010: Annie was getting a little stronger each day, as reflected in her weight gain. Her weight was now 86 pounds, and we were starting to make meaningful progress.

Total Homecare was still heavily involved in her care and making a huge difference.

We saw Dr. Moore Sr. today for the first time in awhile, and he was pleasantly surprised with her progress. He was all smiles while examining her, as he knew that she'd be around to fight another day. He set up an appointment for Annie to see Dr. Moore Jr. on April 19th, 2010. That would be the week of her one-year anniversary, post stem-cell transplant. He also noted that he would see her in three months.

April 19, 2010: We had a nice visit with Dr. Moore Jr. today. This was one-year post stem-cell transplant, and Annie was officially one year old today.

He noted, "She seems to be doing well, but remains debilitated as she always has been and is in a wheelchair." He stated that the recent bone marrow aspiration he completed on Annie in March 2010 indicated that she was in a major partial remission, and showing no evidence of recurrence.

When we were leaving his office, he put a big smile on his face and told Annie, "I would not have given you six months after transplant."

Coming from a brilliant oncologist spoke volumes to Annie and made her day special. Not only was she one year old today, she was still in remission. That was a good first birthday present.

1 Year Post Stem-Cell Birthday Card

One evening in early May, Annie was lying on her bed while I was in the process of changing her ostomy bag. We were watching the television when one of the local weathermen interrupted programming with a tornado warning for our area. Apparently there was a rotating wall cloud heading in our direction. When the sirens went off, Annie started to panic, and wanted to go to our basement. I tried to calm her, but she was frightened, and insisted on going to the basement. I had to wrap a towel around her, and have her hold her hand over the stoma with enough pressure to catch any leakage. I wheeled her to the stairway, put my left hand on the railing, right arm around her waist, and navigated her down 14 steep steps. I was able to change the bag downstairs while she rested comfortably. Our basement is set up like an apartment, is ten feet below ground level, and provides safety from tornadoes. My point is, even people with terminal cancer want to live as long as they can. In their mind, there's always this miracle pill just around the corner, or some sort of drug, that might just save them.

June 6, 2010: Today Annie and I went to the Wichita Arena with our daughter and grandkids to see our grandson Andrew graduate from high school. This picture of Annie and Andrew wouldn't exist if I'd put her on hospice back in February, 2010.

Annie & Andrew Standing in a crowd

June 8, 2010: We drove up to the cancer center today to get the result of Annie's most recent 24 hour urinalysis. We were taken back to one of the patient rooms where Annie's vitals were checked, and we waited to see Dr. Moore Sr. When he walked in, I think Annie and I both knew something wasn't right, as he wasn't his usual bubbly self.

He told her as gently as he could that her cancer was back, and we were now facing a dilemma. He noted, "I could put her on intermittent high-dose Decadron, 40 milligrams weekly, and it might control or slow the myeloma recurrence; but the effects would likely give her diabetic problems, leg weakness problems, and a negative protein balance with more osteoporosis."

I believe Annie and I both understood the magnitude of what we'd just been told. She didn't want all the side effects, which included very swollen facial features, referred to as the "moon face," and in general, she would also be feeling unwell. At the moment she was feeling better, despite what appeared to be a recurrence of her multiple myeloma.

It was further noted that, "Her back pain is now getting worse again, including the right hip where the prosthesis is; but her weight is much better, and is now ninety-six pounds."

I suspected the tumors were starting to form in her spine and hip once again; but as unhealthy as Annie was, there would be no more X-rays or scans looking for the cancer.

Another one of those timeless questions came out on this day. I asked Dr. Moore Sr., "What happens if Annie does not start the Decadron today?"

Dr. Moore Sr. replied, "Just buying some time Bob."

Annie's sister Wendy was put on the steroids for her cancer, and Annie always described her face to me as massive; and she didn't want that. I think she knew in the long run it wasn't going to help her anyway.

Later on in the visit, Dr. Moore Sr. visited with Dr. Moore Jr. about getting the ileostomy reversed. When Dr. Nold did the surgery, he told Annie when her weight reached one hundred pounds, and if she was still well, he'd reverse it. In other words, hook her intestines back up so she could have normal bowel movements.

Not quite sure of the date, but it was during the month of July that Annie's weight reached ninety-eight pounds. We went to see Dr. Nold, and he was able to pull her peg tube out; and there would be no more tube feeding as Annie would be on an oral diet only. That was bittersweet for her, as the cancer was becoming part of our conversation again.

August 31, 2010: Today Annie went over to visit Dr. Moore Sr. in regards to a 24 hour check of her urine he performed a few days earlier. He wanted to see how much abnormal protein was in her urine. In his notes from this day, he found it to be quite elevated at 10,400 mg/L. That number was just under what it was when she was first diagnosed. Her protein outputs from her malignant plasma cells were basically unchanged. He told us that based on the results of her 24 hour urine study, the myeloma was trucking right along.

I was shocked and surprised when Annie asked him, "How much time do I have left?"

He pulled his stool over close to her and looked her straight in the eyes and said, "Maybe five or six months, but I'm not God."

Surprisingly Annie took the news in stride. We were on the verge of a major relapse, which was my greatest fear. Her weakened state left little options for treatment, if any. He decided to hold off on any treatment today.

In his prognosis notes, there was one big "red herring," and he knew it and so did I! If her platelets failed her, as they'd been doing all along, the journey could be much shorter. I don't think Annie realized that, and it wasn't ever mentioned to her.

I knew this day was coming, but we weren't prepared. It seemed to me after coming so far, and beating the odds so many times, we were caught off guard. It was only in April that she was showing no signs of cancer.

We both sensed we were now entering some very troubled waters, but no matter what, we would fight this battle together and somehow make the most out of each day. Giving in to the cancer was not an option.

Before we left his presence, he called Dr. Nold and talked with him about reversing the ileostomy. Apparently Dr. Nold didn't want to reverse the procedure now, as all the information at the moment indicated the cancer was back. Dr. Moore Sr. set us up an appointment to see Dr. Nold so we could discuss the matter.

September 1, 2010: We had a visit with Dr. Nold today. He explained the situation to Annie, telling her that when he got a comprehensive report on the stage of her cancer, he'd make a decision then. I knew the bag would never come off, as Annie was in trouble.

September 9, 2010: Dr. Moore Sr. called Annie back to his office, telling her he needed to know exactly where she was with the cancer. That would allow him to set up his treatment strategies, if possible. This was a tough day for Annie, as she had a bone marrow aspiration, with the understanding that most likely the news would be very bad.

Based on previous experience, I knew the multiple myeloma was probably already out of control.

September 12, 2010: Beverly and her friend Kathy came over this morning to pick up Annie and take her to Victory in the Valley. Victory in the Valley is a charitable organization deeply involved with cancer patients and their loved ones.

Over the past few months Annie had made close to 60 fleece tie blankets. Many were made for family members, some for friends, but mostly for the "Adults" and the "Children of Cancer." Annie always had a special place in her heart for the children, and always gave to the children's cancer charities.

When she was able, I'd take her to the fabric store and help her purchase the fabric. She was a very creative person, and had a way with mixing and matching colors. She could make an adult six or seven foot blanket in about three or four hours. She whipped out the children's blankets rather quickly. When she was unable to make the trip to the fabric shop, I'd go for her. I wasn't that creative, but no matter what fabric I brought home, or how mismatched it might be, she always thanked me and told me how beautiful it was.

Annie was obviously living in grace, and knew she didn't have a lot of time left; but in her own special way, she just wanted to give back to people she felt were less fortunate than her. With a warm calmness in my heart, I can tell you that Annie did feel very fortunate for all the love she received from the people she met within her cancer family, and from those on the outside.

In this picture, Annie is at Victory in the Valley with her friend Kathy on her right and Beverley on her left. In front of her is but a few of the blankets she delivered that day for the "Children of Cancer."

Annie, Kathy and Beverly at Victory in the Valley

September 18, 2010: Annie was standing in front of the dining room mirror this morning, leaning on her wheelchair putting lotion on her face. Somehow she lost her balance, fell and broke her pinky finger on her right hand. I was in the other room at the time, but heard her fall. I ran to her, and found her lying on her side on the dining room floor. I made a quick visual check of her body, and noticed her pinky finger protruding out in a way that let me know it was broken. She had a small cut on her chin, and one on the side of her face. The pupils in her eyes looked normal, giving me the initial indication that she had suffered no major head trauma. I told her she was okay, but her pinky finger was broken. I pulled the wheelchair over to her, and slowly but gently picked her up and sat her back in the wheelchair. I called Melissa, and about one half hour later Dr. Klein came over and placed her finger in a sports bandage.

It was very important when Annie fell, that as her caregiver, I made a visual assessment of her before moving her into the wheelchair. If the pupils of her eyes had been dilated, or she was complaining of back, neck or head pain, I would have made her as comfortable on the floor as possible without moving her and called for the paramedics.

September 22, 2010: We went back to Dr. Moore Sr.'s office for the results of her latest bone marrow aspiration; here is a quote from the results. "Mrs. Harrison is seen in follow-up for results of her bone marrow. Now she has 80 percent plasma cells. She is in relapse." He further states, "Her back is hurting more, and she feels tired all the time." He noted that she had received two units of packed red blood cells today, and tomorrow she would receive a PICC line, as she was going to need many transfusions. He said he wanted to start treatment with a very low dose of Velcade, chemotherapy, but wait until he sees her next week and make a decision. He decided to start her on Amicar, 500 milligram tablets, to help her blood clot. Her platelets were critical low at 10,500; with her inability to respond to platelet transfusions and her bone marrow being eighty percent cancer, what would her odds be of surviving this unforgiving situation she was in? It was no longer a matter of if, but when. With that amount of cancer, her bone marrow isn't going to produce many platelets on its own.

What I got from this appointment today was Annie's worst nightmare. I knew beyond any doubt the cancer couldn't be stopped, and that we were most likely out of any realistic options.

On the drive home, once again it was very quiet, and it seemed as though we were living in a surreal world. I think on this day the door leading to the mystery of "Life After Death" was now slowly opening for Annie. I knew there would be no realistic way of denying her entry this time. Although Annie wasn't about giving up, she'd fought a long, hard battle, and was now tired and getting very weak.

October 5, 2010: Dr. Moore Sr.'s strategy today was to start her on high-dose Decadron, 40 milligrams a day. During her examination he noticed four scabbed-over sores, each about half the size of a dime. When he saw them he said, "Oh no, when did you get them?"

Annie apparently had shingles, which can be deadly to myeloma patients. Unfortunately, he'd no longer be able to give her Decadron as it's a steroid, and could make the shingles worse. Instead, he placed her on a very low dose of IV Velcade, less than 1 milligram. He really didn't want to do the Velcade at the moment, even in a very small dose, as it might affect the platelets. It could also possibly help, but was more like a roll of the dice, and he had no idea how they would fall.

Dr. Moore Sr. was very fond of Annie, and loved her fighting spirit. Her attitude was always positive, and she was gracious to all the help she received from him and other medical personnel. She never complained and usually smiled, even through many traumatic events. That sort of personality grows on people, especially doctors. He discussed the use of Velcade with her, and told her it might or might not work, but she wanted to try it. I think she knew she was out of options as her platelets were now 2,000. He also decided to put her on a course of Acyclovir for the shingles, even though he said it was probably too late in the treatment for anti-viral medication to make a difference.

When Dr. Moore Sr. had the discussion with Annie on using low dose Velcade, I could clearly see in his eyes and his body language that he knew the situation with Annie was grave, but he desperately wanted to help her, knowing he had no viable weapons to use. Still, he had to try for her.

Platelets were always going to be her problem, and I knew that. What I didn't know at the time was that platelets only live in the blood stream from five to nine days, then die off automatically. With the chemotherapy potentially killing off most of the platelets she had left, coupled with the fact that they're dying naturally, and most likely not many are being produced by the bone marrow, things were worse than I had thought. I had trouble wrapping my head around that scenario; and this situation became known to me as the "curse of her isoantibodies." That wasn't supposed to happen.

October 12, 2010: Today, when we arrived at Dr. Moore Sr.'s office, he had a little surprise for us. Her platelets were 3,300, a jump of 1,300, so he decided to try the Velcade for another week.

Also, he noted, "She is feeling fine and her shingles are drying up."

That was a blessing! He checked her body thoroughly for any bleeding, but didn't see any.

October 16, 2010: Annie and I took a drive out to Mid Continent Airport in Wichita to pick up her sister Lesley from California. I had called Lesley a few days earlier and told her I thought it was time she started making her way out here. When we got to the airport, I got Annie out of the car, into the wheelchair, and pushed her inside where she waited until I parked the car. Annie was very excited and really looking forward to this visit with her sister.

Rather than talk about our ride home, I'd like to share a letter Lesley wrote me a short time after Annie's death:

> "I flew to Kansas to see Annie, not knowing it would be the last time I ever saw her. Bless her heart she was at the airport waiting for me. Shock roared through my heart. Holding back the tears and trying to be peppy and smile, and not let on the disbelief, of what I saw the cancer had done to Annie, sitting there in her wheelchair still smiling. Thanking me in the car ride home for coming out. A big shock that night at dinner too; Annie forgot who I was. I was sitting next to her, and she looked up at Melissa and asked, Is this one of your friends, Melissa? Cause she keeps watching me eat, and I don't know her. Thank God, Melissa got through to Annie that it was me."

To me, that was the child in Annie again. It was like she had regressed back to a child, and Melissa was able to snap her out of it. It seemed at times Annie just wanted to get out of the cancer world, and away from the pain and suffering. I think in some sort of way, it was a gift she acquired from her spiritual journey. I really don't know how else to explain her ability to change personalities so rapidly.

Another thing Lesley wrote, that was clearly a gift to me, from Annie. Lesley, Annie, and I were at the infusion center getting her platelets, and apparently as I was walking away, doing a silly little dance for Annie, she said that Annie leaned over to her and said, "I love that man, Lesley, he is so good to me." It made me cry, and is now a cherished memory.

October 19, 2010: We went to Dr. Moore Sr.'s office today and got her lab results. Her HGB and WBC was low, and her platelets had fallen to 1,000. She would be getting two units of red blood cells today and one unit of platelets tomorrow.

He noted, "I am stopping the Velcade, and if her platelets don't come up, I will start transfusions on a daily basis, which of course is going to bring back her isoantibodies." Basically, that means the platelets will be recognized as foreign to her body and be destroyed; and that's why she always had trouble taking platelets.

I was completely in tune with what Dr. Moore Sr.'s strategy was. There was no hope for Annie, as she was way too frail and weak, and couldn't handle what would be normal multiple myeloma maintenance treatment for patients in relapse.

October 20, 2010: We went over to the infusion center today and had one unit of platelets. Lesley was with us, providing sisterly love for her sister. Annie was in a bad situation and being blocked now at every angle as her cancer was totally compromising her bone marrow, and she couldn't grow enough new platelets to make a difference. She couldn't receive chemotherapy, as it would kill any platelets she had left, and with the isoantibodies the transfused platelets weren't going to work either. All Dr. Moore Sr. could do was to give it his best shot.

At this point I knew Annie didn't have much time left, and we were all powerless to help her. It was very painful to watch, as she had fought so hard for so long. But, instead of dwelling on the negative, we still tried to have as normal of a life as possible and have some fun.

We waited for the results that day, and received a pleasant surprise. Her platelets climbed to 7,000, which was still critically low. We had a jubilant celebration inside the infusion center, as I held her and shed some tears for her happiness; but I knew the truth. With her isoantibodies, that boost would be gone by tomorrow. But at this moment in time she was feeling very upbeat, and we were going to savor the moment.

Nobody was going to take that from her. When I got her in the car as we were preparing to depart the infusion center, a picture was taken of that precious moment. Her happiness was so clear to see.

Annie Sitting in the car Smiling,

October 21, 2010: Lesley, Annie, and I had a lovely day today; but when late afternoon started rolling around, Annie wanted to go shopping. Lesley and I were against the idea, due to her being at such a high risk of bleeding, but we put big smiles on our faces and took her out. She knew Lesley was leaving in two days, and this might be their last chance to go shopping together. I couldn't deny her that simple pleasure.

We left our home around 4 P.M., arriving at Target in Derby about twenty minutes later. Once she got near the ladies clothing, she seemed to want one of everything for her and Lesley. Her child like personality that she'd been developing was in full force tonight. She was having a blast. We left Target and headed for Kohl's, which was one of her favorite shops. She started getting carried away in there too. I started pushing the wheelchair almost under the clothes racks so she couldn't see anything. It took her a while, but she caught on.

She said, "Bobby, how come you keep parking me under these clothes?"

"Just trying to have a bit of fun Annie," I replied.

"Well, I don't think it's funny, I want to shop." So she shopped and shopped until her cart was full.

When we got to the checkout counter, Annie had one of those little scratch cards to get her percentage off. When she scratched her card, it came up 15 percent off. She said, "Oh, darn it. I was hoping for more."

The attendant behind the counter, after she rang the items up, asked Annie for her card, which turned out to be a very precious moment. The attendant said, "Darn it, I hit the wrong key and gave you 30 percent off." Annie was so excited; and it was probably one of her most pleasant last memories. She was grinning from ear to ear.

I was standing behind Annie while that was going on, and at one point watched Lesley lean over, give Annie a hug, then wipe her mouth, while telling her she had some food on a tooth and she just wanted to wipe it off.

When we got home, and Annie was inside the house, I went to the car and retrieved all their goodies. Lesley was laying the clothes all over the room, which for some reason was making us all laugh. Annie would say, "Oh look, I can make two outfits out of this set," and, "This goes with this, and that goes with that."

I was just enjoying watching them.

A short time later Annie sat down beside me and thanked me, while smiling. That's when I saw the blood all over her top teeth. She was bleeding! I didn't panic, as in my mind I'd trained for this day for a long time, and knew what to do. I got up calmly, walked over to the kitchen counter, retrieved the pre-positioned flashlight and checked her upper gums. They were seeping blood, which was running down her upper teeth. Then I checked under her tongue, which was okay. Under the top and bottom lips there were a few blood blisters, about the size of pencil erasers. I checked the inside of her cheeks and they had a few dime sized blood blisters on them. The last places to look were the roof of her mouth and back of her throat. There was nothing on the roof of her mouth, but there were a couple of dime-sized sores on the back of her throat, and I could see the blood running down her throat from where food had opened them up on its way down. The visual of her mouth literally sucked the life out of me, but I couldn't let her know that.

I simply said to her in a soft voice, "Annie, you are starting to bleed, and I need to take you to the hospital."

She said, "No! I don't want to go."

She started getting very anxious, and again in a soft voice I told her to stop worrying.

I said, "Annie this is not the bleeding Dr. Moore Sr. talks about. This in itself isn't an emergency, but you do need to be further evaluated for the possibility of a transfusion."

Once again, her reply was, "I'm not going to go to the hospital."

I was upset as I wanted her evaluated, but I said okay, knowing that a multitude of things had to be going on in her mind at the moment, and although I didn't agree, I would honor her wishes. Lesley tried a couple of times to get her to go to the hospital too, but she refused.

At that point there was nothing else I could do, so I went to the market to get some food for dinner.

I hadn't been gone five minutes when my cell phone rang. Lesley called and asked me to come back home, as Annie apparently had a change of heart and wanted to go to the hospital.

I told Lesley I'd go ahead and get the food, and to tell Annie I'd be home in a few minutes and would place a call to the on-duty oncologist for guidance on the bleeding. Annie was okay with that, however, I knew what he was going to say. As soon as I got home I made the call, and about twenty minutes or so later Dr. Reddy called me back.

"I understand your wife is bleeding."

"She's not actually bleeding now, but the blood blisters are there and she was bleeding."

He replied, "We have to try to get her some platelets."

I told him platelets don't work for her.

He said, "It doesn't matter, we have to try."

I asked him if it would be appropriate for me to call the paramedics, as I didn't want her sitting in the emergency room.

He said, "I understand. It would be appropriate to call emergency services."

I placed the call and EMS arrived shortly thereafter, took Annie's vital signs, and transported her to the hospital.

Lesley and I followed them to the hospital in my vehicle. Lesley told me something on the way to the hospital that I didn't know. She said Annie had some blood flowing from one of her nostrils, and out of one of her ears after I left to go get the food.

No wonder Annie changed her mind. That can quickly become a serious event, but regardless, hoping against all hope, I wanted her to try some more platelets. I already knew if she started bleeding internally, it couldn't be stopped by anyone; but depending on the severity of the bleeding, new platelets, if they worked, might stop it.

Here's a message for most people in that situation. As I've said before, it's reasonably rare for a person to bleed to death from low platelets caused by cancer. Reason being, their bodies normally accept platelet transfusions. This event meant Annie was starting to bleed. She had to have platelets, but the question was, would they work?

This beautiful day we were having has now turned out to be very long and traumatic. At this moment, Annie's survival was certainly in question, as normally when one starts to bleed, such as Annie, the end is very near.

When we arrived at the hospital it was around 9:00 P.M. and Annie was taken straight back to one of the rooms. Within minutes there was much activity in Annie's room. She received an IV placement, and was immediately hooked up to 1,000 cc of fluid. They drew her blood to have it typed, crossed and matched, and then ordered her platelets. Prior to the transfusion the blood count showed her platelets were 1,000; and only yesterday her platelets had moved up to 7,000. That speaks volumes to the situation we were in, and it appeared her isoantibodies were destroying all our hopes and dreams. There was nothing anyone could do, but keep trying.

After Annie received her platelets, the decision was made to put her in the ICU for observation due to her high risk of bleeding. Apparently, the platelets she received didn't work. I didn't bother to get the actual number. Just the words 'they're still very critically low' is all I needed to hear.

Lesley and I stayed up most of the night while in the ICU watching over and loving on Annie. Eventually, Lesley curled up in a recliner near Annie's bed and took a nap. I sat in a chair near her bedside, placed a hand on her leg so I'd be disturbed if she moved, and then laid my head on my arm and had a short nap.

October 22, 2010: This morning around 9:00 A.M. things started to move rather fast. Melissa showed up just after 9:00 A.M. She wasn't with us last night as I didn't call her. I knew this could be the beginning of the end, but I didn't think it was time to get everyone worried.

During the night, I had been watching her ostomy bag for any signs of internal bleeding, and didn't see any. Lesley and I did the bedpan, so we were watching the urine as well; and it was still clear. When the time came it would most likely be internal bleeding, and we would see the blood in the urine or bag; however, the other possibility would be a brain hemorrhage, which we wouldn't know about until it happened.

Around 11:00 A.M. Dr. Dang was in consultation with other doctors about Annie's condition. Apparently all were in agreement that she was in end-stage multiple myeloma and the family needed to proceed with hospice.

Not long after their meeting, I was called over to Dr. Dang's desk, still in the ICU. She broke down their strategy to me, and I think mentally my mind just froze. I told her to give me a few minutes to make a decision, while I took a walk and thought about it.

I walked over to Annie's room and told Melissa not to let anyone touch her until I got back. As I walked and got more oxygen to my brain, the picture of what Dr. Dang wanted to do was becoming clear. She wanted to put her on the tenth floor for comfort care. Please don't get me wrong, I believe Dr. Dang was correct in her thoughts, but I was not going to let her die in the hospital. I knew Annie was going to pass soon, but the bleeding had stopped. So I made a calculated decision that Annie wouldn't be going up to the tenth floor under any circumstances. I'd agree to hospice at my home, as long as Annie was not told by anyone. I'd tell her when I felt the time was right.

I was putting my newly found faith on the line that I was doing the right thing. If she started bleeding, it would be a nightmare, and Annie would be fully aware of her circumstances until she passed. I know I was taking a huge risk, but that's what Annie would have wanted—to die on her and her creator's terms.

I knew that when a patient has a bleed out (medical term), the blood can come from all crevices of their body, and projectile vomiting of blood is not uncommon.

When I got back in the area, I walked over to Dr. Dang's desk. She was staring at me as I walked towards her, and I told her of my decision; but as before, she didn't agree.

"Annie is not going to wake up. She needs hospice now."

"She will wake up." I walked over to Annie's room with Dr. Dang following me.

When we walked in, Melissa was lying on the bed next to her momma, cleaning the blood off her teeth with a soft rubber sponge. It scared Annie, seeing me and the doctor together. Annie asked me very softly, "Is everything okay?"

I was looking Dr. Dang straight in the eyes when I replied to Annie, "Everything is just fine. We'll be leaving here for home about 2:00 P.M."

Dr. Dang replied by saying that she'd go ahead and get the discharge papers in order.

I knew she'd be calling hospice as well, so I went back over to her desk and asked her to have a hospice representative at my home around 5:00 P.M.

Sometimes you have to negotiate with hospital personnel in a way that lets them know that they are doing what's best for the family. Dr. Dang was doing the right thing, and our only dispute was where the hospice would be. We resolved that issue together. Yes, we'd be getting hospice, but it would now be in our home on my terms, which is what I wanted. I'd be the one to tell Annie about hospice when the time was right.

While in the hallway I bumped into a nurse I knew and she wanted to know how Annie was doing. When I told her she was going on hospice, she looked at me and said, "Oh no!"

It was then that I realized most people don't know in layman's terms what hospice really is. In the state of Kansas, I knew hospice nurses would not be allowed to administer any life sustaining fluids, to include blood or platelets. However, she was allowed all medications taken orally. Some people actually get better while on hospice and are taken off, so the word hospice didn't scare me as I had control over Annie's care. If I had let her go to the tenth floor of the hospital for hospice, sometimes they are actually talking about comfort care. Comfort care is supposed to be the later stages of hospice, when all indications are that the patient is clearly on their way out. Hospice then steps in and starts giving the patient morphine and other medications to help them stay calm and pass peacefully. The person in charge, whoever it is, makes the final decision on when to start comfort care.

In Annie's case it would be me, so I thought!

I went over and gave Annie a hug, and told her I was going to have Dr. Dang set up an appointment with the paramedics to take her home, and that they should be here around 2:00 P.M. Dr. Dang already knew that, but I wanted to make sure everything was running smoothly.

A short time later, when Lesley was sitting with Annie, Melissa and I were in the hallway outside Annie's room. I asked Melissa how she woke her momma.

She said she laid beside her momma, started cleaning her teeth, and her eyes popped open. She told me Annie's first words were, in a very excited voice, "I've done it again!" Meaning, she survived another event. She then asked Melissa, "Do they know what's wrong with me?"

Melissa told her "No," but they kept her in the ICU overnight for observation.

Annie asked her if she was going home, and Melissa said yes, but didn't know when. Melissa knew I would never let her momma stay in the hospital on hospice. Annie was really fearful of dying in the hospital. That was one of Annie's mother's greatest fears too, but in her case it happened. I basically swore an oath that I would not let that happen to Annie. I was keeping my word under some very stressful circumstances.

The paramedics arrived around 2:00 P.M. Annie was put on the gurney, strapped down, and we were on our way home. We were all very excited.

When we got home it was around 3:00 P.M. Annie was all smiles and happy to be home. Apparently Melissa called one of her work mates at some point, and told them her momma was coming home to hospice.

What a night this turned out to be. Around 4:30 P.M. Michelle, one of Melissa's work mates, arrived with several deli trays loaded with food. It looked like we were going to have a party. Shortly after she arrived, many of the girls got off work from Family Medicine East. They just started showing up and partied with Annie. She sat on her hospital bed loving it. That was probably as happy as I'd seen her over the thirty-month illness. Annie was truly graceful under such extraordinary circumstances, which in part helped make this an amazing evening, and allowed the newly found child in Annie to have one of her finest hours.

Annie at Her Hospice Party with Melissa

During the festive event, the hospice nurse showed up. I was informed by Melissa that I owed her momma an explanation. I cleared the living room of people, then went over and sat beside her on the bed.

She asked me, "What is going on?"

I told her nothing was going on that she needed to worry about. I explained to her that I negotiated with Dr. Dang, who was in consultation with other doctors who were all in agreement; you needed to be on hospice. So I agreed to hospice to get you home without a struggle or red tape.

I immediately saw the worry and disappointment come across her face; but as I gently squeezed her hand, and told her not to worry, she started relaxing again.

As we talked, the nurse was doing the forms, which I signed a little later. Annie was now officially on hospice. Not long after I signed the papers the nurse left and told us she would be back tomorrow to visit with us about the policies and procedures of hospice.

I told Annie, "As things are at the moment you make your own decisions." I promised her this was a formality and no one was going to touch her. I did make her laugh when I told her, "You can't be sitting up partying one moment then put on comfort care the next." She loved that, and seemed to relax even more.

I knew I was being a bit deceptive, but sometimes it can be a delicate balancing act between honoring the doctors' wisdom, and the wishes of the patient. I always did what I thought was best for Annie and rarely second guessed myself. I knew with all the negative information coming in, the bleeding, and then hospice, Annie had to feel as if her life was out of control. My job was to get her to refocus, in understanding that I was in control, and I would be the one to decide when it was time to start comfort care. I was performing a delicate balancing act at the moment; but I'd been doing that for twenty-nine months, and it was nothing new or complicated to me. As long as I maintained control, without flinching, she would see that and be able to relax.

Annie knew hospice and comfort care were two different entities. She also knew that before hospice could do comfort care she had to be on hospice, which she now was. Comfort care is what I called "end of life care." Once started, there is no turning back and the patient will pass from the administration of liquid morphine over time, or perhaps die from their specific illness or another related illness. No death certificate will say, 'morphine induced death.'

All I could do now was play it by ear. It would now be a minute by minute, hour by hour vigil. I emptied her ostomy pouch several times a day and always checked her urine for blood. I'd have a good idea when the time was near. I knew I was playing with fire, but it was not a game. At the moment, I didn't have the power to choose death over life, and that was exactly as it should be. I loved Annie more than most people will understand, and felt I was being guided, or my decisions were being influenced by a greater power. The rest of our journey needed to be focused on loving Annie, helping her relax, and making her comfortable.

October 23, 2010: Today was a bittersweet day, as Lesley had to return home and get back to work. Annie was truly going to miss her, but thankful for the time they had together. I assumed, as did Lesley, that Annie didn't have much time left, but we really had no way of knowing for sure. Lesley worked for the Los Angeles school district, and without certainty that Annie's death was imminent, she had to return home.

Personally, I think it was a blessing for Lesley. She loved Annie dearly, and watching her pass away, in my opinion, was a memory she didn't need. She would be able to hang onto the fun times we all had during her visit, and the good memories they made. This picture of Lesley and Annie was taken during the visit.

Lesley and Annie in her wheelchair.

This afternoon a hospice nurse came over to talk to us. She had a bag in her hand that held the liquid morphine, liquid Xanax, and liquid Atropine, which would be the comfort care medications I would be using when the time came. One of the first things she did after our warm greeting was to explain to me how to use the medications. The nurse sat on our sofa, while Annie and I sat across from her on the hospital bed. Things were going fine for a while, and then we hit some turbulence.

She said, "I'll be coming over twice a week to check on Annie."

I asked her what she'd be doing when she comes over.

She stated that she'd be checking her vital signs and general health.

I asked her what I was supposed to do if Annie started having a major bleeding event.

She replied, "Just give me a call me and I'll come over."

I said, "You're over twenty minutes away, and if it's in the middle of the night, probably longer."

"You can go ahead and start her on the morphine as you are a competent caregiver."

This is what I told the nurse in general terms.

If Annie starts a major bleed in the middle of the night, there will be no need to call you as it will be too late. All I will be able to do is hold her and love her through it. As far as her vitals go, I can do that, I do it all the time. I already knew she couldn't have platelets or blood, which was an issue to me, but not going to change my decision on hospice. What was boggling my mind was that there was one hundred and sixty-eight hours in a week, and if I was only going to see the nurse for two hours a week, what did I need hospice for? What were the odds of a major event, which I knew was coming, happening while she wasn't here? My calculations put it at 98 percent. This all evolved because I was a competent caregiver. I may be competent, but I'm still human, and I was very worried and afraid of what potentially would be a very traumatic event. I had never seen a person bleed to death from cancer, but Annie's nurse and good friend Beverly had seen a few. My goal was not to let that happen, but it seemed I was going to be on my own. Apparently, I would have to make the decision when to start comfort care based on what I knew. One thing I knew for sure; I was comfortable with the decisions I'd made thus far, so I was just going to have to use my best judgment.

It's difficult having an end of life conversation when the person that's going to pass is your loving wife, and she's sitting right beside you. Yes, I could have found a better way, such as taking the conversation outside, perhaps on the phone, or even another room. But, what's the point? At this point there is no point. Annie knows that the train has left the station and is not coming back. It was now time to be honest, and somehow find the courage and wisdom, to put forth a plan built on integrity to help her through what to her must be very traumatic times. I surely was feeling the chaos and trauma, so what must she be feeling? All I knew at this moment was that I had to somehow take control of this situation.

I thought hospice would be playing a much greater role in her care, and that I'd see the nurse on a regular basis; moreover, she'd help me make that death verses life decision. She could warn me of any impending signs that I may have missed, and I could take the appropriate action.

It wasn't going to work that way for me. I was starting to see that I was clearly going to be on my own with Annie, and to start preparing myself for the tough decision I would soon be making. At that moment something very strange happened to me. It was like something slapped me on the back of my head, and said, "What are you making such a fuss about, I will let you know when it's time." Maybe the mysterious voice, which may have been my emotions, helps explain the reasoning behind what I was about to do.

I said to the nurse, "I'm going to put everything on hold for now. We'll see Dr. Moore Sr. on Tuesday, and I want his advice."

The nurse said we could no longer see Dr. Moore Sr. as Annie was now on hospice and their responsibility.

I guess I was just having trouble letting go of Annie, as at the moment everything was so conflicting. So I told the nurse, regardless of the consequences, I was taking Annie to see Dr. Moore Sr. on Tuesday morning. I knew it could potentially create an insurance issue, or she could have a catastrophic event over the next couple of days.

Once again, I was playing with fire, but the pieces to this puzzle weren't falling into place. At the moment Annie was aware of her circumstances and was not bleeding. I couldn't just put her to sleep! In my heart, I knew I was making the right decision for Annie, and no matter what happened I was at peace with it. Annie never said a word; she just sat and listened. I knew what Annie wanted.

I made the statement a couple of times before that 'a part of Annie was becoming a child.' After the nurse left, I wheeled her into the dining room to sit at the dining room table with me.

She looked at me, and in her excited little voice said, "Bobby, if I take my medicine I'll get better, won't I?" Then again, "Won't I Bobby?"

"That's the plan Annie."

Her statement overwhelmed me. All I felt was a sensation of total love for the person that just spoke to me. From that point on, every time she took on her child-like personality, I called her "Little Annie." I knew Little Annie was out there, as she had popped out a few times before. But not to this extent! Now I would be watching for her. What a treasured moment!

October 25, 2010: Today we had to go over to Heartland Cardiology to see Dr. Farhat. Her heart was working fine with no real problems; but he was concerned about her platelet count. Dr. Farhat and Annie visited for a while about the hospice issue and her general health and wellbeing.

His comment on hospice was, "It's a choice that we all might have to make someday, and it's going to always be on an individual basis and circumstances."

Then he looked at Annie and basically asked her if she knew why she was still alive. She just stared at him and he pointed at me. He told her, "There is no doubt in my mind."

Just imagine, I had the Power of Attorney allowing me, in certain circumstances, to decide if she should live or die. That's dangerous! I guess what I'm saying to you is, if you give someone a Power of

Attorney, like the one I had, make sure you know them well and trust them. Write a note, or just make it clear what your wishes are. Annie trusted me, and I never let her down.

By the way, our last summer together, as it turned out, was the best summer of my life! One I shall never forget. That one decision I made in February allowed us to love each other "One more time."

Bob & Ann Standing together

October 26, 2010: We made it! We were going to see Dr. Moore Sr. This is kind of how our life had been the past thirty months. When we got there, we went straight back for a CBC, and then back to the waiting area.

When the nurse came to get us and I was wheeling Annie into her room, I noticed Sarah, Dr. Moore Sr.'s nurse, standing down the hallway near Dr. Moore Sr.'s office. She was looking over her shoulder at Annie and me with her hand behind her back, waving at us. I remember thinking that was rather odd.

Apparently this morning Dr. Moore Sr. was in a staff meeting, and one of the other oncologists walked over to him and said he was sorry to hear about Mrs. Harrison passing away while she was in the hospital, and while he was out of town. As you can imagine, he took the news a little hard.

When he got to his office that morning, he went straight to Sarah and told her the news. He asked her to call me for confirmation.

She said she wasn't going to call me; if Ann did pass away, Bob would be grieving, and she wasn't going to bother me.

According to Sarah, that went on until lunch time. She told me Dr. Moore Sr. finally gave up saying, "We'll just have to wait and see if she shows for her 1:00 P.M. appointment."

Sarah said, "I guess we will."

What Dr. Moore Sr. didn't know was that Sarah immediately checked with someone after he initially spoke to her, so she knew Annie was alive. She was just having some fun with her boss.

When Dr. Moore Sr. came into the room, he was laughing and grinning from ear to ear.

He said, "Hi, Momma!"

He then asked her if she wanted the good news or bad news first. Annie said she wanted the bad news first.

He told her rather nonchalantly, with a strangely curious look on his face, that her platelets were "0;" that she didn't have any.

He carefully examined her mouth, and could see where she'd been bleeding, but wasn't bleeding at the moment. He basically said that she had a relapse from her transplant, and failed her reintroduction of a very low dose of Velcade. He further stated that he was sending us over for a transfusion of platelets, and if they didn't work he'd have her there the next day on an outpatient basis. He also told her that he had ordered the blood bank to resurrect the HLA compatible list and to get HLA donors in for her. HLA platelets are a close match to hers, and she'd had them before. They would usually give her a little boost, but it seemed to disappear overnight.

I think I had just sat in on one of the most amazing conversations, or lack thereof, I'd ever heard. He just casually told her she had no platelets, and she took it like it was no big deal. For that moment it seemed like their minds were locked together like, "So what? What else is new?" I was speechless. I guess I expected a stronger reaction from both of them. But that wasn't the case. It was just 'business as usual.' I didn't even know there was such a thing as "0" platelets.

At this point, I walked Dr. Moore Sr. through my conversation with hospice. I told him the only way Annie could have transfusions was to withdraw from hospice. I don't think he knew she was on hospice. He was a wonderful, caring doctor, and kept good eye contact, listening to me carefully, making sure he understood what I was saying. Once I finished, I felt a great relief come over me. I was out of the equation for the moment.

He asked Annie if she understood what he and I had just talked about.

Her answer was a straight forward and simple, "Yes."

He then asked her what she wanted to do.

She said, "I want to fight."

He put his right hand up to his face, thumb under his chin, with his fingers sticking up and whispered to her, "Bob should open up a hospice, he is really good."

With that, I told him I would call hospice and withdraw Annie before we got to the infusion center.

He got up to leave, and then started laughing. He said, "Ann, do you want the good news now?"

She wiggled in her chair a bit with anxious excitement saying "Yes."

I looked at her---the sparkle in her eyes was priceless.

He said, "Well, the good news is that you're still alive." He stood in front of her and told her the story of her supposed death. We all had a good laugh! That was fun, and we all really needed it.

That was always the thing about Annie. She wanted to fight the disease, and I knew it. I also knew she needed to tell someone competent other than me—someone that was nonbiased. He let her make her choice and she made it. I was now released from the decision making process on whether she'd go on comfort care or not—at least for the time being. Yes, she had "0" platelets, and desperately needed the count to come up. She knew that, however, she only had two choices at this point. Fight on, or go on comfort care. I was going to fight for her no matter what, and it made me feel once again that the right decision was made. The only difference was "She made it."

Dr. Moore Sr. was not opposed to hospice; but he was a believer in folks not dying prematurely. At the moment all the signs and science dictated that at some point she was going to start bleeding and bleed to death. I think he felt as I. We'd deal with that problem when it happened. With immediate intervention I should be able to slow down or stop the process. I'm sure that based on the "0" platelet count, we could have scared her into comfort care, but that is not humane. I knew this sort of thing happened quite often, and sometimes wondered how many people died needlessly at the time. Looking back to February 2010, based on sound medical advice, Annie shouldn't even be here. But she's here, and my intentions were to keep her alive as long as I could, and love her through this mess we were in.

After we left the cancer center, I called hospice and withdrew Annie. While Annie was getting platelets, I called her case manager in Colorado and explained the situation to her. She knew me well, and my commitment to Annie's best interests was never questioned. She was okay with Annie's decision.

Kenny Chesney, a famous country singer, wrote a song with the lyrics, "Everybody wants to go to heaven, but nobody wants to go now." Annie was a classic example of that song.

After the transfusion, we had to wait an hour for the results of the platelet count to come back. They were at 3,000, which was more than I expected, but nowhere near enough to make a difference. The nurse at the infusion center told us to be back tomorrow morning for more platelets.

October 27, 2010: Annie received another unit of platelets today. When the results of the count came back, they remained unchanged—still 3,000.

These were very sad times for Annie and me, and it appeared we were fighting a losing battle. She also received one unit of red blood cells, and would get another unit when we came over tomorrow for more platelets. This was all being caused by the cancer in the bone marrow. With no treatment options available, transfusions become useless. In other words, the patient becomes refractory, and transfusions no longer work. Her body would become resistant to whatever they tried.

In the beginning it was difficult for me to understand how a woman that seemingly did most things right regarding her health, was diagnosed with such a rare cancer. Now, piled on top of that, it seemed the thing that was going to bring her down was the rarest form of death by that same disease. There were so many "what ifs" going around in my mind, it was difficult to focus at times.

This picture of Annie, Melissa, and I was taken at the infusion center, on this day.

Annie, Melissa, and Bob

That evening, I was sitting at the dining room table and saw Annie shuffling to the bathroom. She didn't walk properly, as she didn't have the strength to lift her legs, so she slid her feet along the carpet. When she came out of the bathroom I looked towards her, and noticed she had a very sad look on her face. I must have said this one hundred times through the course of her illness, always with a soft voice.

"What's going on, Annie?" Her little lips were puckering up as if she was going to cry. I walked over to her and put my arms around her.

She said, "My urine is full of blood." I didn't say anything at that moment as there was nothing reassuring I could say.

I took her hand and helped her over to her bed. I then told her I would place a call to the on-duty oncologist, and see what he thought. I spoke to Dr. Reddy again. I told him what happened, and was curious as to the cause.

He said he didn't know, but that internal bleeding can be caused by many things. However, he made it clear that she was now most likely starting to bleed internally.

I simply told Annie he didn't know what the cause was and that we needed to keep an eye on it.

Normally, she always let me check the urine after she went to the bathroom. For whatever reason, this time she didn't let me check the urine. I guess she didn't want me to see the blood.

I knew now, beyond a doubt, we were approaching "end times" for Annie, and going to the hospital was not an option, as they couldn't help her either. Even if you have normal platelets, with internal bleeding, they have to open you up and stop the bleeding. There was literally nothing anyone could do for Annie.

October 28, 2010: Today Annie received a unit of HLA platelets. While we were waiting for the results to come back, they started transfusing her second unit of blood. Her platelet results were catastrophic under the circumstances. They were now at 1,000. While she was sleeping and getting the rest of her blood transfusion, I checked her ostomy bag. My heart sunk when I got the visual of the bag; it was full of the dark red blood. I motioned for the nurse to come over. When she looked at the bag, I could see her eyes swell, and with a sad look on her face she said very softly, "Oh no."

I found myself in a real dilemma. When Annie woke up, I needed to take her to the bathroom and unload the contents of the bag. I knew she was going to see the blood as I drained the bag, but that was another one of those sad realities of cancer, that there was no way to avoid. When I unloaded the bag, as always, I was on my knees holding the container for the contents to flow in. As I looked up at her and into her eyes, I could see that she was starring at the blood, and I think perhaps trying to come to terms with her mortality. She didn't make a comment, nor did I. There wasn't a single word of comfort or encouragement I could give her at the moment.

When we left the infusion center, the air in the car was so thick I believe I could have cut it with a knife. I think we both knew the blood we saw in the ostomy bag had just set the stage for what was to come. We were now navigating our way through a new frontier, and our fear of the unknown was driving our emotions.

That evening, when I unloaded and changed her bag, all I saw was blood.

October 29, 2010: We went back to the infusion center for more platelets. The results of her count came back at 1,000. There was to be no more miracles.

It was on this day, while Annie was receiving her platelets at the infusion center, that she asked me another timeless question in a very soft voice. "Bobby, can I die at home?" I gave her a big hug and told her that'd be my promise to her. We both had lots of tears, as did a couple of the nurses attending to her.

After that gentle conversation, our emotions had waned and she started staring at me.

She asked me to look into her eyes, and tell her what I see.

After a moment of silence I responded; I see sadness, humanity, and love.

She then asked me to look deeper.

I replied, "Annie I don't know what I'm supposed to be looking for."

Her next words, once again, were, "Look deeper."

As I stared into her eyes, her eyes were locked onto mine.

Annie, "I see your soul."

She asked me what that meant.

After a pause I replied, "I see what you are, what you've been, and I know where you're going."

With those words, she started teaching me.

"Bobby, I know I don't have much time left; promise me you'll surround yourself with people who love and care about you. If you do meet someone, make sure she loves you and has a kind heart."

I knew what she meant as she'd made this statement months before. But unlike then, I couldn't tell her to stop worrying and that everything was going to be okay.

At that point, I asked one of the nurses to keep an eye on Annie while I went outside to get some fresh air. I really couldn't have cared less about the air, but I needed to clear my head. I just didn't know where to put all this information. It was as if there was a cob web of stuff circling in my mind. But, as I pulled away from those thoughts, I instinctively knew my focus had to be on Annie, and I was going to pull my socks up, go back in that room, and take care of her.

All through my life I watched sad and tragic stories of people dying in movies. I never once considered that'd be Annie and me. If you love someone today, try to love them more tomorrow. This stuff does happen, it really does.

I can't describe accurately how I felt seeing the blood in her pouch yesterday, knowing what I knew. It's one of those times when you want to pick the person up, wrap your arms around them and never let go. So much love!

October 30, 2010: Today, we went back to the infusion center for more platelets, and was told that after this batch there were no orders for more. We were to go see Dr. Moore Sr. on Monday for a CBC. I'm sure he was going to give her the grim outlook and in his own way say good-bye to her. I didn't stay around this day for the platelet results as it no longer mattered. Every time I changed her bag, it was predominately blood.

Things were now starting to pile up on Annie and me. The conversation with Annie about comfort care was now becoming a necessity. I didn't know how Annie was feeling inside, but I knew it was an awkward time. She didn't cry over her new reality; and really didn't talk about it. We did the only thing we could do at the moment; get on with our day. Annie was a proud woman, and even in the face of extreme adversity, always held her head high.

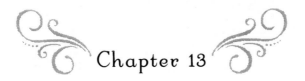

Chapter 13

Halloween Day

O ctober 31, 2010: Annie woke up this morning not feeling very well. All the anxiety around getting blood and platelets the past week was taking its toll on her. But, as always, she found a way to bring out her beautiful smile and made the best of each day. Annie was never one to dwell on the negatives. She was always trying to stay on the positive side of life. I think in this case Annie was starting to accept the reality that she'd soon be starting a new life.

The newly found child inside of her, Little Annie, was really excited for the trick-or-treat event. I can honestly say, throughout our marriage, that Halloween night was never a big deal. We gave out candy, made sure our children had a good evening, and that was about it. For whatever reason, this was a big night for her and it appeared she was going to make the most of it.

That evening Melissa took a picture of her sitting at the dining room table in her wheelchair. She was wearing this frightening mask, playing with the grandchildren—happy, and making them laugh. Annie had the uncanny ability of making each and every one of them seem like they were her favorite. But the truth is, she adored them all. She was so elegant in communicating such happiness and love to us all that night.

Halloween Picture of Annie

Maybe her mannerisms on that night are why the Bible speaks to God's grace. I wondered if this was what it's all about. Does that mean it allowed Annie to be graceful in her final days? Sure seems that way. Although very excited, there was a very strong sense of calmness around her.

I try to imagine how she must have been feeling; and deep down in her thoughts, what must have she been thinking? Getting platelets nearly every day and being told they weren't working. Annie knew if she could have successfully taken platelets a couple of months ago, none of this would be happening now. But for this day, she seemed to be putting all that behind her, and was intent on having fun with the grandkids.

Later on in the evening she went back to her hospital bed, and I propped her up on the bed by putting three pillows behind her back. I then went to the cupboard, pulled out three large boxes of gumballs I had stashed earlier, and gave them to her. I told her not to give them to the grandkids until they were in costume. She stuffed them under her pillows and sat on the bed, so excited and beaming over the fact that she had those boxes of gumballs for the grandkids.

At that moment she was so much like a child. Over the years, Annie always got down on the floor to play with the grandkids, trying to get down to their level. That isn't what Annie was doing tonight; and for this moment in time, she was "Little Annie," one of them. The three grandkids came in the room, made her laugh, and played with her. It was fun watching her dig those gumballs out from under her pillows then passing them on. It seemed to be one of those "Look what I've got for you moments"—full of excitement and love.

Once we were on our own, I sat in the wheelchair beside her bed. We chatted about the evening and how much fun it was. My daughters and grandkids all participated that night in such a positive way, it made me proud. I knew the grandchildren were worried about their nanny too; but sometimes, we as adults have to be strong and make the best of a bad situation. We do it for the children.

She had her medications, and shortly thereafter fell asleep. As it'd been over the past several days, each time I checked her ostomy bag, I always had a nervous anticipation about what I was going to see. I was living on hope too. That night when I checked her ostomy bag, it was still filling with blood, which always gave me one of those helpless, breathless feelings. I changed the bag while she was resting peacefully.

It's a difficult place to be, when you've traveled a journey through cancer with someone you really love, who fought an epic battle, and in the end it all comes down to two lingering question. How long will it take for her to bleed to death; and would I be strong enough to let her go gracefully? At that moment, those were simply questions without answers. I knew there'd be no more blood or platelet transfusions; and I also knew she'd be going home soon to what she felt would be a better place.

Regardless, she went to sleep happy, and I can say from the bottom of my heart, *that was a good night!* We were all so blessed, to have her in true form, for one last time. We had the added gift of seeing "Little Annie!" She was a blast—so full of laughter, love and spirit. As I watched her lying on the bed, I knew this night that I loved her more than life, and would have gladly traded places with her or went with her if I could. She'd suffered enough!

My emotions and imagination were trying to get the best of me, but deep down inside my soul, I knew these were just thoughts, and not possible. My sad reality was; *I would soon have to learn how live on my own without her.*

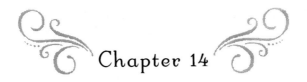

Chapter 14

Going Home

November 1, 2010: It was around 7:00 A.M. and I was lying on the sofa when I heard her sweet little voice say, "Bobby I don't feel well."

I jumped up and came out to the dining room table where she was sitting in her wheelchair. I guess, for whatever reason, this was how it was supposed to be. It was so unusual for her to get up without me knowing it. She said she got up around 6:00 A.M., had a cup of coffee, then wheeled herself to the kitchen sink where she washed her hair and brushed her teeth.

I said to her in a soft voice, "What's going on Annie?"

She looked so sad as if she knew what I was going to say. She started pulling her nightdress up, wanting to show me her ostomy pouch.

I was just staring at her rolled up tissue on the dining room table; and as I unrolled it, I discovered that it was full of bloody mucus. On previous occasions, if there was blood, it would usually be light pink. I knew from the tissue that her lungs were filling with blood, and if I didn't act soon she'd go into full respiratory failure or have a brain hemorrhage. I needed to start preparing her for comfort care; but with my emotions now overwhelming me, I was in a dilemma. How do you tell a loved one it's time to die? I tried to stay as calm as I could for the moment. Dr. Moore Sr. previously told me when the process started my timing would be critical. Worse case would be a bleed out, which would be a very traumatic event, and Annie would be fully aware the whole time. As I said before, all I'd be able to do was hold her tight and love her through it.

I will never forget these words or this conversation.

She looked at me and said, "What am I going to do?" Her eyes were directing mine to her ostomy pouch.

All I saw was blood in the pouch.

I simply said, "At this point Annie, there's nothing we can do."

She asked me if she could go to the hospital. I told her we couldn't, and reminded her of the promise I made her. If we go to the hospital, there's nothing they can do, and they won't let you come home.

She replied, "So this is it?"

"I believe it is Annie."

She laid her little head back onto the wheelchair and closed her eyes.

I asked her if she would like a Xanax, and she answered, "Yes, please."

So I gave her a Xanax tablet.

At this point, I could never describe how I was feeling. Everything was so conflicted. Annie loved life so much, and I wanted it for her. But I knew we were in a race with the clock. Once again, I felt that the train had left the station; and this time it was flying out of control down the tracks. There was no way to stop it now. We'd used up what I was now believing to be all of Annie's miracles, and she would soon be going home.

I suppose to keep hope alive, and to confirm my intuition, I asked her if she'd like to go see Dr. Klein.

Her answer was a simple nod, "Yes."

There were times in her illness when she'd hear bedside talk, and start thinking the worst. I promised her at some point in the illness, after I had command of and understood her cancer, when it was time I'd be the first one to let her know. On several occasions, when she was having difficulties and getting anxious, my simple reassuring words, "This isn't it, Annie, we're going to get through this one," would calm and relax her. She trusted me, and knew I would always be honest with her when the time came. I was her soul mate, and it needed to come from me. I knew she only had a few days left a couple of weeks ago, but as she had such a good Halloween evening last night, this morning caught me off guard. It must have been the calm before the storm.

It was about 8:30 A.M. and Annie had fallen asleep. I called Melissa and told her it was time, but Momma would like to go see Dr. Klein. Melissa came straight home to her momma, we got her bundled up, and Melissa pushed her in the wheelchair to the car. I helped her in as I always did, and then we took the short five minute drive over to Family Medicine East.

Melissa must have told her colleagues that we were on our way, as when we got there, the room was ready for us. Melissa wheeled her momma in, while I walked beside Annie.

Not long after we entered the room, a nurse came in and drew her blood. We really didn't need to do that, but we did it for her. The platelets were just under 3,000; she was in the process of bleeding to death. We had to move fast to prevent her from suffering a catastrophic event.

After looking at the blood test results, Dr. Klein came in and kissed her on the forehead.

Dr. Klein, in a very sincere voice, asked her what he could do to help her.

She simply said, "Tell me this isn't happening."

He explained to her that we'd reached the end of what medical technology can do.

Annie asked him, "Is that the bottom line?" He nodded his head to indicate it was.

At that point, I lost control of my emotions. I left the room, walked straight to Melia's office, who's the clinical coordinator.

I told her I couldn't give Annie the morphine for comfort care, explaining that I fought for thirty months to keep her alive, I wasn't going to be the one.

In a rather stern voice she told me I had no choice!

My response was, "I don't care, I'm not going to do it."

Dr. Klein apparently overheard our conversation, and came walking up.

He told me I had to give her the morphine.

I snapped back, "I can't."

Melissa came running up, gave me a stern look, and told me Momma was looking for me.

Melia awkwardly explained to Melissa what our discussion was about.

Melissa's eyes seemed to be questioning the reality of the moment as she looked at Melia and said, "I'll do the comfort care."

In words that only a loving daughter can speak, Melissa quietly and calmly said, "My momma brought me into this world, and I can help her out."

Those words made me shudder, as the realization that we were now officially on a slippery slope to death was settling in.

Melissa and I walked back to the room to find Annie with her head lying back in her wheelchair, staring at the ceiling. We both gave her a loving hug, and were just getting ready to push her out of the room when the door came open. I guess the news traveled fast throughout the clinic as there was a long line outside the door of staff members waiting to see Annie. One at a time they entered the room. All of them gave her a hug, some said they loved her, some gave her a kiss, and of course, some simply gave her a loving hug in silence. There were lots of tears; but none of them said good-bye as they didn't have too. Annie knew what they were doing.

I know, even though she didn't say it, and under very difficult circumstances, through her tears she felt honored.

On our way home, Annie was sitting in the front seat wrapped up in her blanket. Melissa was in the back seat, sitting forward, with her arms wrapped around her momma. Annie just stared out the window as if looking at nature and life in general for the last time. It was a somber drive home.

I think Annie was tired of fighting cancer, and living in a very diseased body; and who wouldn't be? Spiritually she was ready to move on to what she believed was a world of no pain or suffering.

Her tears were easy to explain. Not only was she leaving the only life she'd ever known, she would be leaving all her loved ones behind, who she knew would experience a deep torment in a way they'd never known before. Grief!

By the time we got home, Victoria and Beverly were sitting at the dining room table. Melissa wheeled her momma to the table, and parked her wheelchair in its familiar place. I walked over to the coffee pot, feeling the uneasiness in the room, and poured Annie a cup of coffee. We must have sat there for an hour or so, as Annie sipped on her coffee, probably sensing this would be the last cup of her beloved coffee she would ever have. The mood was so awkward; and none of us really knew what to say. I had called Beverly that morning and asked her to come over, as I knew Annie would need her.

I remember Melissa kneeling down beside her momma, rubbing her legs and holding her hands.

Her momma looked at her, and spoke these words with so much grace, love, and elegance. "Remember Mel, you were always my 'peace'."

A few minutes later, Annie gave us all a gift when she looked at Melissa and peacefully said, "Let's get started."

Annie, in one of her final gestures of grace, had just let us all off the hook. The final decision had just been made, and Annie, in her wisdom, was getting ready to start her new journey to "Life After Death."

She knew she was running out of time, as every time she coughed it was bloody phlegm.

I wheeled her into the living room and helped her onto the hospital bed, with Melissa, Victoria, and Beverly following.

Once I got her sitting up comfortably, she looked at me and softly said, "How long will it take me to die, one or two days?"

My reply was a soft and sad, "I don't know Annie."

That question will haunt me for the rest of my life. It's the kind of statement I will take to my grave. It's difficult to understand how a person, being so aware of their situation, can keep their poise while staring certain death in the face. How do you do that? Annie was so graceful in dying and in death.

A few minutes later her nephew Andre, who was due in tomorrow afternoon, called her from England. Their conversation wasn't very long, but it covered the most important aspect of life. They spoke their love for each other, in a very personal and meaningful way. I remember her telling him she'd try to hold on until he got there.

The conversation was very painful to listen to, as Annie really loved him, and had taken on the role as his surrogate mom when his mother Wendy passed a few years earlier from cancer.

Not long after she spoke with Andre, we laid her down. The visual of her lying there, and knowing that when she took her first syringe of morphine there would be no turning back, was taxing every emotion in my body. I knew I was on the verge of an emotional breakdown, but somehow I had to stay focused on helping Annie through these troubled waters. I even tried to talk Melissa and Beverly into giving her morphine and Xanax in tablet form; but I knew I just was stalling for more time. Bless their hearts, they tried for me, but she couldn't swallow. It was apparent that her throat was closing down, and her breathing was becoming labored. Yet another sign that her body was starting to shut down. Annie was on her way out of all this pain and suffering; and I knew in my heart there was nothing I could do. I couldn't save her.

I asked for some private time with Annie, and then laid my chest across hers, put my arms around her, and lost it. I cried like a baby, as I was so hurt. I know it sounds like it's all about me, but that isn't even close to the truth. Over the course of the illness, Annie and I became one. I hurt for her because she had to die, and for me, I was losing the love of my life. While I was crying, all I could feel was her right hand with the sports bandage on, rubbing me up and down my back. Annie was dying and comforting me. I gave her everything I had for thirty months. In return, she gave me enough love to sustain me forever, and some of my most incredible memories.

As I rose up off of her chest, I looked her in the eyes, told her I loved her, and she said, "I love you too." I rubbed my hand across her forehead, letting it gently slide down over her hair. After a soft and tender kiss, I turned and disappeared into the dining room.

I truly believe in some way, beyond the imagination of many, *I was kissed by an Angel.*

After I left the room, Melissa walked back into the room, told her momma she loved her, and immediately started comfort care. The time was 2:00 P.M.

Melissa would be giving Annie 20 milligrams of liquid morphine, and 1 milligram of liquid Xanax, placed inside her mouth, near her cheek and down by her tongue; and it had to be administered on the hour, every hour, using a small syringe like instrument. We also had a bottle of liquid Atropine to give her when the "death rattle" started.

When Melissa started comfort care, I was standing a few feet behind her by Victoria, and Beverly was sitting beside the bed in the wheelchair holding Annie's hand.

She said to Annie, "Ann, you know what will happen when I let go of your hand?"

Annie responded, "Jesus will take my hand."

Beverly said, "Absolutely! Praise the Lord!"

Annie trusted me more than anyone, but it was appropriate that Beverly start her on her new journey to eternal life. After all, she was Annie's "Angel."

Unlocking the great mystery of "Life After Death" isn't easy. But I believe throughout this story and chapter, what you've seen and will continue to see, may give some of you pause for thought. In Annie's mind she was going to heaven. Faith is very powerful, and in its truest form can be especially helpful to those fighting terminal diseases. She certainly appeared to be at peace with her decision to get started on her new journey. Annie had already been to hell and back with her cancer. In my opinion, after all the suffering, it doesn't seem right or make sense that the only thing left for the sufferer is a six foot hole in the ground. Surely there is more to life than just death. If the hole in the ground is truly the answer, then what is our purpose for even being here. There is none!

The one thing Melissa did that really pleased me, was how she spoke to her momma when she was giving her comfort care. The first few doses she'd tell her momma, "The dose I'm giving you is the same as dad gives you and won't hurt you; and it will help your breathing and relax you. So please Momma, don't worry."

Melissa's statement was factually true in the short term; but in the long term, Annie would start her new journey.

There were seven family members at our home, including me. Andrew and Hannah are Melissa's older children, 18 and 16, respectively. Eli is Victoria's son; and he was 11. He stayed upstairs most of the time playing video games. Then of course there was Beverly. We classify her as family.

We made a family agreement that Annie would have someone in the wheelchair at her bedside at all times, and holding her hand as much as possible. We just took turns as needed or wanted. Melissa would administer all the medications.

Over the first couple of hours of comfort care, every now and then Annie would wake up, raise herself up off the bed a bit, smiling and trying to laugh. She couldn't speak, but her mumblings were of a person trying to join in on a conversation. I was starting to realize she was hearing what we were saying. I asked myself, how could that be? She had enough morphine in her system that she shouldn't be waking up at all. So all of a sudden, what we said and didn't say became very important. Annie seemed to be happy, so we needed to carry on and speak in the same dialogue and manner we'd been speaking. There would be no crying, but if one of us needed to cry, we would cry with silent tears. Annie didn't need to hear a bunch of sad people sitting around her bed crying. That would make her sad, and in a sense spoil the peaceful journey she was on. Annie would want to pass over in peace, and we all became committed in making sure that she did.

Once again, Annie came through like a trooper. She gave us another gift, by letting us know in the only way she could, that everything was okay.

She was getting ready to start her new journey to "Life After Death," and appeared to be happy. Morphine in liquid form helps the patient relax, which calms the breathing, and it would also slow the bleeding process down. Annie was breathing well and obviously not anxious.

November 2, 2010: Just after midnight, I was sitting in the dining room when Melissa called out, "Dad, something is wrong with Momma."

She came running into the dining room looking for the flashlight, saying momma's head just started shaking. I jumped up, gave her the flashlight, and followed her back to Annie. Melissa scanned her eyes, and they were unresponsive. We noticed that her left cheek near the left side of her mouth had dropped a bit. It was obvious she just had a brain hemorrhage. We were expecting it, but nonetheless, that was a painful moment. We knew it was coming, which was part of our urgency for starting comfort care. But it didn't change things, as Melissa still had to stay on schedule with the morphine and Xanax. It was more important now than ever.

Within about fifteen minutes Annie started the death rattle, which was very distressing to listen to. I gave Melissa the Atropine to administer to her momma, and it worked perfectly. Over a short period of time Annie completely relaxed again.

Without the liquid morphine, Annie would have suffered a great deal of pain from the hemorrhage; but as it happened, she didn't appear to suffer at all. Her face still had a relaxed look, and was not distorted.

As I write this story, it's almost as if it were textbook perfect in places. It really was! Never underestimate the power of the creator. I was now of the opinion that our reward for taking care of Annie through her journey as we did is quite easy to understand. We were able to hold and love her until the last possible moment. We weren't lucky; and I believe this was how it was meant to be.

I asked myself this question several times after Annie started her spiritual journey. *What would be the benefit of Annie getting saved, if there were none?* That question has now been answered.

Around 2:00 A.M. or so, I went over and took Melissa's place in the wheelchair. She'd just given her momma her next dose of medication. I told her to get on the sofa and take a nap, and I'd wake her up at 3:00 AM when the next dose was due. Melissa needed some rest, so I gave Annie her 3:00 A.M. medication. Watching Melissa's strength and courage, giving her momma the drugs knowing full well what the outcome was going to be, made me strong again.

I knew Melissa would carry the sad memory of giving her momma comfort care the rest of her life, there was no getting around that. But I could help her out, and give her little breaks.

By now, I knew from the heart what comfort care was. When administered properly, and especially by a loving family, the loved one can pass over in peace.

Dying is such a personal experience, and in general I think the world can be very cold when dealing with terminally ill patients and loved ones. I know the hospitals and hospice do care about the patients, but you still have to remember the bottom line; it's about money. What we did for Annie was purely about *love*.

Melissa woke up and gave the 4:00 A.M. medications to her momma. I had just got back in the kitchen when Melissa called for me.

"Dad, Momma is trying to call out your name! She wants you!"

I went straight to her, and as soon as I saw her, I knew she was a bit restless. I sat down in the wheelchair, and put her hand in mine. I started kissing her hand, then whispering words of love to her in her ear. She calmed down almost immediately, and her breathing became less labored. I tried to pull my hand away from hers so I could lie down beside her, but she wouldn't let go of my hand. With help from Melissa, I still managed to get up on the bed and lie down beside her. When I did that, she released her grip. I was able to lie close to her, tell her how much I loved her, thank her for being my wife, and kiss her beautiful face. It was a beautiful, emotional, precious few minutes; and I fell asleep loving her.

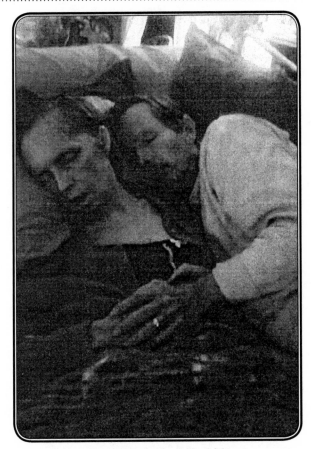

Annie & Me on bed End Times

When I awoke, it was a couple hours later, and someone showed me a beautiful picture of us lying together. Victoria took the picture over Melissa's protests. Victoria lived and worked in Georgia, and had been out three times while her mom was ill. She and I talked several times a week and I always kept her updated. I also promised her when things were bad, I'd send for her. She didn't know my rules of not letting anyone take a picture of Annie when her condition was compromised. As it turned out, the picture is a national treasure to me; and one I shall always cherish.

Not long after I got off the bed, Melissa was leaning over near her momma's face and quietly singing, "Que Sera Sera, whatever will be will be, the future is not ours to see, Que Sera Sera." When she pulled her face away, Annie had tears running down her cheeks. That was a gut wrenching moment! When a person is in a deep coma, as was Annie's case, sometimes they do indeed hear our voices. The song had been a family tradition for a long time. Annie's mom used to sing it to her as a child and Annie sang it to her daughters when they were children. Now Melissa was singing it to her momma, and obviously Annie was hearing her.

It was very difficult for me to comprehend what had just happened. Annie had been on heavy drugs now for almost eighteen hours. It really didn't make any sense to me, but it was apparent that Annie was a gift to us, and one that just kept on giving. Acknowledging Melissa's song with her tears was absolutely priceless to that child. Under very traumatic circumstances, it really doesn't get any better than that.

Through the early afternoon hours we kept on holding her hand, and loving on her as best as we could. Around 3:30 P.M. I received a phone call from Dandurand's Pharmacy. They called to tell me Annie's medications were ready for pickup. I told them I was on home delivery, but apparently they didn't get the prescription in time for them to make the 3:00 P.M. delivery. That put me in a bad position, as we couldn't afford to let Annie run out of medication. But not being able to release the drugs to anyone but me meant I'd have to leave the house. This late in her comfort care I didn't want to leave home.

Around 3:45 P.M. we received a call from Andre. They were having equipment problems with the airplane, so he'd not be in until 5:00 P.M. I knew he anxiously wanted to get here to say good-bye to Annie, and I really had no reason at the moment to believe he wouldn't make it on time.

When Melissa started comfort care, I had no idea she sent Andre a text message telling him to prepare himself. She wasn't sure how long the process would take. Sometimes it takes two or three days, or maybe longer. We had no way of knowing.

Around 3:50 P.M. I was sitting in the wheelchair by Annie, explaining to her why I had to go pick up her medications. By that time I wasn't sure she even heard me. There were no signs of stress on her face, and she seemed comfortable. I left almost immediately, but was concerned that she might have problems while I was gone. I really didn't want to leave her, as she trusted me and responded well to my voice.

My ride to the pharmacy seemed like it took forever, but in reality it was only fifteen or twenty minutes. When I arrived, I felt a rush of anxiety shoot through my body when I saw the line of folks filling prescriptions. After a long, agonizing fifteen minutes, when I got to the counter the pharmacist walked over and put the medications in front of me. He apparently knew who I was. At that precise moment, my cell phone rang. It was Melissa shouting in the phone that Momma was gone. She had so much pain in her voice when saying, "Daddy, she waited for you to leave!"

I just looked at the pharmacist and said, "I no longer need the meds. My wife just passed away." He just stared at me; I think he already knew what the conversation was about.

He simply said, "Get going." I ran out the door as quickly as I could and started the long drive home.

I think Annie's passing while I was gone was how it was meant to be. I wasn't supposed to see her die, as our thirty-month journey together was about living. I already had too many traumatic memories locked in my mind, so I believe she spared me that burden.

On my drive home, I called Melissa back to see if she had made the appropriate notifications. She had to call 911 for the paramedics, and contact Dr. Klein.

Not too long before I got home, Melissa called me and said the fire department personnel and paramedics were there and wanting to resuscitate Momma. Melissa told them she was a DNR, but they needed the paperwork; and with the overload going on in her head, she was having trouble locating it.

I told her to try to hold them off, as I'd be there in a couple of minutes with a copy from my wallet.

She told them, but they said they couldn't wait for me, which upset me, but I understood. As she'd been transported to the hospital many times by the paramedics, one of the paramedics that came in behind the others recognized her from previous visits and was able to confirm the DNR. There was also a two-by-three-inch red-and-white sticker on our front door that said, "File of Life." That meant, "Do not resuscitate." I suspect Melissa or someone was holding the door open when they came in our home, so they didn't see it. Of course, we didn't think of it either. They were just trying to do their job.

I knew whatever they did wouldn't hurt her, and that it wouldn't have worked anyway. She was starting a new journey to a place far away from all the pain and suffering. It was now time for a deep, eternal love.

Annie's reasoning for the DNR was simple. She didn't want to come back to a body with more broken ribs. Her ribs were so compromised by the cancer that pushing on her chest would have been a painful disaster for her.

When I arrived home, there was a fire truck or two, the paramedics, and a police car. When the family does comfort care and doesn't use hospice, it's my understanding that emergency services are told to advise the police department of the death. Officer Mattson was the responding officer, and was very polite, courteous, and professional in his investigation. In the state of Kansas you can legally do the comfort care for your loved one. Your state may have different laws, so make sure you know what you're doing. When the police officer arrives at your doorstep, he'll do a thorough investigation. If you, as the caregiver, think it is time for comfort care, get the doctor's confirmation before you start. I'm sure as the doctor probably knows the patient, it could be done over the phone. A doctor will come to your home after the patient passes, give the pronounced time of death, and the police officer will file his report on the death based on the doctor's input. In our case Annie's family doctor came over; but had it been a different doctor with no knowledge of Annie's illness, I would simply have referred the officer to Dr. Klein.

When I got out of my vehicle and started walking toward the house, Melissa came running out crying, in obvious pain. I gave her a big hug, and while crying with her, I simply said, "It's going to be okay, sweetie." As we walked back to the house, I was able to acknowledge the fire department and paramedics as they were preparing to leave.

Once I got inside, it was like being in a fog. I walked straight over to Annie, raised her up so I could lay her body across my lap, and cradle her head in my arms. When I kissed her I could feel the warmth of her lips, and as I held her cheek to cheek, I had a strong sensation of wanting to hold onto her forever.

Melissa had the blanket raised, and was rubbing her momma's legs, while telling me how beautifully warm they were.

I was not in shock, as I believed I was given ample warning this day was coming soon. I was pleased that the suffering was over, and felt comfortable about the new journey she was on. But, on the other hand, selfishly, the pain and hurt of knowing I'd have to live the rest of my life without her was a bit unbearable at this moment. I just wanted her back! I can say this without any reservation. If I could have her back, even as she was, I would love and take care of her until the end of my mortal stay on this earth. That would be my promise to her.

When Dr. Terry Klein arrived, he walked over to Annie and checked her pulse. The pronounced time of death was 4:52 P.M., November 2nd, 2010. He visited with the police officer, and confirmed he knew we were doing comfort care for Annie.

I remember while holding Annie, that Victoria was sitting on the floor near the head of the bed, rocking back and forth while crying. Melissa was doing her best trying to help the police officer with his investigation. I believe he stayed just over an hour. Hannah and Andrew left to go to the airport and pick up Andre, shortly after their nanny passed. They both adored their nanny, and after watching her pass, it must have been a difficult drive.

Hannah told me that she and Andrew waited in the airport lounge for Andre, and as he walked up, he could see that they'd both been crying. Andre knew immediately that Annie was gone. Andrew told me they just stood where they were, made a circle, hugged each other and shedding some tears.

Andre arrived at our home around 5:30 P.M. I asked everyone to leave the room so he'd have some quiet time with Annie. I looked in the room at him; he was kneeling beside the bed, hands and fingers clasped together on the bed with his forehead on his hands. I understood his sadness. He'd lost his mom in December 2001. Now, the second most important person in his life was gone too. He was definitely in pain and showing signs of emotional distress.

I'm not sure what time it was but Sarah from next door came over, and took charge of Annie. She and Melissa cut Annie's nightdress off and gave her a nice bed bath, and dressed her in one of her favorite nightdresses. In her healthy days, Annie was always meticulously clean when she went out. This would be her final outing, and although different, she looked beautiful.

After everything started calming down, Melissa told me her momma took two deep breaths with a sigh, then her eyes opened wide. Victoria was holding her mom's hand when she passed away. She told me her eyes were sparkling, as if she'd seen something very beautiful.

Not long after Annie died, Janet from next door, and Annie's "Angel" Beverly and her husband Gene showed up. Gene led the family in prayer, as Beverly was too upset.

The paramedics, fire department, and Dr. Klein told the family how peaceful Annie looked. There were no signs of stress on her face, which validated my thoughts that if there is such a thing as a peaceful death, we'd just witnessed one.

Annie was very graceful throughout her journey, which I believe allowed her to die with peace in her heart.

At this point so many things were filtering through my mind. I wondered if maybe all the struggles she had with the cancer, and its wretched side effects, just wore her out and she was ready to pass over to the other side. Or, was it simply that her creator was fulfilling his promise to her. I knew as a physical being I would never be able to resolve that question as it entered into the world of the unknown;

however, to Annie the question was answered earlier in her journey, and from her perspective I knew it was all about faith.

A few days prior to Annie's death, I'd asked Melissa to stop by the funeral home and make them aware of our situation. I wanted her to get all contact information so we were prepared, and make it easier for me to fulfill Annie's core wishes.

At some point, Watson Funeral Home was notified of Annie's death and arrived around 6:00 P.M. The gentlemen that came over representing the funeral home were Larry Sutherland and Matt Speer. Those two gentlemen were incredible, and met all our needs and more. They were patient, compassionate, and very professional in their duties. I was as protective of Annie in death, as I was in life, but soon realized I didn't have to say anything to them. They treated her like a princess or one of their own. They gave us all the time we needed to say good-bye to her, while standing in the background like a couple of Honor Guards. When we were through saying good-bye to Annie, I asked Larry what the remainder of the process was. He told me they'd get her ready and on their way out, we could say our last good-bye. When they were through getting her ready, it appeared she was in some sort of body bag, which had a beautiful heavy burgundy blanket draped over the top, leaving her head exposed for viewing. They then moved her over near the front door, where we all took a turn at saying our last good-bye to her. Once everyone had a chance to wish her farewell, she left our home for the last time. Melissa and I escorted her to the hearse.

I held Melissa tight as we watched the black hearse pull out of the driveway, heading down the road. The visual for my daughter and me will live in our memories forever. That's when it finally sunk in and I knew our lives would forever be changed.

It was a sad reality for me, as Annie and I had spent over half of our lives together, and never once thought this could happen to one of us. Well it happened, and in the process really rocked my world. I'm now of the understanding of just how vulnerable and fragile life really is. I didn't just lose a spouse, I lost a child too. I was also in love with "Little Annie." Once again I must reiterate that *if you love someone today, try to love them more tomorrow.*

That was a bad night for many reasons; and even though I had accepted the fact that she was gone, the thought of her lying alone and cold in the morgue was troubling me. That's just a sad reality of life and death. But, it made me more determined than ever to honor her core wishes. I needed to get her out of the morgue and back home as quickly as I could.

I only had two instructions for Watson Funeral Home. These were also two of Annie's wishes as said by her, "Don't let me lie around in the morgue, and have me cremated as quickly as you can."

Fifteen hours after she left our home she was cremated.

Thanks to a great team effort at Watson Funeral Home, her ashes were handed over to me at about the 36th hour from the time she left our home. Her ashes were in a beautiful ebony container which would have pleased Annie. Some of us put little love notes inside the container that would be placed with her in her final place of rest.

The morning after Annie passed away, Andre and I went to the funeral home. I had Doug Watson, the owner, and his office manager, Chancy, help me with the logistics of getting Annie's ashes back to England. They handled all the TSA paperwork, ordered the death certificates, and notified other pertinent agencies to include the Social Security Administration of her death.

When Andre left for home, Annie's ashes would be going home with him.

November 10, 2010: Andre flew Annie's ashes back home to England, and with the TSA paperwork in hand, he had no problems with customs officials. He said he was able to keep her with him at all times. It was so important to me that this part of her journey went flawless.

Just over a week later, Annie's ashes were sprinkled in the Chelmsford Crematorium's Rose Garden. That fulfilled two more of her wishes. Getting her ashes back home quickly and sprinkled in the rose garden with her mother and two sisters.

In the old days they literally sprinkled the ashes. They don't do that anymore, although they still call it sprinkling of the ashes.

I would soon be traveling to visit Annie, and I couldn't wait! While there, I plan to make a plaque for the crematorium's wall and add her name to the book of remembrances. I could have made the trip sooner; however, Annie and I always knew when the time came, Andre would be here to take her ashes home.

Approximately three weeks after Annie passed away, I made the journey to the cancer center to see Dr. Moore Sr. Once I arrived, I walked by reception and went straight back to the nurses' station. None of the nurses had seen me since she passed away, and were overwhelming with their condolences. They all thought very highly of Annie and felt her loss too.

I asked Sarah if I could see Dr. Moore Sr., she said I could, and had a nurse escort me to a private room next door to the doctor's office. I sat and waited for about fifteen minutes until he came in. He listened intently while I explained to him how she died. When I was through, he put a beautiful smile on his face and said, "They know when it's time, don't they! I always thought they did, but now you've confirmed it." He went on to say that under the circumstances her death was a blessing as she died of low platelets and not multiple myeloma. He told me multiple myeloma is a horrible excruciating death, and during the process, if the patient rolls over in bed, or has to be moved, bones simply break causing an almost uncontrollable pain. So it would appear that Annie was spared a very painful death.

May 2, 2011: I flew out of McConnell Air Force Base for England at 5:00 P.M. The flight took approximately eight hours and was very interesting, as during the journey I got to see the sun set in the west and rise in the east. We landed at RAF Mildenhall in England at 7:00 A.M., May 3rd, 2011.

From RAF Mildenhall, I hired a taxi to take me to Annie's hometown of Chelmsford, Essex, England. It was about a seventy-mile drive, but went by quickly as luckily I had a very attentive taxi driver, whom I had a wonderful chat with about my beautiful English lady. He enjoyed the story and gave me some wonderful positive feedback.

The ride also gave me time to check my emotions, as I'd made that journey many times before in 1971. As a young Sergeant, I was stationed at RAF Lakenheath, which is next door to RAF Mildenhall. I made that drive almost every day to go spend time with Annie when we were dating. A lot had changed with the new highways, but I still went through some small villages and saw some familiar sights.

I arrived at Andre's house around 10:00 A.M., and after a warm greeting and a couple cups of coffee, we walked to town where I rented a car. While doing the paperwork, he asked me if I was ready to visit the crematorium. With anxious anticipation, I told him I was ready.

We left the car rental agency, and drove straight to the crematorium. It was around noon when we arrived at their gates. As you turn off the roadway into the crematorium grounds, you're immediately surrounded by beautiful trees and gardens. I was a bit disappointed as the roses were just starting to bloom, but that was only for a fleeting second or two, as my goal was to find Annie. As we wound our way down the narrow roadway, we started seeing people everywhere. A large funeral had just ended, which made things feel a bit awkward at first. But as I settled in and refocused on my goal, I could feel the excitement racing through me as we got closer to her site. Still, I was able to see the pain on some of the faces, as I navigated the vehicle through the crowd.

As I parked the vehicle, it became apparent we'd be walking through a crowd of grieving people. As we walked through the crowd I was nervous, but it went well. Many of the people acknowledged us as if they knew why we were there; and of course we returned the courtesy. As Andre guided me over to Annie's site, I looked back and noticed that many of the people were watching us. I guess the look on our faces must have made the nature of our visit obvious. We walked between the rose bushes, and about five feet away lying on the ground was a red rose that Andre had put there last week. He then pointed to a spot about six feet away where there was another red rose. That's where his mom Wendy was resting. Annie would have been pleased being so close to her sister Wendy.

As I looked down on Annie's site, I could clearly make out the shovel marks from what looked to be an eight by twelve-inch dig. As I got down on my knees, with my right hand index finger I was able to trace the outline of her site. I put my hand, palm down on top of her sight and said a few words. I stood up with tears in my eyes, and said to Andre, "She's not there!"

He just stared at me; but I knew immediately that all my questions had now been answered. Annie was tucked away safely in my heart, and in that better place she called "Heaven." She was safe!

As we walked away, Andre confided in me. He said he felt the same way when his mother was placed there.

It was a comforting feeling, knowing that when I left for home in a few days everything was going to be okay.

May 5, 2011: Andre and I went back to the crematorium, this time with Joe, one of Annie's good friends. When Annie passed, I called him in England and gave him the sad news. He asked me, and I made him a promise, that I'd get in touch with him when I arrived and he could come to the crematorium with me. Joe helped us start our antiques journey in the mid-1970s. He wanted to see her site, and leave her some flowers, as did I. He also wanted to be there when I ordered her plaque and entered her name in the Book of Remembrance. After we drove away, we went out and had a wonderful English Country Pub lunch, and of course, we had a pint of ale to go with it. It was a good day.

I was in England a total of six days, and only went to Annie's site those two times. In the future when I go there, it'll be out of respect, as I won't be looking for her. I know where she is, and going to stay. I will tell you a little secret; Annie not being there was a blessing. I was so worried and afraid that I was going to leave England and feel like I was leaving her behind. That would have been a heavy burden for me to carry.

While I was in England I had this plaque made to place on the "Wall of Remembrance," in the Rose Garden.

Annie's Plaque

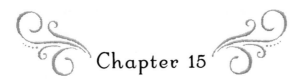

Chapter 15

Unlocking the Mystery

In Annie's case, the most important day of her life was her last day on earth as a physical being. I think writing this book has taught me many things, some of which I still don't fully understand.

Still, I can't deny what I saw. When Annie passed, with her newly found spiritualism, she was ready to make the leap to "Life After Death." Her creator promised her a brighter new world, one of no suffering, and full of promise and love. I wasn't sure that was the case, but as I look back on her story, I can clearly see Annie was looking for an alternative to quite simply being placed in the ground for all eternity.

On August 15th, 2008, while in a coma, she felt something she never wanted to feel again. As you saw in her story, she was offered a different path than the one she was on, and took it. We can't fault her for that. We'd all like more, in one form or another. So the mystery really isn't a mystery at all. It's simply a choice given to each one of us. Annie's Story defines that choice.

Anyone diagnosed with a terminal illness will likely go through many changes, which will allow their mind to explore areas of opportunities that were always there but never acknowledged. If you're ever in that situation, don't be afraid to open your heart and see what's out there waiting for you. In Annie's case, what did she have to lose? What's the worst that could happen if she was wrong? She'd simply be lying in the ground along with the other non-believers.

Annie made the right choice for her, and who knows, she may be laughing as I speak to you, or maybe not. I know this, we can't criticize her spiritualism as she died with a smile on her face and love in her heart for the new journey she was embarking on. For me, the person that suffered her loss the most, it doesn't get any better than that.

My path has now been defined by her journey, and I'll do the best I can to get there. I believe I'll see her one day in some form, and I'm looking forward to that day. A non-believer might say to me, "I feel so sorry for you, you're in for a big surprise." That is the point of this conversation; I won't be surprised. If you're right I'll just be dead. Unlocking the mystery of life after death was about Annie's spiritual journey to "Life After Death."

Watching my little atheist transform into a person full of hope and love for what was to come after she left her physical body was amazing. I have no doubt when Annie died she wasn't surprised. At the end, it's either all or nothing. Annie wanted it all and I believe she got it. It's rather like Annie was handed a key to unlock the mystery and didn't hesitate. She was very fearful of the dark, until she got the key and started peering through the crack. It slowly changed her life and way of thinking. Whatever she was seeing will forever remain a mystery. My assumption is that it was something very special and beautiful, as she never looked back or changed course throughout her journey.

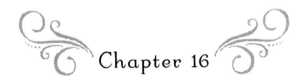

Chapter 16

The Night We Met

Letter to Heaven

Hi babe, it's the 25th of March 2011, and I'm really struggling tonight and missing you. I try to get on with my life; but each time I do, I end up right back in the same place, looking for you. When I get a hug, it's not your hug. When we embraced, it always felt so perfect. I'll admit to you though, over our thirty month journey through cancer, each time I held you in my arms, I was always fearful to let go. I never knew from one day to the next when I'd held you in my arms for the last time.

I still have vivid memories of the night we met. It was in March 1971, at RAF Wethersfield, England. My buddies and I decided to go to the club for a few drinks and a little fun. I was sitting with them, when I noticed this beautiful young lady at the table to my right and just a bit back from us. I had no idea that night would change my life forever. I kept sneaking little glances your way, you had such natural beauty. Your hair was in pigtails, you had on a muted-color maxi dress, with sandals that laced up your legs. I could tell you weren't happy with your date, but couldn't approach you out of respect.

At some point, I decided to go get me another drink. The bar was very crowded, so I scampered off to the bathroom. I couldn't believe my eyes when I walked into the lobby and you were standing there with my friend Jay. I walked right up behind you and was standing there when you said to Jay, "Can you give me a ride home? I'm not happy."

Jay, being the intellectual person that he was, had a way of thinking before he spoke. When you said those words and he opened his mouth rather slowly to reply, that was my opening. I leaned forward just a bit over your shoulder and said, "I will!" You turned around, looked at me, and gave me the most beautiful smile I'd ever seen. I remember taking hold of your hand, and we ran out of the club together, like a couple of kids.

I've told you this story before, but I just want you to know that I still love you in death as I did in life.

What I didn't know, was you'd been watching me too. One evening about halfway through your illness, I was sitting on the sofa and you were sitting up in your hospital bed. I asked you to tell me a story, and to my surprise, your story started with the night we met. You'd never told me this story before, and I loved it when you told me you'd been watching this good-looking "bloke," but never tried to get his attention because you didn't think you had a chance.

"Why did you wait so long to tell me this?" Your words are the missing piece of the puzzle. Our journey through life started that night. The smile you gave me when we met, I shall never forget.

Annie, remember the poem I wrote you on Christmas Eve in 1971. We were going to spend the evening together and do some Christmas shopping and follow your dad's tradition of going to the market and getting all our goodies and a tree. I was put on standby that night and restricted to the base. You were sixty miles away, and I wasn't there to enjoy the festivities or help you. I was missing you then, but it's on a much higher level now. So the poem is still appropriate and shall be tucked away in my heart and in my memory, until it fades.

To you my love:

Christmas comes but once a year
Bringing all its gifts so dear,
The gift of Love the gift of Life
I'd like to make this girl my wife,
Because I can't come
and touch her where she stands,
My gift will be my heart
This pen will be my hand.

Annie & Bob 1972

Chapter 17

Self-Help Measures

August 25, 2012: After writing Annie's story, and still struggling with my grief, I'd like to share some of the things that were important to me and helped me gain control over my emotions.

The first two month after Annie's death, it was obvious to me that I needed some professional help. After the 30 month extraordinary journey I took with Annie, many days running on adrenaline, I was feeling as if I had hit a brick wall. My world seemed to stop, leaving me with only a sense of being. It was a strange feeling, one I didn't know, and I wasn't sure how to deal with it. As subtle thoughts of suicide started creeping into my thought process, I made an appointment to see Dr. Bud Bryant, Psychologist. For the first several months, it was two visits a week, then slowly changed to one visit a week. He brought direction and stability to me, helping me understand that all the trauma I saw Annie go through was piling on top of me and my brain had no way to digest all the negative events. He helped me start seeing all the beautiful memories we made together, and over time, the good memories started overshadowing the bad.

On a day in November 2012, I was standing in the kitchen fixing me something to eat. I found myself singing happily, oblivious to my grief. When I realized that I was singing, I felt really weird and had to go sit down at the dining room table. I shed some tears, and found that I was trying to get back to the darkness where I felt I belonged.

That's where Annie was; in a dark corner in my mind. Realizing I had no choice, I crawled and scratched my way out of grief; although it wasn't immediately apparent, I was able to bring Annie with me. My sunshine was now hers too.

I still see Dr. Bryant once a week, as he's being mindful that I don't have a relapse. Yes, that is possible in grief.

August 25, 2012: After writing Annie's story, and still struggling with my grief, I'd like to share some of the things that were important to me and helped me gain control over my emotions.

On September the 4th 2011, I was having a particularly bad night. So I went online and started searching, uncertain of what I was looking for. I was visiting the website of the crematorium in England where Annie's ashes were sprinkled. I spotted a little box, Forevermissed.com at the bottom right side of my page. It was an advertisement for placement of online memorials. Endless possibilities just started radiating through my mind. I didn't have a clue that the decision I made that night would change my life forever. Every day I spent time on the site leaving tributes, telling stories, and sharing pictures of Annie as she was when fighting cancer, and before. As time passed, I'd get up each morning, say hi to her, and always be there in the evening before I went to bed tucking her in. One of the things I noticed over time was when I looked at her, I no longer had that extreme sense of sorrow, and the pain had turned into an ache.

I instinctively knew I had a platform to help me come to terms with her death. As I believe the amount of love you have for a person drives your grief, Annie's online memorial became a grief buster for me. To this day, I still look at her memorial four or five times a day, with an overwhelming sense of pride and love for this amazing person gifted to me for thirty-nine years.

Of course, I'm sharing her with the world. Through emails from visitors of Annie's online memorial, I've been able to communicate with folks in her native England, and have received several emails from different parts of this country and others. Most have their own unique story to tell of a loss. It's usually the loss of a parent, child, spouse, or a sibling. I always respond, and have made a few meaningful friendships.

Annie is now receiving over 2,000 visitors a month to her site. It started slow, just 30 visitors a month for the first few months. It seems her "star" has lit up the sky, and in death as in life, people just seem to be drawn to her. Annie has received over 27,000 visitors.

If you're interested in meeting Annie, and viewing the ultimate in online memorials, log onto www.forevermissed.com and click on her picture. Or when you get to the site just use the search bar and enter annie-barber-harrison to pull up her memorial. Annie's online memorial has been rated as one of the top on-line memorials in the world; it was created out of love with the intention of leaving her legacy and helping others through their loss.

In January 2013, I received an email from West Point Monuments, a large granite company in Nebraska. They have teamed up with Forevermissed.com and are in the process of creating SmartMemorials, which are high tech, innovative, and certain to play a role in many of the memorials created for our loved ones over the next few months, and beyond. SmartMemorials are already in place in parts of the country. The process is unique, and offers the bereaved a 3 1/2 by 5 inch plaque with a smart tag at the base. In addition the bereaved receives an individual smart tag, and a memory card. It's a simple process; an online memorial is set up at Forevermissed.com, then through technology is transferred to the smart tag. The plaque comes with a lifetime warranty, is weather proof, and has adhesive on the back and will stick to any monument, or stand. Any person with a smart phone can scan the plaque, smart tag, or memory card to access the person's individual story at Forevermissed.com. When I visited Annie in England, it was only natural to look around, walk through the cemetery, then leaving with more questions than answers. I would love to have known who some of those people were, and their story. I've opened the door on Annie; I want everybody humanly possible to meet and get to know her.

In the next few months, SmartMemorials will be hyper-linked around the world. Annie will be one of the on-line memorials they will be using as their model for the new high tech memorials.

The significance of a SmartMemorial is very apparent when dealing with grief. In my case, dealing with Annie's cancer for 30 months allowed me to become addicted to her through our extraordinary way of life. There were times when I needed to detox. When I was away from home and started missing Annie, I'd pull my memory card out of my wallet and scan the smart tag on the back of the card with my smart phone. In seconds I was visiting with her and getting my emotions in check, and in turn being reminded of just how precious life is.

SmartMemorials

Social networking has also helped me tremendously. My daughter signed me up on Facebook shortly after Annie passed. I didn't know this, but Annie told Melissa she was worried about the deep loneliness she feared I would experience when she was gone. She asked Melissa to help me reconnect with old friends, and make new ones. To get me started, Melissa set me up with sixty of her friends, which were people I already knew.

My very first post was an emotional post about Annie. The response I received from that post was overwhelming, and for the first time I realized I was not alone. I now have over four-hundred friends, and through them I found a way to help me heal by telling them stories about Annie. Now many of them know and love her too. It not only helped me deal with my tragedy, it also helps others deal with their losses too. If you would like to submit a friend request to me, I would be honored. Simply search Facebook for Bob Harrison, Wichita, Kansas to submit the request.

In May 2012, I started building an inspirational cancer Facebook page for Annie. It's growing, but it takes time for the word to get out as it mainly links to my Facebook friends. My attempt through Annie's page is to inspire others, give them some self-help measures, tell them some beautiful stories, as well as talk about the down side of cancer and the effects it has on loved ones. One of the things I stress is that *you're not alone.*

Cancer isn't only difficult, it creates a very challenging environment for the loved ones left behind. Cancer has a way of sucking the life out of a patient and makes an attempt to swallow up everything around it. As tough as it is, you'll move on in time. As I've learned, the time is when we decide, or the emotional drag on our body becomes so great we start moving on as our survival mechanism kicks in. It's important that one's grief is not defined by others.

If you have a Facebook page, just go to the white search bar and type in the link, www.facebook.com/BloodCancerAnnie, or use one of the internet search engines. If you've lost a loved one, or are grieving, you'll find this page helpful and quite possibly comforting.

If you like, you can share your loved one on there with their own unique story, to include posting a photograph. Annie would like that.

The Leukemia & Lymphoma Society was a great help to me as well. The following is an overview of the assistance they provide, but they offer so much more.

Within the first three weeks of Annie's diagnosis, I received a call from a gentleman in Long Island, New York. He was asked to get in touch with me by the Leukemia & Lymphoma Society. He said his wife had been suffering with multiple myeloma for the past five years, and he was going to be my buddy and help me through Annie's journey. He helped me through the important initial stages, but as time went by, his wife started taking a turn for the worse and our conversations ended. He'd already given me what I needed, and for that I am thankful.

Also, the society provides modest financial help for the patients, as well as a twenty-four hour a day hotline, offering telephone support and counseling when needed. Over our thirty month journey, I had numerous calls from the Leukemia & Lymphoma Society, checking on Annie and seeing if they could be of help in any way.

When a person is diagnosed with a blood cancer, their life quickly spirals out of control. The caring phone calls make a difference, and help bring some sense of normality to an otherwise abnormal new world. For those of you entering the world of blood cancer, go to www. LLS.Org or call toll free at 1-800-955-4572 and discover a breath of fresh air. They will help you answer some of the many questions circling in your mind, in regards to your disease. You'll be able to receive literature on the exciting new breakthroughs in research and development of new drugs, and the specific effects they can have on your blood cancer. The literature will include treatment strategies available, options such as clinical trials, and most of all, help the patient and family understand the benefits of a strong support system.

I felt the most appropriate way to turn the page on this chapter in my life was to share my thoughts on Annie's new found spiritualism, and the effect it had on me. I guess, if I'd been told at some point in Annie's journey with cancer she'd become a Christian, I'd never entertained such a thought. It wasn't possible! But indeed, it happened.

It left me with a real sense of lacking the inner peace I saw in her. Some folks had their doubts about her new found faith, as they were non-believers. It didn't bother me, as we all know life is about choices; Annie truly was a person who believed in love, compassion, and kindness towards others. That's what her creator was all about; so making the leap to Christianity isn't that difficult to understand. In my opinion, it would have been a terrible shame if her life had stayed on the course it was on. Heaven was calling her, and sent Beverly, one of the nicest most precious ladies I have ever known, to rescue her.

Beverly is spiritually gifted; she never has an unkind word to say about anyone. Over time, others have heard about the gift she helped Annie obtain, and have contacted me, asking if it would be possible to speak to her. The answer is always yes. She's a servant of the Lord, but it doesn't matter who or what the person's beliefs are, she provides comfort during the storm. And I mean this with every fiber in my body, *she really does.*

In March 2013 while I was in California, I got a call from my friend Steve. One of his good friends had just been put on hospice and was dying from cancer. He had known Annie and me for years, and knew about Beverly. He asked me if I thought Beverly would come over to his friend's home. Two days after I heard from Steve, Beverly made that drive to his friend's home, late in the evening in heavy snow. That was a difficult journey for Beverly as she lives in the country and is 73 years old. Before she made the trip she called me and said, "Bob, I must be out of my mind, driving in this weather. But when I get a calling, I have to go." And she did! Steve was there when she arrived, and said everyone in this large family was mesmerized by her presence. Steve told me that a calmness came over that home that hadn't been there since his friend got sick. In her own spiritual way, she made a difference for that family, and they still speak of her presence.

In October 2011, after giving it much thought, and not attending church for over 50 years, I decided to go to church. I tried a couple of churches, but they were the wrong fit for me. I had basically given up when my daughter suggested the Aviator Church in Derby, Kansas. I started attending and found the message quite refreshing, and on a level that that I could relate to. It brought back many memories of my childhood, as mom and dad always took us to church each Sunday.

So I've hung in there, mostly in the shadows, but listening carefully to Pastor Joe's message.

I've started reading the Bible, and am now starting to understand that what happened to Annie was no accident. In my opinion, she was selected by a higher power to receive "Life After Death."

Annie set the bar very high for me, but I'm learning to take baby steps, one step at a time, and I shall just have to wait and see where they take me. Who knows, maybe I'll make the grade and see what the mystery to unlocking "Life After Death" is all about. I'd like that! *My Annie knows!*